Applying Math with Pyth

Practical recipes for solving computational math problems using Python programming and its libraries

Sam Morley

BIRMINGHAM - MUMBAI

Applying Math with Python

Commissioning Editor: Ravit Jain
Acquisition Editor: Pratik Tandel
Content Development Editor: Divya Vijayan
Senior Editor: Hayden Edwards
Technical Editor: Deepesh Patel
Copy Editor: Safis Editing
Project Coordinator: Kinjal Bari
Proofreader: Safis Editing
Indexer: Rekha Nair
Production Designer: Jyoti Chauhan

First published: July 2020

Production reference: 1300720

Published by Packt Publishing Ltd.
Livery Place
35 Livery Street
Birmingham
B3 2PB, UK.

ISBN 978-1-83898-975-0

www.packt.com

For my parents...

Contributors

About the author

Sam Morley is an experienced lecturer in mathematics and a researcher in pure mathematics. He is currently a research software engineer at the University of Oxford working on the DataSig project. He was previously a lecturer in mathematics at the University of East Anglia and Nottingham Trent University. His research interests lie in functional analysis, especially Banach algebras. Sam has a firm commitment to providing high-quality, inclusive, and enjoyable teaching, with the aim of inspiring his students and spreading his enthusiasm for mathematics.

I would like to thank my friends and colleagues at the University of East Anglia for their support and encouragement while writing this book. I would also like to thank my editorial team and the technical reviewers for their hard work.

About the reviewers

Bryan Johns is an experienced data scientist and mathematician. Since completing his PhD in mathematics, Bryan has been working as a data scientist, where he has been using Python to deliver machine learning solutions to some of today's most intractable business problems. Bryan has worked in the financial services and consulting industries, as well as serving as a data science mentor for the next generation of data scientists. In his free time, Bryan enjoys surfing, skiing, sailing, and other activities that start with "s." Bryan lives in San Diego, California, with his wife, one-year-old son, and two mischievous cats.

Valeriy Babushkin is the senior director of data science at X5 Retail Group, where he leads a team of 80+ people in the fields of machine learning, data analysis, computer vision, natural language processing, R&D, and A/B testing. Valeriy is a Kaggle competition grandmaster and attending lecturer at the National Research Institute Higher School of Economics and the Central Bank of Kazakhstan. He is a technical reviewer of *AI Crash Course* and *Hands-On Reinforcement Learning with Python, Second Edition*, published by Packt.

Packt is searching for authors like you

If you're interested in becoming an author for Packt, please visit `authors.packtpub.com` and apply today. We have worked with thousands of developers and tech professionals, just like you, to help them share their insight with the global tech community. You can make a general application, apply for a specific hot topic that we are recruiting an author for, or submit your own idea.

Table of Contents

Preface

Python is a powerful and flexible programming language that is fun and easy to learn. It is the programming language of choice for many professionals, hobbyists, and scientists. The power of Python comes from its large ecosystem of packages and friendly community, and from its ability to communicate seamlessly with compiled extension modules. This means that Python is ideal for solving problems of all kinds, and mathematical problems in particular.

Mathematics is usually associated with calculations and equations, but in reality, these are very small parts of a much larger subject. At its core, mathematics is about solving problems, and the logical, structured approach to solutions. Once you explore past the equations, calculations, derivatives, and integrals, you discover a vast world of beautiful, elegant structures.

This book is an introduction to solving mathematical problems using Python. It provides an introduction to some of the basic concepts from mathematics – and how to use Python to work with these concepts – and templates for solving a variety of mathematical problems across a large number of topics within mathematics. The first few chapters focus on core skills such as working with NumPy arrays, plotting, calculus, and probability. These topics are very important throughout mathematics, and act as the foundation for the rest of the book. In the remaining chapters, we discuss more practical problems, covering topics such as data analysis and statistics, networks, regression and forecasting, optimization, and game theory. We hope that this book provides a basis for solving mathematical problems and the tools for you to further explore the world of mathematics.

Who this book is for

Readers will need to have a basic knowledge of Python. We don't assume any knowledge of mathematics, although readers who are familiar with some basic mathematical concepts will better understand the context and details of the techniques we discuss.

What this book covers

`Chapter 1`, *Basic Packages, Functions, and Concepts*, introduces some of the basic tools and concepts that will be needed in the rest of the book, including the main Python packages for mathematical programming, NumPy and SciPy.

`Chapter 2`, *Mathematical Plotting with Matplotlib*, covers the basics of plotting with Matplotlib, which is useful when solving almost all mathematical problems.

`Chapter 3`, *Calculus and Differential Equations*, introduces topics from calculus such as differentiation and integration, and some more advanced topics such as ordinary and partial differential equations.

`Chapter 4`, *Working with Randomness and Probability*, introduces the fundamentals of randomness and probability, and how to use Python to explore these ideas.

`Chapter 5`, *Working with Trees and Networks*, covers working with trees and networks (graphs) in Python using the NetworkX package.

`Chapter 6`, *Working with Data and Statistics*, gives various techniques for handling, manipulating, and analyzing data using Python.

`Chapter 7`, *Regression and Forecasting*, describes various techniques for modeling data and predicting future values using the Statsmodels package and scikit-learn.

`Chapter 8`, *Geometric Problems*, demonstrates various techniques for working with geometric objects in Python using the Shapely package.

`Chapter 9`, *Finding Optimal Solutions*, introduces optimization and game theory, which use mathematical methods to find the best solutions to problems.

`Chapter 10`, *Miscellaneous Topics*, covers an assortment of situations that you might encounter while solving mathematical problems using Python.

To get the most out of this book

The only requirement throughout this book is a recent version of Python, at least Python 3.6, but a higher version is preferable. Some readers might prefer to use the Anaconda distribution of Python, which comes with many of the packages and tools required in this book. If this is the case, you should use the `conda` package manager to install the packages. Python is supported on all major operating systems – Windows, macOS, and Linux – and on many platforms. The following table covers the main libraries and their versions used at the time of writing this book:

Software/libraries covered in the book	**Version**	**Chapter**
Python	3.6 or higher	All
NumPy	1.18.3	All
SciPy	1.4.1	All

Matplotlib	3.2.1	All
Pandas	1.0.3	6 - 10
Bokeh	2.1.0	6
Scikit-Learn	0.22.1	7
Dask	2.18.1	10
Apache Kafka	2.5.0	10

If you are using the digital version of this book, we advise you to type the code yourself or access the code via the GitHub repository (link available in the next section). Doing so will help you avoid any potential errors related to the copying and pasting of code.

Some readers may prefer to work through the code samples in this book in a Jupyter notebook rather than in a simple Python file. There are one or two places in this book where you may need to repeat plotting commands. These places are marked in the instructions.

Download the example code files

You can download the example code files for this book from your account at `www.packt.com`. If you purchased this book elsewhere, you can visit `www.packtpub.com/support` and register to have the files emailed directly to you.

You can download the code files by following these steps:

1. Log in or register at `www.packt.com`.
2. Select the **Support** tab.
3. Click on **Code Downloads**.
4. Enter the name of the book in the **Search** box and follow the onscreen instructions.

Once the file is downloaded, please make sure that you unzip or extract the folder using the latest version of:

- WinRAR/7-Zip for Windows
- Zipeg/iZip/UnRarX for Mac
- 7-Zip/PeaZip for Linux

The code bundle for the book is also hosted on GitHub at `https://github.com/PacktPublishing/Applying-Math-with-Python`. In case there's an update to the code, it will be updated on the existing GitHub repository.

We also have other code bundles from our rich catalog of books and videos available at `https://github.com/PacktPublishing/`. Check them out!

Code in Action

Code in Action videos for this book can be viewed at `https://bit.ly/2ZQcwIM`.

Conventions used

There are a number of text conventions used throughout this book.

`CodeInText`: Indicates code words in text, database table names, folder names, filenames, file extensions, pathnames, dummy URLs, user input, and Twitter handles. Here is an example: "The `decimal` package also provides a `Context` object, which allows fine-grained control over the precision, display, and attributes of `Decimal` objects."

A block of code is set as follows:

```
from decimal import getcontext
ctx = getcontext()
num = Decimal('1.1')
num**4  # Decimal('1.4641')
ctx.prec = 4 # set new precision
num**4  # Decimal('1.464')
```

When we wish to draw your attention to a particular part of a code block, the relevant lines or items are set in bold:

```
from numpy import linalg

A = np.array([[3, -2, 1], [1, 1, -2], [-3, -2, 1]])
b = np.array([7, -4, 1])
```

Any command-line input or output is written as follows::

```
python3.8 -m pip install numpy scipy
```

Bold: Indicates a new term, an important word, or words that you see on screen. For example, words in menus or dialog boxes appear in the text like this. Here is an example: "Select **System info** from the **Administration** panel."

Warnings or important notes appear like this.

Tips and tricks appear like this.

Sections

In this book, you will find several headings that appear frequently (*Getting ready*, *How to do it...*, *How it works...*, *There's more...*, and *See also*).

To give clear instructions on how to complete a recipe, use these sections as follows:

Getting ready

This section tells you what to expect in the recipe and describes how to set up any software or any preliminary settings required for the recipe.

How to do it...

This section contains the steps required to follow the recipe.

How it works...

This section usually consists of a detailed explanation of what happened in the previous section.

There's more...

This section consists of additional information about the recipe in order to make you more knowledgeable about the recipe.

See also

This section provides helpful links to other useful information for the recipe.

Get in touch

Feedback from our readers is always welcome.

General feedback: If you have questions about any aspect of this book, mention the book title in the subject of your message and email us at `customercare@packtpub.com`.

Errata: Although we have taken every care to ensure the accuracy of our content, mistakes do happen. If you have found a mistake in this book, we would be grateful if you would report this to us. Please visit `www.packtpub.com/support/errata`, selecting your book, clicking on the Errata Submission Form link, and entering the details.

Piracy: If you come across any illegal copies of our works in any form on the Internet, we would be grateful if you would provide us with the location address or website name. Please contact us at `copyright@packt.com` with a link to the material.

If you are interested in becoming an author: If there is a topic that you have expertise in, and you are interested in either writing or contributing to a book, please visit `authors.packtpub.com`.

Reviews

Please leave a review. Once you have read and used this book, why not leave a review on the site that you purchased it from? Potential readers can then see and use your unbiased opinion to make purchase decisions, we at Packt can understand what you think about our products, and our authors can see your feedback on their book. Thank you!

For more information about Packt, please visit `packt.com`.

1 Basic Packages, Functions, and Concepts

Before getting started on any practical recipes, we'll use this opening chapter to introduce several core mathematical concepts and structures and their Python representations. In particular, we'll look at basic numerical types, basic mathematical functions (trigonometric functions, the exponential function, and logarithms), and matrices. Matrices are fundamental in most computational applications because of the connection between matrices and solutions of systems of linear equations. We'll explore some of these applications in this chapter, but matrices will play an important role throughout this book.

We'll cover the following main topics in this order:

- Python numerical types
- Basic mathematical functions
- NumPy arrays
- Matrices

Technical requirements

In this chapter, and throughout this book, we will use Python version 3.8, which is the most recent version of Python at the time of writing. Most of the code in this book will work on recent versions of Python from 3.6. We will use features that were introduced in Python 3.6 at various points, including f-strings. This means that you may need to change `python3.8`, which appears in any terminal commands to match your version of Python. This might be another version of Python, such as `python3.6` or `python3.7`, or a more general command such as `python3` or `python`. For the latter commands, you need to check that the version of Python is at least 3.6 by using the following command:

```
python --version
```

Python has built-in numerical types and basic mathematical functions that suffice for small applications that involve only small calculations. The NumPy package provides a high performance array type and associated routines (including basic mathematical functions that operate efficiently on arrays). This package will be used in many of the recipes in this chapter and the remainder of this book. We will also make use of the SciPy package in the latter recipes of this chapter. Both can be installed using your preferred package manager, such as `pip`:

```
python3.8 -m pip install numpy scipy
```

By convention, we import these package under a shorter alias. We import `numpy` as `np` and `scipy` as `sp` using the following `import` statements:

```
import numpy as np
import scipy as sp
```

These conventions are used in the official documentation for these packages, along with many tutorials and other materials that use these packages.

The code for this chapter can be found in the `Chapter 01` folder of the GitHub repository at `https://github.com/PacktPublishing/Applying-Math-with-Python/tree/master/Chapter%2001`.

Check out the following video to see the Code in Action: `https://bit.ly/3g3eBXv`.

Python numerical types

Python provides basic numerical types such as arbitrarily sized integers and floating-point numbers (double precision) as standard, but it also provides several additional types that are useful in specific applications where precision is especially important. Python also provides (built-in) support for complex numbers, which are useful for some more advanced mathematical applications.

Decimal type

For applications that require decimal digits with accurate arithmetic operations, use the `Decimal` type from the `decimal` module in the Python Standard Library:

```
from decimal import Decimal
num1 = Decimal('1.1')
num2 = Decimal('1.563')
num1 + num2  # Decimal('2.663')
```

Performing this calculation with float objects gives the result 2.6630000000000003, which includes a small error arising from the fact that certain numbers cannot be represented exactly using a finite sum of powers of 2. For example, 0.1 has a binary expansion 0.000110011..., which does not terminate. Any floating-point representation of this number will therefore carry a small error. Note that the argument to `Decimal` is given as a string rather than a float.

The `Decimal` type is based on the IBM General Decimal Arithmetic Specification (`http://speleotrove.com/decimal/decarith.html`), which is an alternative specification for floating-point arithmetic that represents decimal numbers exactly by using powers of 10 rather than powers of 2. This means that it can be safely used for calculations in finance where the accumulation of rounding errors would have dire consequences. However, the `Decimal` format is less memory efficient, since it must store decimal digits rather than binary digits (bits), and are more computationally expensive than traditional floating-point numbers.

The `decimal` package also provides a `Context` object, which allows fine-grained control over the precision, display, and attributes of `Decimal` objects. The current (default) context can be accessed using the `getcontext` function from the `decimal` module.
The `Context` object returned by `getcontext` has a number of attributes that can be modified. For example, we can set the precision for arithmetic operations:

```
from decimal import getcontext
ctx = getcontext()
num = Decimal('1.1')
num**4  # Decimal('1.4641')
ctx.prec = 4 # set new precision
num**4  # Decimal('1.464')
```

When we set the precision to `4`, rather than the default `28`, we see that the fourth power of 1.1 is rounded to 4 significant figures.

The context can even be set locally by using the `localcontext` function, which returns a context manager that restores the original environment at the end of the `with` block:

```
from decimal import localcontext
num = Decimal("1.1")
with localcontext() as ctx:
    ctx.prec = 2
    num**4  # Decimal('1.5')
num**4  # Decimal('1.4641')
```

This means that the context can be freely modified inside the `with` block, and will be returned to the default at the end.

Fraction type

Alternatively, for working with applications that require accurate representations of integer fractions, such as when working with proportions or probabilities, there is the `Fraction` type from the `fractions` module in the Python Standard Library. The usage is similar, except that we typically give the numerator and denominator of the fraction as arguments:

```
from fractions import Fraction
num1 = Fraction(1, 3)
num2 = Fraction(1, 7)
num1 * num2  # Fraction(1, 21)
```

The `Fraction` type simply stores two integers, the numerator and the denominator, and arithmetic is performed using the basic rules for the addition and multiplication of fractions.

Complex type

Python also has support for complex numbers, including a literal character to denote the complex unit `1j` in code. This might be different from the idiom for representing the complex unit that you are familiar with from other sources on complex numbers. Most mathematical texts will often use the symbol i to represent the complex unit:

```
z = 1 + 1j
z + 2  # 3 + 1j
z.conjugate()  # 1 - 1j
```

Special "complex number" - aware mathematical functions are provided in the `cmath` module of the Python Standard Library.

Basic mathematical functions

Basic mathematical functions appear in many applications. For example, logarithms can be used to scale data that grows exponentially to give linear data. The exponential function and trigonometric functions are common fixtures when working with geometric information, the *gamma function* appears in combinatorics, and the *Gaussian error function* is important in statistics.

The `math` module in the Python Standard Library provides all of the standard mathematical functions, along with common constants and some utility functions, and it can be imported using the following command:

```
import math
```

Once it's imported, we can use any of the mathematical functions that are contained in this module. For instance, to find the square root of a non-negative number, we would use the `sqrt` function from `math`:

```
import math
math.sqrt(4)  #  2.0
```

Attempting to use the `sqrt` function with a negative argument will raise a ValueError. The square root of a negative number is not defined for this `sqrt` function, which deals only with *real numbers*. The square root of a negative number—this will be a complex number—can be found using the alternative `sqrt` function from the `cmath` module in the Python Standard Library.

The trigonometric functions, sine, cosine, and tangent, are available under their common abbreviations `sin`, `cos`, and `tan`, respectively, in the `math` module. The `pi` constant holds the value of π, which is approximately 3.1416:

```
theta = pi/4
math.cos(theta)   # 0.7071067811865476
math.sin(theta)   # 0.7071067811865475
math.tan(theta)   # 0.9999999999999999
```

The inverse trigonometric functions are named `acos`, `asin`, and `atan` in the `math` module:

```
math.asin(-1)  # -1.5707963267948966
math.acos(-1)  # 3.141592653589793
math.atan(1)  # 0.7853981633974483
```

The `log` function in the `math` module performs logarithms. It has an optional argument to specify the base of the logarithm (note that the second argument is positional only). By default, without the optional argument, it is the *natural logarithm* with base *e*. The *e* constant can be accessed using `math.e`:

```
math.log(10) # 2.302585092994046
math.log(10, 10) # 1.0
```

The `math` module also contains the function `gamma`, which is the gamma function, and the function `erf`, the Gaussian error function, which is important in statistics. Both of these functions are defined by integrals. The gamma function is defined by the integral

$$\Gamma(s) = \int_0^\infty t^{s-1} e^{-t} \, \mathrm{d}t$$

and the error function is defined by

$$\mathrm{erf}(x) = \frac{2}{\sqrt{\pi}} \int_0^x e^{-t^2} \, \mathrm{d}t$$

The integral in the definition of the error function cannot be evaluated using calculus, and instead must be computed numerically:

```
math.gamma(5) # 24.0
math.erf(2) # 0.9953222650189527
```

In addition to standard functions such as trigonometric functions, logarithms, and exponential functions, the `math` module contains various number of theoretic and combinatorial functions. These include the functions `comb` and `factorial`, which are useful in a variety of applications. The `comb` function called with arguments n and k returns the number of ways to choose k items from a collection of n without repeats if order is not important. For example, picking 1 then 2 is the same as picking 2 then 1. This number is sometimes written ^nC_k. The factorial called with argument n returns the factorial $n! = n(n-1)(n-2)\ldots1$:

```
math.comb(5, 2)  # 10
math.factorial(5)  # 120
```

Applying the factorial to a negative number raises a `ValueError`. The factorial of an integer n, coincides with the value of the gamma function at $n + 1$; that is,

$$\Gamma(n+1) = n!$$

The `math` module also contains a function that returns the *greatest common divisor* of its arguments called `gcd`. The greatest common divisor of a and b is the largest integer k such that k divides both a and b exactly:

```
math.gcd(2, 4)  # 2
math.gcd(2, 3)  # 1
```

There are also a number of functions for working with floating-point numbers. The `fsum` function performs addition on an iterable of numbers and keeps track of the sums each step to reduce the error in the result. This is nicely illustrated by the following example:

```
nums = [0.1]*10  # list containing 0.1 ten times
sum(nums)  # 0.9999999999999999
math.fsum(nums)  # 1.0
```

The `isclose` function returns `True` if the difference between the arguments is smaller than the tolerance. This is especially useful in unit tests, where there may be small variations in results based on machine architecture or data variability.

Finally, the `floor` and `ceil` functions from `math` provide the floor and ceiling of their argument. The *floor* of a number x is the largest integer f with $f \leq x$, and the *ceiling* of x is the smallest integer c with $x \leq c$. These functions are useful when converting between a float obtained by dividing one number by another and an integer.

The `math` module contains functions that are implemented in C (assuming you are running CPython), and so are much faster than those implemented in Python. This module is a good choice if you need to apply a function to a relatively small collection of numbers. If you want to apply these functions to a large collection of data simultaneously, it is better to use their equivalents from the NumPy package, which are more efficient for working with arrays. In general, if you have imported the NumPy package already, then it is probably best to always use NumPy equivalents of these functions to limit the chance of error.

NumPy arrays

NumPy provides high performance array types and routines for manipulating these arrays in Python. These arrays are useful for processing large datasets where performance is crucial. NumPy forms the base for the numerical and scientific computing stack in Python. Under the hood, NumPy makes use of low-level libraries for working with vectors and matrices, such as the **Basic Linear Algebra Subprograms** (**BLAS**) package, and the **Linear Algebra Package** (**LAPACK**) contains more advanced routines for linear algebra.

Traditionally, the NumPy package is imported under the shorter alias `np`, which can be accomplished using the following `import` statement:

```
import numpy as np
```

In particular, this convention is used in the NumPy documentation and in the wider scientific Python ecosystem (SciPy, Pandas, and so on).

The basic type provided by the NumPy library is the `ndarray` type (henceforth referred to as a NumPy array). Generally, you won't create your own instances of this type, and will instead use one of the helper routines such as `array` to set up the type correctly. The `array` routine creates NumPy arrays from an array-like object, which is typically a list of numbers or a list of lists (of numbers). For example, we can create a simple array by providing a list with the required elements:

```
ary = np.array([1, 2, 3, 4])  # array([1, 2, 3, 4])
```

The NumPy array type (`ndarray`) is a Python wrapper around an underlying C array structure. The array operations are implemented in C and optimized for performance. NumPy arrays must consist of homogeneous data (all elements have the same type), although this type could be a pointer to an arbitrary Python object. NumPy will infer an appropriate data type during creation if one is not explicitly provided using the `dtype` keyword argument:

```
np.array([1, 2, 3, 4], dtype=np.float32)
# array([1., 2., 3., 4.], dtype=float32)
```

Under the hood, a NumPy array of any shape is a buffer containing the raw data as a flat (one-dimensional) array, and a collection of additional metadata that specifies details such as the type of the elements.

After creation, the data type can be accessed using the `dtype` attribute of the array. Modifying the `dtype` attribute will have undesirable consequences since the raw bytes that constitute the data in the array will simply be reinterpreted as the new data type. For example, if we create an array using Python integers, NumPy will convert those to 64-bit integers in the array. Changing the `dtype` value will cause NumPy to reinterpret these 64-bit integers to the new data type:

```
arr = np.array([1, 2, 3, 4])
print(arr.dtype) # dtype('int64')
arr.dtype = np.float32
print(arr)
# [1.e-45 0.e+00 3.e-45 0.e+00 4.e-45 0.e+00 6.e-45 0.e+00]
```

Each 64-bit integer has been re-interpreted as two 32-bit, floating-point numbers, which clearly gives nonsense values. Instead, if you wish to change the data type after creation, use the `astype` method to specify the new type. The correct way to change the data type is shown here:

```
arr = arr.astype(np.float32)
print(arr)
# [1. 2. 3. 4.]
```

NumPy also provides a number of routines for creating various standard arrays. The `zeros` routine creates an array, of the specified shape, in which every element is `0`, and the `ones` routine creates an array in which every element is `1`.

Element access

NumPy arrays support the `getitem` protocol, so elements in an array can be accessed as if it were a list and support all of the arithmetic operations, which are performed component-wise. This means we can use the index notation and the index to retrieve the element from the specified index as follows:

```
ary = np.array([1, 2, 3, 4])
ary[0]  # 1
ary[2]  # 3
```

This also includes the usual slice syntax for extracting an array of data from an existing array. A slice of an array is again an array, containing the elements specified by the slice. For example, we can retrieve an array containing the first two elements of `ary`, or an array containing the elements at even indexes, as follows:

```
first_two = ary[:2]  # array([1, 2])
even_idx = ary[::2]  # array([1, 3])
```

The syntax for a slice is `start:stop:step`. We can omit either, or both, of `start` and `stop` to take from the beginning or the end, respectively, of all elements. We can also omit the `step` parameter, in which case we also drop the trailing `:`. The `step` parameter describes the elements from the chosen range that should be selected. A value of `1` selects every element or, as in the recipe, a value of `2` selects every second element (starting from `0` gives even-numbered elements). This syntax is the same as for slicing Python lists.

Array arithmetic and functions

NumPy provides a number of *universal functions* (ufunc), which are routines that can operate efficiently on NumPy array types. In particular, all of the basic mathematical functions discussed in the *Basic mathematical functions* section have analogues in NumPy that can operate on NumPy arrays. Universal functions can also perform *broadcasting*, to allow them to operate on arrays of different—but compatible—shapes.

The arithmetic operations on NumPy arrays are performed component-wise. This is best illustrated by the following example:

```
arr_a = np.array([1, 2, 3, 4])
arr_b = np.array([1, 0, -3, 1])
arr_a + arr_b  # array([2, 2, 0, 5])
arr_a - arr_b  # array([0, 2, 6, 3])
arr_a * arr_b  # array([ 1, 0, -9, 4])
arr_b / arr_a  # array([ 1. , 0. , -1. , 0.25])
arr_b**arr_a  # array([1, 0, -27, 1])
```

Note that the arrays must be the same shape, which means have the same length. Using an arithmetic operation on arrays of different shapes will result in a `ValueError`. Adding, subtracting, multiplying, or dividing by a number will result in array where the operation has been applied to each component. For example, we can multiply all elements in an array by `2` by using the following command:

```
arr = np.array([1, 2, 3, 4])
new = 2*arr
print(new)
# [2, 4, 6, 8]
```

Useful array creation routines

To generate arrays of numbers at regular intervals between two given end points, you can use either the `arange` routine or the `linspace` routine. The difference between these two routines is that `linspace` generates a number (the default is 50) of values with equal spacing between the two end points, including both endpoints, while `arange` generates numbers at a given step size up to, but not including, the upper limit. The `linspace` routine generates values in the closed interval $a \leq x \leq b$ and the `arange` routine generates values in the half-open interval $a \leq x < b$:

```
np.linspace(0, 1, 5)  # array([0., 0.25, 0.5, 0.75, 1.0])
np.arange(0, 1, 0.3)  # array([0.0, 0.3, 0.6, 0.9])
```

Note that the array generated using `linspace` has exactly 5 points, specified by the third argument, including the two end points, `0` and `1`. The array generated by `arange` has 4 points, and does not include the right end point, `1`; an additional step of 0.3 would equal 1.2, which is larger than 1.

Higher dimensional arrays

NumPy can create arrays with any number of dimensions, which are created using the same `array` routine as simple one-dimensional arrays. The number of dimensions of an array is specified by the number of nested lists provided to the `array` routine. For example, we can create a two-dimensional array by providing a list of lists, where each member of the inner list is a number, such as the following:

```
mat = np.array([[1, 2], [3, 4]])
```

NumPy arrays have a `shape` attribute, which describes the arrangement of the elements in each dimension. For a two-dimensional array, the shape can be interpreted as the number of rows and the number of columns of the array.

NumPy stores the shape as the `shape` attribute on the array object, which is a tuple. The number of elements in this tuple is the number of dimensions:

```
vec = np.array([1, 2])
mat.shape  # (2, 2)
vec.shape  # (2,)
```

Since the data in a NumPy array is stored in a flat (one-dimensional) array, an array can be reshaped with little cost by simply changing the associated metadata. This is done using the `reshape` method on a NumPy array:

```
mat.reshape(4,)  # array([1, 2, 3, 4])
```

Note that the total number of elements must remain unchanged. The matrix `mat` originally has shape `(2, 2)` with a total of 4 elements, and the latter is a one-dimensional array with shape `(4,)`, which again has a total of 4 elements. Attempting to reshape when there is a mismatch in the total number of elements will result in a `ValueError`.

To create an array of higher dimensions, simply add more levels of nested lists. To make this clearer, in the following example, we separate out the lists for each element in the third dimension before we construct the array:

```
mat1 = [[1, 2], [3, 4]]
mat2 = [[5, 6], [7, 8]]
mat3 = [[9, 10], [11, 12]]
arr_3d = np.array([mat1, mat2, mat3])
arr_3d.shape  # (3, 2, 2)
```

Note that the first element of the shape is the outermost, and the last element is the innermost.

This means that adding an additional dimension to an array is a simple matter of providing the relevant metadata. Using the `array` routine, the `shape` metadata is described by the length of each list in the argument. The length of the outermost list defines the corresponding `shape` parameter for that dimension, and so on.

The size in memory of a NumPy array does not significantly depend on the number of dimensions, but only on the total number of elements, which is the product of the `shape` parameters. However, note that th e total number of elements tends to be larger in higher dimensional arrays.

To access an element in a multi-dimensional array, you use the usual index notation, but rather than providing a single number, you need to provide the index in each dimension. For a 2 × 2 matrix, this means specifying the row and column for the desired element:

```
mat[0, 0]  # 1 - top left element
mat[1, 1]  # 4 - bottom right element
```

The index notation also supports slicing in each dimension, so we can extract all members of a single column by using the slice `mat[:, 0]` like so:

```
mat[:, 0]
# array([1, 3])
```

Note that the result of the slice is a one-dimensional array.

The array creation functions, `zeros` and `ones`, can create multi-dimensional arrays by simply specifying a shape with more than one dimension parameter.

Matrices

NumPy arrays also serve as *matrices*, which are fundamental in mathematics and computational programming. A *matrix* is simply a two-dimensional array. Matrices are central in many applications, such as geometric transformations and simultaneous equations, but also appear as useful tools in other areas such a statistics. Matrices themselves are only distinctive (compared to any other array) once we equip them with *matrix arithmetic*. Matrices have element-wise addition and subtraction operations, just as for NumPy arrays, a third operation called *scalar multiplication*, where we multiply every element of the matrix by a constant number, and a different notion of *matrix multiplication*. Matrix multiplication is fundamentally different from other notions of multiplication, as we will see later.

One of the most important attributes of a matrix is its shape, defined exactly as for NumPy arrays. A matrix with m rows and n columns is usually described as an $m \times n$ matrix. A matrix that has the same number of rows as columns is said to be a *square* matrix, and these matrices play a special role in the theory of vectors and matrices.

The *identity matrix* (of size n) is the $n \times n$ matrix where the (i, i)-th entry is 1, and the (i, j)-th entry is zero for $i \neq j$. There is an array creation routine that gives an $n \times n$ identity matrix for a specified n value:

```
np.eye(3)
# array([[1., 0., 0.],
#        [0., 1., 0.],
#        [0., 0., 1.]])
```

Basic methods and properties

There are a large number of terms and quantities associated with matrices. We only mention two such properties here, since they will be useful later. These are the *transpose* of a matrix, where rows and columns are interchanged, and the *trace* of a square matrix, which is the sum of the elements along the *leading diagonal*. The leading diagonal consists of the elements a_{ii} along the line from the top left of the matrix to the bottom right.

NumPy arrays can be easily transposed by calling the `transpose` method on the `array` object. In fact, since this is such a common operation, arrays have a convenience property `T` that returns the transpose of the matrix. The transposition reverses the order of the shape of a matrix (array), so that rows become columns and columns become rows. For example, if we start with a 3×2 matrix (3 rows, 2 columns), then its transpose will be a 2×3 matrix, such as in the following example:

```
mat = np.array([[1, 2], [3, 4]])
mat.transpose()
# array([[1, 3],
#        [2, 4]])
mat.T
# array([[1, 3],
#        [2, 4]])
```

Another quantity associated with matrices that is occasionally useful is the *trace*. The trace of a square matrix A, with entries as in the preceding code, is defined to be the sum of the elements along the leading diagonal, which consists of the elements starting from the top left diagonally to the bottom right. The formula for the trace is given as

$$\mathrm{trace}(A) = \sum_{i=1}^{n} a_{i,i}$$

NumPy arrays have a `trace` method that returns the trace of a matrix:

```
A = np.array([[1, 2], [3, 4]])
A.trace()  # 5
```

The trace can also be accessed using the `np.trace` function, which is not bound to the array.

Matrix multiplication

Matrix multiplication is an operation performed on two matrices, which preserves some of the structure and character of both matrices. Formally, if A is an $l \times m$ matrix, and B is an $m \times n$ matrix, say

$$A = \begin{pmatrix} a_{1,1} & a_{1,2} & \cdots & a_{1,m} \\ a_{2,1} & a_{2,2} & \cdots & a_{2,m} \\ \vdots & \vdots & \ddots & \vdots \\ a_{l,1} & a_{l,2} & \cdots & a_{l,m} \end{pmatrix} \text{ and } B = \begin{pmatrix} b_{1,1} & b_{1,2} & \cdots & b_{1,n} \\ b_{2,1} & b_{2,2} & \cdots & b_{2,n} \\ \vdots & \vdots & \ddots & \vdots \\ b_{m,1} & b_{m,2} & \cdots & b_{m,n} \end{pmatrix}$$

then the matrix product C of A and B is an $l \times n$ matrix whose (p, q)-th entry is given by

$$c_{p,q} = \sum_{i=1}^{m} a_{p,i} b_{i,q}$$

Note that the number of columns of the first matrix **must** match the number of rows of the second matrix in order for matrix multiplication to be defined. We usually write AB for the matrix product of A and B, if it is defined. Matrix multiplication is a peculiar operation. It is not *commutative* like most other arithmetic operations: even if AB and BA can both be computed, there is no need for them to be equal. In practice, this means that the order of multiplication matters for matrices. This arises from the origins of matrix algebras as representations of linear maps, where multiplication corresponds to the composition of functions.

Python has an operator reserved for matrix multiplication `@`, which was added in Python 3.5. NumPy arrays implement the operator to perform matrix multiplication. Note that this is fundamentally different from the component-wise multiplication of arrays `*`:

```
A = np.array([[1, 2], [3, 4]])
B = np.array([[-1, 1], [0, 1]])
A @ B
# array([[-1, 3],
#        [-3, 7]])
A * B # different from A @ B
# array([[-1, 2],
#        [ 0, 4]])
```

The identity matrix is a *neutral element* under matrix multiplication. That is, if A is any $l \times m$ matrix, and I is the $m \times m$ identity matrix, then $AI = A$. This can be easily checked for specific examples using NumPy arrays:

```
A = np.array([[1, 2], [3, 4]])
I = np.eye(2)
A @ I
# array([[1, 2],
#        [3, 4]])
```

Determinants and inverses

The *determinant* of a square matrix is important in most applications because of its strong link with finding the inverse of a matrix. A matrix is *square* if the number of rows and columns are equal. In particular, a matrix that has a non-zero determinant has a (unique) inverse, which translates to unique solutions of certain systems of equations. The determinant of a matrix is defined recursively. For a 2 × 2 matrix

$$A = \begin{pmatrix} a_{1,1} & a_{1,2} \\ a_{2,1} & a_{2,2} \end{pmatrix}$$

the *determinant* of A is defined by the formula

$$\det A = a_{1,1}a_{2,2} - a_{1,2}a_{2,1}$$

For a general $n \times n$ matrix

$$A = \begin{pmatrix} a_{1,1} & a_{1,2} & \cdots & a_{1,n} \\ a_{2,1} & a_{2,2} & \cdots & a_{2,n} \\ \vdots & \vdots & \ddots & \vdots \\ a_{n,1} & a_{n,2} & \cdots & a_{n,n} \end{pmatrix}$$

where $n > 2$, we define the submatrix $A_{i,j}$ for $1 \leq i, j \leq n$, to be the result of deleting the ith row and jth column from A. The submatrix $A_{i,j}$ is an $(n-1) \times (n-1)$ matrix, and so we can compute the determinant. We then define the determinant of A to be the quantity

$$\det A = \sum_{j=1}^{n} (-1)^{1+j} a_{1,j} \det A_{1,j}$$

In fact, the index 1 that appears in the preceding equation can be replaced by any $1 \leq i \leq n$ and the result will be the same.

The NumPy routine for computing the determinant of a matrix is contained in a separate module called `linalg`. This module contains many common routines for *linear algebra,* which is the branch of mathematics that covers vector and matrix algebra. The routine for computing the determinant of a square matrix is the `det` routine:

```
from numpy import linalg
linalg.det(A)   # -2.0000000000000004
```

Note that a floating-point rounding error has occurred in the calculation of the determinant.

The SciPy package, if installed, also offers a `linalg` module that extends NumPy's `linalg`. The SciPy version not only includes additional routines, but it is also always compiled with BLAS and LAPACK support, while for the NumPy version, this is optional. Thus, the SciPy variant may be preferable, depending on how NumPy was compiled, if speed is important.

The *inverse* of an $n \times n$ matrix A is the (necessarily unique) $n \times n$ matrix B, such that $AB = BA = I$, where I denotes the $n \times n$ identity matrix and the multiplication performed here is matrix multiplication. Not every square matrix has an inverse; those that do not are sometimes called *singular* matrices. In fact, a matrix is non-singular (that is, has an inverse) if, and only if, the determinant of that matrix is not 0. When A has an inverse, it is customary to denote it by A^{-1}.

The `inv` routine from the `linalg` module computes the inverse of a matrix, if it exists:

```
linalg.inv(A)
# array([[-2. , 1. ],
#        [ 1.5, -0.5]])
```

We can check that the matrix given by the `inv` routine is indeed the matrix inverse of `A` by matrix multiplying (on either side) by the inverse and checking that we get the 2×2 identity matrix:

```
Ainv = linalg.inv(A)
Ainv @ A
# Approximately
# array([[1., 0.],
#        [0., 1.]])
A @ Ainv
# Approximately
# array([[1., 0.],
#        [0., 1.]])
```

There will be a floating-point error in these computations, which has been hidden away behind the `Approximately` comment, due to the way that matrix inverses are computed.

The `linalg` package also contains a number of other methods such as `norm`, which computes various norms of a matrix. It also contains functions for decomposing matrices in various ways and solving systems of equations.

There are also the matrix analogues of the exponential function `expm`, the logarithm `logm`, sine `sinm`, cosine `cosm`, and tangent `tanm`. Note that these functions are not the same as the standard `exp`, `log`, `sin`, `cos`, and `tan` functions in the base NumPy package, which apply the corresponding function on an element by element basis. In contrast, the matrix exponential function is defined using a "power series" of matrices

$$\exp(A) = \sum_{k=0}^{\infty} \frac{A^k}{k!}$$

where A is an $n \times n$ matrix and A^k is the kth *matrix power* of A; that is, the A matrix multiplied by itself k times. Note that this "power series" always converges in an appropriate sense. By convention, we take $A^0 = I$, where I is the $n \times n$ identity matrix. This is completely analogous to the usual power series definition of the exponential function for real or complex numbers, but with matrices and matrix multiplication in place of numbers and (regular) multiplication. The other functions are defined in a similar fashion, but we will skip the details.

Systems of equations

Solving systems of (linear) equations is one of the main motivations for studying matrices in mathematics. Problems of this type occur frequently in a variety of applications. We start with a system of linear equations written as

$$\begin{aligned} a_{1,1}x_1 + a_{1,2}x_2 + \cdots + a_{1,n}x_n &= b_1 \\ a_{2,1}x_1 + a_{2,2}x_2 + \cdots + a_{2,n}x_n &= b_2 \\ &\vdots \\ a_{n,1}x_1 + a_{n,2}x_2 + \cdots + a_{n,n}x_n &= b_n \end{aligned}$$

where n is at least two, $a_{i,j}$ and b_i are known values, and the x_i values are the unknown values that we wish to find.

Before we can solve such a system of equations, we need to convert the problem into a matrix equation. This is achieved by collecting together the coefficients $a_{i,j}$ into an $n \times n$ matrix and using the properties of matrix multiplication to relate this matrix to the system of equations. So, let

$$A = \begin{pmatrix} a_{1,1} & a_{1,2} & \cdots & a_{1,n} \\ a_{2,1} & a_{2,2} & \cdots & a_{2,n} \\ \vdots & \vdots & \ddots & \vdots \\ a_{n,1} & a_{n,2} & \cdots & a_{n,n} \end{pmatrix}$$

be the matrix containing the coefficients taken from the equations. Then, if we take $\mathbf{x}$ to be the unknown (column) vector containing the x_i values and $\mathbf{b}$ to be the (column) vector containing the known values b_i, then we can rewrite the system of equations as the single matrix equation

$$A\mathbf{x} = \mathbf{b}$$

which we can now solve using matrix techniques. In this situation, we view a column vector as an $n \times 1$ matrix, so the multiplication in the preceding equation is matrix multiplication. To solve this matrix equation, we use the `solve` routine in the `linalg` module. To illustrate the technique, we will solve the following system of equations as an example:

$$\begin{aligned} 3x_1 - 2x_2 + x_3 &= 7 \\ x_1 + x_2 - 2x_3 &= -4 \\ -3x_1 - 2x_2 + x_3 &= 1 \end{aligned}$$

These equations have three unknown values, x_1, x_2, and x_3. First, we create the matrix of coefficients and the vector **b**. Since we are using NumPy as our means of working with matrices and vectors, we create a two-dimensional NumPy array for the matrix A and a one-dimensional array for **b**:

```
import numpy as np
from numpy import linalg

A = np.array([[3, -2, 1], [1, 1, -2], [-3, -2, 1]])
b = np.array([7, -4, 1])
```

Now, the solution to the system of equations can be found using the `solve` routine:

```
linalg.solve(A, b)  # array([ 1., -1., 2.])
```

This is indeed the solution to the system of equations, which can be easily verified by computing `A @ x` and checking the result against the `b` array. There may be a floating-point rounding error in this computation.

The `solve` function expects two inputs, which are the matrix of coefficients A and the right-hand side vector **b**. It solves the system of equations using LAPACK routines that decompose matrix A into simpler matrices to quickly reduce to an easier problem that can be solved by simple substitution. This technique for solving matrix equations is extremely powerful and efficient, and is less prone to the floating-point rounding errors that dog some other methods. For instance, the solution to a system of equations could be computed by multiplying (on the left) by the inverse of the matrix A, if the inverse is known. However, this is generally not as good as using the `solve` routine since it may be slower or result in larger numerical errors.

In the example we used, the coefficient matrix A was square. That is, there are the same number of equations as there are unknown values. In this case, the system of equations has a unique solution if (and only if) the determinant of this matrix A is not 0. In cases where the determinant of A is 0, one of two things can happen: the system can have no solution, in which case we say that the system is *inconsistent*; or there can be infinitely many solutions. The difference between a consistent and inconsistent system is usually determined by the vector **b**. For example, consider the following systems of equations:

$$\begin{aligned} x + y &= 2 \\ x + y &= 2 \end{aligned} \qquad \begin{aligned} x + y &= 1 \\ x + y &= 2 \end{aligned}$$

The left-hand system of equations is consistent and has infinitely many solutions; for instance, taking $x = 1$ and $y = 1$ or $x = 0$ and $y = 2$ are both solutions. The right-hand system of equations is inconsistent, and there are no solutions. In both of the above, the `solve` routine will fail because the coefficient matrix is singular.

The coefficient matrix does not need to be square for the system to be solvable. For example, if there are more equations than there are unknown values (a coefficient matrix has more rows than columns). Such a system is said to be *over-specified* and, provided that it is consistent, it will have a solution. If there are fewer equations than there are unknown values, then the system is said to be *under-specified.* Under-specified systems of equations generally have infinitely many solutions if they are consistent, since there is not enough information to uniquely specify all the unknown values. Unfortunately, the `solve` routine will not be able to find solutions for systems where the coefficient matrix is not square, even if the system does have a solution.

Eigenvalues and eigenvectors

Consider the matrix equation $A\mathbf{x} = \lambda\mathbf{x}$, where A is a square ($n \times n$) matrix, $\mathbf{x}$ is a vector, and λ is a number. Numbers λ for which there is an $\mathbf{x}$ that solves this equation are called *eigenvalues*, and the corresponding vectors $\mathbf{x}$ are called *eigenvectors*. Pairs of eigenvalues and corresponding eigenvectors encode information about the matrix A, and are therefore important in many applications where matrices appear.

We will demonstrate computing eigenvalues and eigenvectors using the following matrix:

$$A = \begin{pmatrix} 3 & -1 & 4 \\ -1 & 0 & -1 \\ 4 & -1 & 2 \end{pmatrix}$$

We must first define this as a NumPy array:

```
import numpy as np
from numpy import linalg
A = np.array([[3, -1, 4], [-1, 0, -1], [4, -1, 2]])
```

The `eig` routine in the `linalg` module is used to find the eigenvalues and eigenvectors of a square matrix. This routine returns a pair `(v, B)` where `v` is a one-dimensional array containing the eigenvalues and `B` is a two-dimensional array whose columns are the corresponding eigenvectors:

```
v, B = linalg.eig(A)
```

It is perfectly possible for a matrix with only real entries to have complex eigenvalues and eigenvectors. For this reason, the return type of the `eig` routine will sometimes be a complex number type such as `complex32` or `complex64`. In some applications, complex eigenvalues have a special meaning, while in others we only consider the real eigenvalues.

We can extract an eigenvalue/eigenvector pair from the output of `eig` using the following sequence:

```
i = 0 # first eigenvalue/eigenvector pair
lambda0 = v[i]
print(lambda0)
# 6.823156164525971
x0 = B[:, i] # ith column of B
print(x0)
# array([ 0.73271846, -0.20260301, 0.649672352])
```

The eigenvectors returned by the `eig` routine are *normalized* so that they have norm (length) 1. (The *Euclidean norm* is defined to be the square root of the sum of the squares of the members of the array.) We can check that this is the case by evaluating in the norm of the vector using the `norm` routine from `linalg`:

```
linalg.norm(x0)  # 1.0  - eigenvectors are normalized.
```

Finally, we can check that these values do indeed satisfy the definition of an eigenvalue/eigenvector pair by computing the product `A @ x0` and checking that, up to floating-point precision, this is equal to `lambda0*x0`:

```
lhs = A @ x0
rhs = lambda0*x0
linalg.norm(lhs - rhs)  # 2.8435583831733384e-15 - very small.
```

The norm computed here represents the "distance" between the left-hand side `lhs` and the right-hand side `rhs` of the equation $A\mathbf{x} = \lambda\mathbf{x}$. Since this distance is extremely small (0 to 14 decimal places), we can be fairly confident that they are actually the same. The fact that this is not zero is likely due to floating-point precision error.

The `eig` routine is a wrapper around the low-level LAPACK routines for computing eigenvalues and eigenvectors. The theoretical procedure for finding eigenvalues and eigenvectors is to first find the eigenvalues by solving the equation

$$\det(A - \lambda I) = 0$$

where I is the appropriate identity matrix, to find the values λ. The equation determined by the left-hand side is a polynomial in λ and is called the *characteristic polynomial* of A. The corresponding eigenvectors can then be found by solving the matrix equation

$$(A - \lambda_j I)\mathbf{x} = \mathbf{0}$$

where λ_j is one of the eigenvalues already found. In practice, this process is somewhat inefficient, and there are alternative strategies for computing eigenvalues and eigenvectors numerically more efficiently.

One key application of eigenvalues and eigenvectors is in *principal component analysis*, which is a key technique for reducing a large, complex dataset to better understand the internal structure.

We can only compute eigenvalues and eigenvectors for square matrices; for non-square matrices, the definition does not make sense. There is a generalization of eigenvalues and eigenvalues to non-square matrices called *singular values*.

Sparse matrices

Systems of linear equations such as those discussed earlier are extremely common throughout mathematics and, in particular, in mathematical computing. In many applications, the coefficient matrix will be extremely large, with thousands of rows and columns, and will likely be obtained from an alternative source rather than simply entering by hand. In many cases, it will also be a *sparse* matrix, where most of the entries are 0.

A matrix is *sparse* if a large number of the elements are zero. The exact number of elements that need to be zero in order to call a matrix sparse is not well defined. Sparse matrices can be represented more efficiently, for example, by simply storing the indexes (i, j) and the values $a_{i,j}$ that are non-zero. There are entire collections of algorithms for sparse matrices that offer great improvements in performance, assuming the matrix is indeed sufficiently sparse.

Sparse matrices appear in many applications, and often follow some kind of pattern. In particular, several techniques for solving **partial differential equations** (**PDEs**) involve solving sparse matrix equations (see `Chapter 3`, *Calculus and Differential Equations)*, and matrices associated with networks are often sparse. There are additional routines for sparse matrices associated with networks (graphs) contained in the `sparse.csgraph` module. We will discuss these further in `Chapter 5`, *Working with Trees and Networks*.

The `sparse` module contains several different classes representing the different means of storing a sparse matrix. The most basic means of storing a sparse matrix is to store three arrays, two containing integers representing the indices of non zero elements, and the third the data of the corresponding element. This is the format of the `coo_matrix` class. Then there are the compressed column CSC (`csc_matrix`) and the compressed row CSR (`csr_matrix`) formats, which provide efficient column or row slicing, respectively. There are three additional sparse matrix classes in `sparse`, including `dia_matrix`, which efficiently stores matrices where the non-zero entries appear along a diagonal band.

The `sparse` module from SciPy contains routines for creating and working with sparse matrices. We import the `sparse` module from SciPy using the following `import` statement:

```
import numpy as np
from scipy import sparse
```

A sparse matrix can be created from a full (dense) matrix, or some other kind of data structure. This is done using the constructor for the specific format in which you wish to store the sparse matrix.

For example, we can take a dense matrix and store it in CSR format by using the following command:

```
A = np.array([[1., 0., 0.], [0., 1., 0.], [0., 0., 1.]])
sp_A = sparse.csr_matrix(A)
```

If you are generating a sparse matrix by hand, the matrix probably follows some kind of pattern, such as the following *tridiagonal* matrix:

$$T = \begin{pmatrix} 2 & -1 & 0 & 0 & 0 \\ -1 & 2 & -1 & 0 & 0 \\ 0 & -1 & 2 & -1 & 0 \\ 0 & 0 & -1 & 2 & -1 \\ 0 & 0 & 0 & -1 & 2 \end{pmatrix}$$

Here, the non-zero entries appear on the diagonal and on either side of the diagonal, and the non-zero entries in each row follow the same pattern. To create such a matrix, we could use one of the array creation routines in `sparse` such as `diags`, which is a convenience routine for creating matrices with diagonal patterns:

```
T = sparse.diags([-1, 2, -1], (-1, 0, 1), shape=(5, 5), format="csr")
```

This will create the matrix T as described previously and store it as a sparse matrix in compressed sparse row CSR format. The first argument specifies the values that should appear in the output matrix, and the second argument is the positions relative to the diagonal position in which the values should be placed. So the 0 index in the tuple represents the diagonal entry, -1 is to the left of the diagonal in the row, and +1 is to the right of the diagonal in the row. The `shape` keyword argument gives the dimensions of the matrix produced, and the `format` specifies the storage format for the matrix. If no format is provided using the optional argument, then a reasonable default will be used. The array `T` can be expanded to a full (*dense*) matrix using the `toarray` method:

```
T.toarray()
# array([[ 2, -1,  0,  0,  0],
#        [-1,  2, -1,  0,  0],
#        [ 0, -1,  2, -1,  0],
#        [ 0,  0, -1,  2, -1],
#        [ 0,  0,  0, -1,  2]])
```

When the matrix is small (as it is here), there is little difference in performance between the sparse solving routine and the usual solving routines.

Once a matrix is stored in a sparse format, we can use the sparse solving routines in the `linalg` submodule of `sparse`. For example, we can solve a matrix equation using the `spsolve` routine from this module. The `spsolve` routine will convert the matrix into CSR or CSC, which may add additional time to the computation if it is not provided in one of these formats:

```
from scipy.sparse import linalg
linalg.spsolve(T.tocsr(), np.array([1, 2, 3, 4, 5]))
# array([ 5.83333333, 10.66666667, 13.5 , 13.33333333, 9.16666667])
```

The `sparse.linalg` module also contains many of the routines that can be found in the `linalg` module of NumPy (or SciPy) that accept sparse matrices instead of full NumPy arrays, such as `eig` and `inv`.

Summary

Python offers built-in support for mathematics with some basic numerical types, arithmetic, and basic mathematical functions. However, for more serious computations involving large arrays of numerical values, you should use the NumPy and SciPy packages. NumPy provides high-performance array types and basic routines, while SciPy provides more specific tools for solving equations and working with sparse matrices (among many other things).

NumPy arrays can be multi-dimensional. In particular, two-dimensional arrays have matrix properties that can be accessed using the `linalg` module from either NumPy or SciPy (the former is a subset of the latter). Moreover, there is a special operator in Python for matrix multiplication, `@`, which is implemented for NumPy arrays.

In the next chapter, we'll get started looking at some recipes.

Further reading

There are many mathematical textbooks describing the basic properties of matrices and linear algebra, which is the study of vectors and matrices. A good introductory text is *Blyth, T. and Robertson, E. (2013). Basic Linear Algebra. London: Springer London, Limited.*

NumPy and SciPy are part of the Python mathematical and scientific computing ecosystem, and have extensive documentation that can be accessed from the official website, `https://scipy.org`. We will see several other packages from this ecosystem throughout this book.

More information about the BLAS and LAPACK libraries that NumPy and SciPy use behind the scenes can be found at the following links: BLAS: `https://www.netlib.org/blas/` and LAPACK: `https://www.netlib.org/lapack/`.

2
Mathematical Plotting with Matplotlib

Plotting is a fundamental tool in all of mathematics. A good plot can reveal hidden details, suggest future directions, verify results, or reinforce an argument. It is no surprise, then, that the scientific Python stack features a powerful and flexible plotting library called Matplotlib.

In this chapter, we will plot functions and data in a variety of styles and create figures that are fully labeled and annotated. We will create three-dimensional plots, customize the appearance of figures, create figures that contain multiple plots using subplots, and save figures directly to files for applications that are not running in an interactive environment.

In this chapter, we will cover the following recipes:

- Basic plotting with Matplotlib
- Changing the plotting style
- Adding labels and legends to plots
- Adding subplots
- Saving Matplotlib figures
- Surface and contour plots
- Customizing three-dimensional plots

Technical requirements

The main plotting package for Python is Matplotlib, which can be installed using your favorite package manager, such as `pip`:

```
python3.8 -m pip install matplotlib
```

This will install the most recent version of Matplotlib, which, at the time of writing this book, is version 3.2.1.

Matplotlib contains numerous sub-packages, but the main user interface is the `matplotlib.pyplot` package, which, by convention, is imported under the `plt` alias. This is achieved using the following import statement:

```
import matplotlib.pyplot as plt
```

Many of the recipes in this chapter also require NumPy, which, as usual, is imported under the `np` alias.

The code for this chapter can be found in the `Chapter 02` folder of the GitHub repository at `https://github.com/PacktPublishing/Applying-Math-with-Python/tree/master/Chapter%2002`.

Check out the following video to see the Code in Action: `https://bit.ly/2ZOSuhs`.

Basic plotting with Matplotlib

Plotting is an important part of understanding behavior. So much can be learned by simply plotting a function or data that would otherwise be hidden. In this recipe, we will walk through how to plot a simple function or data using Matplotlib.

Matplotlib is a very powerful plotting library, which means it can be rather intimidating to perform simple tasks with it. For users who are used to working with MATLAB and other mathematical software packages, there is a state-based interface called `pyplot`. There is also an object-orientated interface, which might be more appropriate for more complex plots. The `pyplot` interface is a convenient way to create basic objects.

Getting ready

Most commonly, the data that you wish to plot will be stored in two separate NumPy arrays, which we will label `x` and `y` for clarity (although this naming does not matter in practice). We will demonstrate plotting the graph of a function, so we will generate an array of `x` values and use the function to generate the corresponding `y` values. We define the function that we will plot as follows:

```
def f(x):
    return x*(x - 2)*np.exp(3 - x)
```

How to do it...

Before we can plot the function, we must generate the `x` and `y` data to be plotted. If you are plotting existing data, you can skip these commands. We need to create a set of the `x` values that cover the desired range, and then use the function to create the `y` values:

1. The `linspace` routine from NumPy is ideal for creating arrays of numbers for plotting. By default, it will create 50 equally spaced points between the specified arguments. The number of points can be customized by providing an additional argument, but 50 is sufficient for most cases:

   ```
   x = np.linspace(-0.5, 3.0)  # 100 values between -0.5 and 3.0
   ```

2. Once we have created the `x` values, we can generate the `y` values:

   ```
   y = f(x)  # evaluate f on the x points
   ```

3. To plot the data, we simply need to call the `plot` function from the `pyplot` interface, which is imported under the `plt` alias. The first argument is the `x` data and the second is the `y` data. The function returns a handle to the axes object on which the data is plotted:

   ```
   plt.plot(x, y)
   ```

4. This will plot the `y` values against the `x` values on a new figure. If you are working within IPython or with a Jupyter notebook, then the plot should automatically appear at this point; otherwise, you might need to call the `plt.show` function to make the plot appear:

   ```
   plt.show()
   ```

If you use `plt.show`, the figure should appear in a new window. The resulting plot should look something like the plot in *Figure 2.1*. The default plot color might be different on your plot. It has been changed for high visibility for this book:

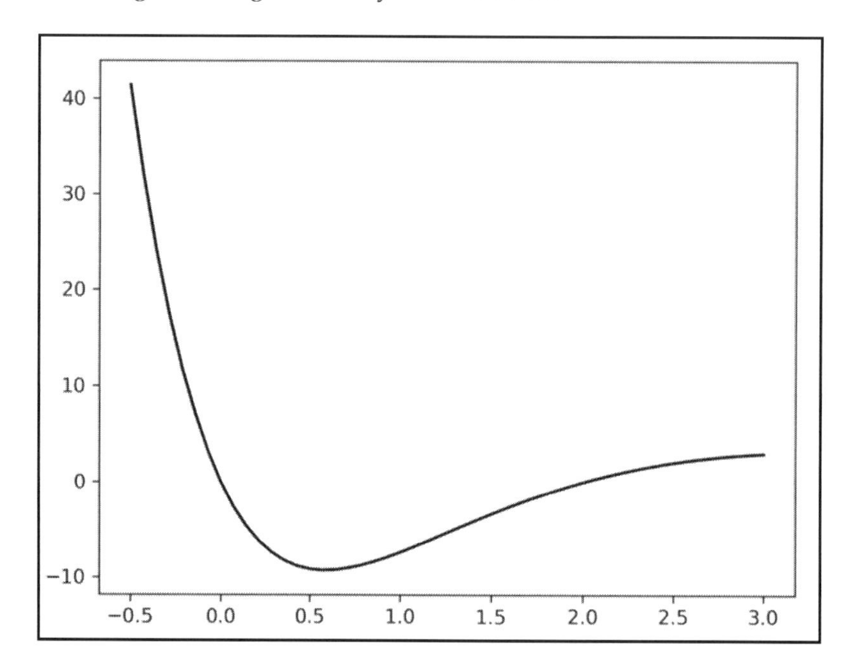

Figure 2.1: Plot of a function produced using Matplotlib without any additional styling parameters

We won't add this command to any further recipes in this chapter, but you should be aware that you will need to use it if you are not working in an environment where plots will be rendered automatically, such as an IPython console or Jupyter Notebook.

How it works...

If there are currently no `Figure` or `Axes` objects, the `plt.plot` routine creates a new `Figure` object, adds a new `Axes` object to the figure, and populates this `Axes` object with the plotted data. A list of handles to the plotted lines is returned. Each of these handles is a `Lines2D` object. In this case, this list will contain a single `Lines2D` object. We can use this `Lines2D` object to customize the appearance of the line later (see the *Changing the plotting style* recipe).

The object layer of Matplotlib interacts with a lower-level *backend*, which does the heavy lifting of producing the graphical plot. The `plt.show` function issues an instruction to the backend to render the current figure. There are a number of backends that can be used with Matplotlib, which can be customized by setting the `MPLBACKEND` environment variable, modifying the `matplotlibrc` file, or by calling `matplotlib.use` from within Python with the name of an alternative backend.

The `plt.show` function does more than simply call the `show` method on a figure. It also hooks into an event loop to correctly display the figure. The `plt.show` routine should be used to display a figure, rather than the `show` method on a `Figure` object.

There's more...

It is sometimes useful to manually instantiate a `Figure` object prior to calling the `plot` routine—for instance, to force the creation of a new figure. The code in this recipe could instead have been written as follows:

```
fig = plt.figure()  # manually create a figure
lines = plt.plot(x, y)  # plot data
```

The `plt.plot` routine accepts a variable number of positional inputs. In the preceding code, we supplied two positional arguments that were interpreted as `x` values and `y` values (in that order). If we had instead provided only a single array, the `plot` routine would have plotted the values against their position in the array; that is, the `x` values are taken to be `0`, `1`, `2`, and so on. We could also supply multiple pairs of arrays to plot several sets of data on the same axes:

```
x = np.linspace(-0.5, 3.0)
lines = plt.plot(x, f(x), x, x**2, x, 1 - x)
```

The output of the preceding code is as follows:

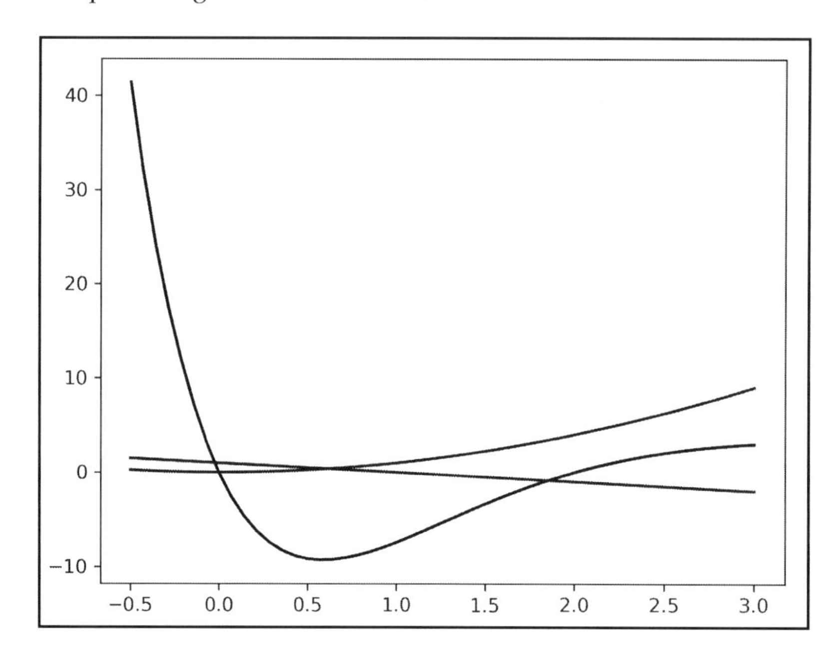

Figure 2.2: Multiple plots on a single figure, produced using a single call to the plot routine in Matplotlib

It is occasionally useful to create a new figure and explicitly create a new set of axes in this figure together. The best way to accomplish this is to use the `subplots` routine in the `pyplot` interface (refer to the *Adding subplots* recipe). This routine returns a pair, where the first object is `Figure` and the second is an `Axes` object:

```
fig, ax = plt.subplots()
l1 = ax.plot(x, f(x))
l2 = ax.plot(x, x**2)
l3 = ax.plot(x, 1 - x)
```

This sequence of commands produces the same plot as the preceding one displayed in *Figure 2.2*.

Matplotlib has many other plotting routines besides the `plot` routine described here. For example, there are plotting methods that use a different scale for the axes, including the logarithmic x or y axes separately (`semilogx` or `semilogy`, respectively) or together (`loglog`). These are explained in the Matplotlib documentation.

Changing the plotting style

The basic style of Matplotlib plots is fine for plotting functions or data that is ordered, but it is less appropriate for plotting discrete data that is not presented in any order. To prevent Matplotlib from drawing lines between each data point, we can change the plotting style to "turn off" the line drawing. In this recipe, we will customize the plotting style for each line on the axes by adding a format string argument to the `plot` method.

Getting ready

You will need to have your data stored in pairs of arrays. For the purposes of this demonstration, we will define the following data:

```
y1 = np.array([1.0, 2.0, 3.0, 4.0, 5.0])
y2 = np.array([1.2, 1.6, 3.1, 4.2, 4.8])
y3 = np.array([3.2, 1.1, 2.0, 4.9, 2.5])
```

We will plot these points against their position in the array (that is, the *x* coordinate will be `0`, `1`, `2`, `3`, or `4`, respectively, for each array).

How to do it...

The easiest way to control the style of a plot is to use a **format string**, which is provided as an optional argument after the *x*-*y* pair or the `y` data in the `plot` command. When plotting multiple sets of data, a different format string can be provided for each set of arguments. The following steps give a general procedure for creating a new figure and plotting data on this figure:

1. We first create the `Figure` and `Axes` objects explicitly using the `subplots` routine from `pyplot`:

   ```
   fig, ax = plt.subplots()
   ```

2. Now that we have created the `Figure` and `Axes` objects, we can plot the data using the `plot` method on the `Axes` object. This method takes the same arguments as the `plot` routine from `pyplot`:

   ```
   lines = ax.plot(y1, 'o', y2, 'x', y3, '*')
   ```

This plots the first dataset (`y1`) with a circle marker, the second (`y2`) with an `x` marker, and the third (`y3`) with a star (`*`) marker. The output of this command is shown in *Figure 2.3*. The format string can specify a number of different marker lines and color styles. The same applies if we instead used the plot routine from the `pyplot` interface, which has the same calling signature as the `plot` method:

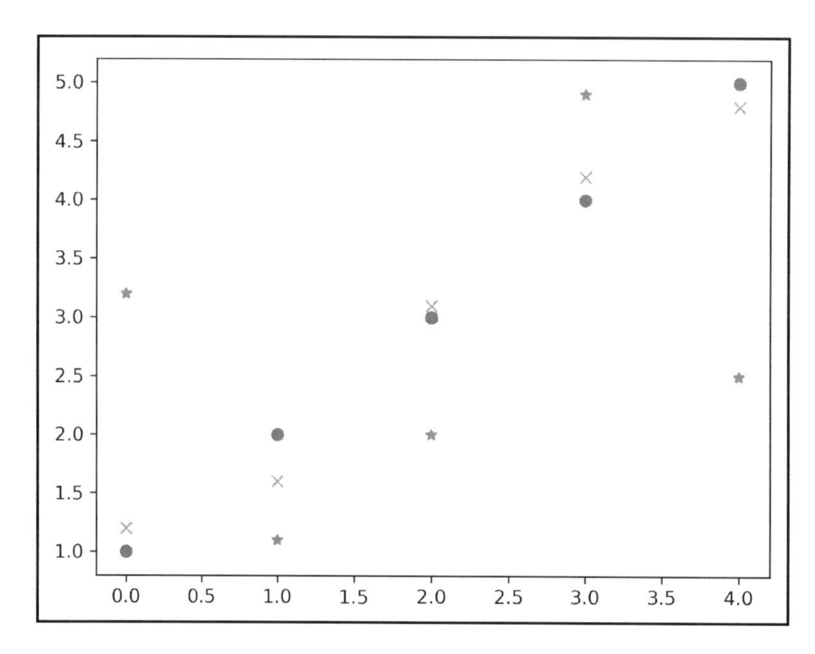

Figure 2.3: Plot of three sets of data, each plotted using a different marker style

How it works...

The format string has three optional parts, each consisting of one or more characters. The first part controls the marker style, which is the symbol that is printed at each data point; the second controls the style of the line that connects the data points; and the third controls the color of the plot. In this recipe, we only specified the marker style, which means that no connecting line is drawn between adjacent data points. This is useful for plotting discrete data where no interpolation between points is necessary. Four line style parameters are available: a solid line (`-`); a dashed line (`--`); a dash-dot line (`-.`); or a dotted line (`:`). Only a limited number of colors can be specified in the format string; they are red, green, blue, cyan, yellow, magenta, black, and white. The character used in the format string is the first letter of each color (with the exception of black), so the corresponding characters are `r`, `g`, `b`, `c`, `y`, `m`, `k`, and `w`, respectively.

For example, if we want to change the marker style only, as we did in this recipe, to a plus character, we would use the `"+"` format string. If we also want to change the line style to a dash-dot line, we would use the `"+-."` format string. Finally, if we also wish to change the color of the marker to red, we would use the `"+-.r"` format string. These specifiers can also be provided in other configurations, such as specifying the color before the marker style, but this might lead to ambiguities in the way Matplotlib parses the format string.

If you are using a Jupyter notebook and the `subplots` command, you must include the call to `subplots` within the same cell as the plotting commands or the figure will not be produced.

There's more...

The `plot` method also accepts a number of keyword arguments that can also be used to control the style of a plot. Keyword arguments take precedence over format string parameters if both are present, and they apply to all sets of data plotted by the call. The keyword to control the marker style is `marker`, the keyword for the line style is `linestyle`, and the keyword for color is `color`. The `color` keyword argument accepts a number of different formats to specify a color, which includes RGB values as a `(r, g, b)` tuple, where each character is a float between `0` and `1` or is a hex string. The width of the line plotted can be controlled using the `linewidth` keyword, which should be provided with a `float` value. There are many other keyword arguments that can be passed to `plot`; a list is given in the Matplotlib documentation. Many of these keyword arguments have a shorter version, such as `c` for `color` and `lw` for `linewidth`.

For example, we could set the color of all of the markers in the recipe by using the `color` keyword argument in the call to `plot` using the following command:

```
ax.plot(y1, 'o', y2, 'x', y3, '*', color="k")
```

The `Line2D` objects returned from calls to the `plot` method (or the `plt.plot` routine) can also be used to customize the appearance of each set of data. For example, the `set_linestyle` method in a `Line2D` object can be used, with the appropriate line style format string, to set the line style.

Other aspects of the plot can be customized by using methods on the `Axes` object. The axes ticks can be modified using the `set_xticks` and `set_yticks` methods on the `Axes` object, and the grid appearance can be configured using the `grid` method. There are also convenient methods in the `pyplot` interface that apply these modifications to the current axes (if they exist).

For example, we modify the axis limits, set the ticks at every multiple of `0.5` in both the x and y direction, and add a grid to the plot by using the following commands:

```
ax.axis([-0.5, 5.5, 0, 5.5]) # set axes
ax.set_xticks([0.5*i for i in range(9)])  # set xticks
ax.set_yticks([0.5*i for i in range(11)] # set yticks
ax.grid()  # add a grid
```

Notice how we set the limits slightly larger than the extent of the plot. This is to avoid markers being placed on the boundary of the plot window.

The `scatter` plotting routine may be better if you wish to plot discrete data on axes without connecting the points with a line. This allows more control over the style of the marker. For example, you can scale the marker according to some additional information.

Adding labels and legends to plots

Every plot should have a title, and the axes should be properly labeled. For plots displaying multiple sets of data, legends are a good way to help the reader quickly identify the marker, the line, and the color of different datasets. In this recipe, we will add axes labels and a title to a plot, and then add a legend to help distinguish between the different sets of data. To keep the code simple, we will plot the data from the previous recipe.

How to do it...

Follow these steps to add labels and a legend to your plots to help distinguish the sets of data that they represent:

1. We first recreate the plot from the previous recipe using the following `plot` command:

    ```
    fig, ax = plt.subplots()
    ax = ax.plot(y1, "o-", y2, "x--", y3, "*-.")
    ```

2. Now, we have a reference to the `Axes` object on which our data is plotted, and so we can start to customize these axes by adding labels and titles. The title and axes labels can be added to a figure by using the `set_title`, `set_xlabel`, and `set_ylabel` methods on the `ax` object created by the `subplots` routine. In each case, the argument is a string that contains the text to be displayed:

```
ax.set_title("Plot of the data y1, y2, and y3")
ax.set_xlabel("x axis label")
ax.set_ylabel("y axis label")
```

   Here, we plot the three datasets with a different style. The marker style is the same as in the previous recipe, but we have added a solid line for the first dataset, a dashed line for the second, and a dash-dot line for the third.

3. To add a legend, we call the `legend` method on the `ax` object. The argument should be a tuple or list containing the description to be placed in the legend for each set of data:

```
ax.legend(("data y1", "data y2", "data y3"))
```

The result of the preceding sequence of commands is shown here:

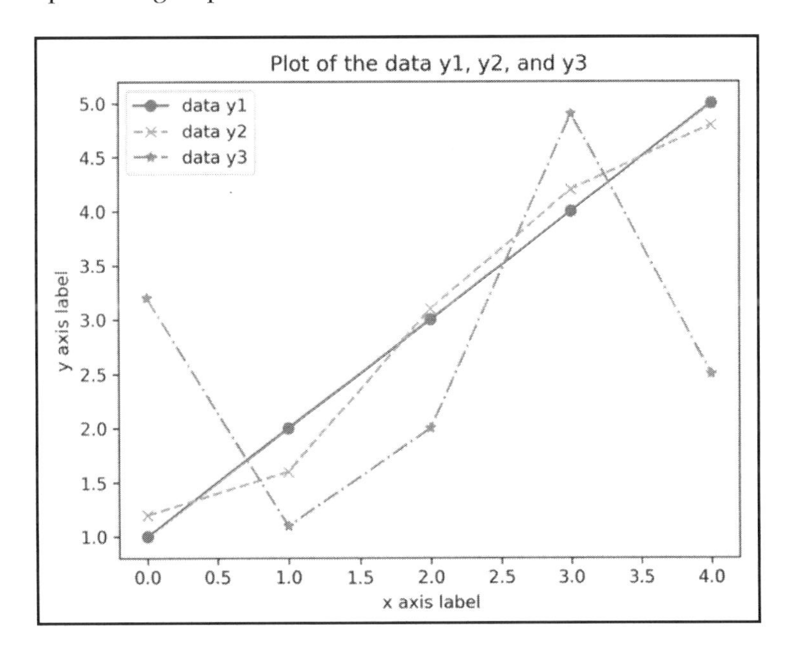

Figure 2.4: A plot with axes labels, a title, and a legend produced using Matplotlib

How it works...

The `set_title`, `set_xlabel`, and `set_ylabel` methods simply add the text argument to the corresponding position of the `Axes` object. The `legend` method, as called in the preceding code, adds the labels to the datasets in the order that they were added to the plot—in this case, `y1`, `y2`, and then `y3`.

There are a number of keyword arguments that can be supplied to the `set_title`, `set_xlabel`, and `set_ylabel` routines to control the style of the text. For example, the `fontsize` keyword can be used to specify the size of the label font in the usual `pt` point measure. The text argument can also be rendered using TeX for additional formatting by supplying `usetex=True` to the routine. The TeX formatting of labels is demonstrated in *Figure 2.5*. This is especially useful if the title or axis label contains a mathematical formula. Unfortunately, the `usetex` keyword argument cannot be used if TeX is not installed on the system—it will cause an error in this case. However, it is still possible to use the TeX syntax for formatting mathematical text within labels, but this will be typeset by Matplotlib, rather than by TeX.

We can use a different font by using the `fontfamily` keyword, the value of which can be the name of a font or `serif`, `sans-serif`, or `monospace`, which will choose the appropriate built-in font. A complete list of modifiers can be found in the Matplotlib documentation for the `matplotlib.text.Text` class.

To add separate text annotations to a plot, you can use the `annotate` method on the `Axes` object. This routine takes two arguments—the text to display as a string and the coordinates of the point at which the annotation should be placed. This routine also accepts the previously mentioned styling keyword arguments.

Adding subplots

Occasionally, it is useful to place multiple related plots within the same figure side by side but not on the same axes. Subplots allow us to produce a grid of individual plots within a single figure. In this recipe, we will see how to create two plots side by side on a single figure using subplots.

Getting ready

You will need the data to be plotted on each subplot. As an example, we will plot the first five iterates of Newton's method applied to the $f(x) = x^2-1$ function with an initial value of $x_0 = 2$ on the first subplot, and for the second, we will plot the error of the iterate. We first define a generator function to get the iterates:

```
def generate_newton_iters(x0, number):
    iterates = [x0]
    errors = [abs(x0 - 1.)]
    for _ in range(number):
        x0 = x0 - (x0*x0 - 1.)/(2*x0)
        iterates.append(x0)
        errors.append(abs(x0 - 1.))
    return iterates, errors
```

This routine generates two lists. The first list contains iterates of Newton's method applied to the function, and the second contains the error in the approximation:

```
iterates, errors = generate_newton_iters(2.0, 5)
```

How to do it...

The following steps show how to create a figure that contains multiple subplots:

1. We use the `subplots` routine to create a new figure and references to all of the `Axes` objects in each subplot, arranged in a grid with one row and two columns. We also set the `tight_layout` keyword argument to `True` to fix the layout of the resulting plots. This isn't strictly necessary, but it is in this case as it produces a better result than the default:

```
fig, (ax1, ax2) = plt.subplots(1, 2, tight_layout=True) # 1 row, 2
columns
```

2. Once the `Figure` and `Axes` objects are created, we can populate the figure by calling the relevant plotting method on each `Axes` object. For the first plot (displayed on the left), we use the `plot` method on the `ax1` object, which has the same signature as the standard `plt.plot` routine. We can then call the `set_title`, `set_xlabel`, and `set_ylabel` methods on `ax1` to set the title and the `x` and `y` labels. We also use TeX formatting for the axes labels by providing the `usetex` keyword argument; you can ignore this if you don't have TeX installed on your system:

```
ax1.plot(iterates, "x")
ax1.set_title("Iterates")
ax1.set_xlabel("$i$", usetex=True)
ax1.set_ylabel("$x_i$", usetex=True)
```

3. Now, we can plot the error values on the second plot (displayed on the right) using the `ax2` object. We use an alternative plotting method that uses a logarithmic scale on the *y*-axis, called `semilogy`. The signature for this method is the same as the standard `plot` method. Again, we set the axes labels and the title. Again, the use of `usetex` can be left out if you don't have TeX installed:

```
ax2.semilogy(errors, "x") # plot y on logarithmic scale
ax2.set_title("Error")
ax2.set_xlabel("$i$", usetex=True)
ax2.set_ylabel("Error")
```

The result of this sequence of commands is shown here:

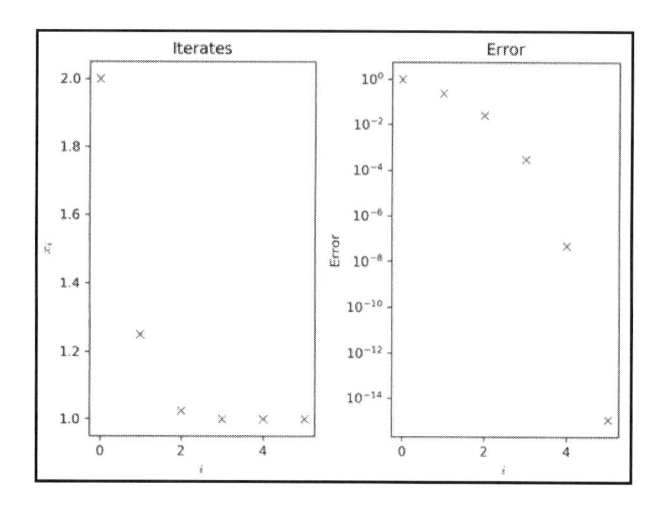

Figure 2.5: Matplotlib subplots

The left-hand side plots the first five iterates of Newton's method and the right-hand side is the approximation error plotted on a logarithmic scale.

How it works...

A `Figure` object in Matplotlib is simply a container for plot elements, such as `Axes`, of a certain size. A `Figure` object will usually only hold a single `Axes` object, which occupies the entire figure area, but it can contain any number of `Axes` objects in the same area. The `subplots` routine does several things. It first creates a new figure and then creates a grid with the specified shape in the figure area. Then, a new `Axes` object is added to each position of the grid. The new `Figure` object and one or more `Axes` objects are then returned to the user. If a single subplot is requested (one row and one column, with no arguments) then a plain `Axes` object is returned. If a single row or column is requested (with more than one column or row, respectively), then a list of the `Axes` objects is returned. If more than one row and column is requested, a list of lists, with rows represented by inner lists filled with the `Axes` objects, will be returned. We can then use the plotting methods on each of the `Axes` objects to populate the figure with the desired plots.

In this recipe, we used the standard `plot` method for the left-hand side plot, as we have seen in previous recipes. However, for the right-hand side plot, we used a plot where the y-axis had been changed to a logarithmic scale. This means that each unit on the y-axis represents a change of a power of 10, rather than a change of one unit, so that `0` represents $10^0 = 1$, `1` represents 10, `2` represents 100, and so on. The axes labels are automatically changed to reflect this change in scale. This type of scaling is useful when the values change by an order of magnitude, such as the error in an approximation, as we use more and more iterations. We can also plot with a logarithmic scale for x only by using the `semilogx` method, or both axes on a logarithmic scale by using the `loglog` method.

There's more...

There are several ways to create subplots in Matplotlib. If you have already created a `Figure` object, then subplots can be added using the `add_subplot` method of the `Figure` object. Alternatively, you can use the `subplot` routine from `matplotlib.pyplot` to add subplots to the current figure. If one does not yet exist, it will be created when this routine is called. The `subplot` routine is a convenience wrapper of the `add_subplot` method on the `Figure` object.

To create a new figure with one or more subplots, you can also use the `subplots` routine from the `pyplot` interface—as we saw in the *Changing the plotting style* recipe—which returns a new figure object and an array of the `Axes` objects, one for each position. All three of these methods require the number of rows and columns for the subplot matrix. The `add_subplot` method and the `subplot` routine also require a third argument, which is the index of the subplot to modify. The `Axes` object of the current subplot is returned.

In the preceding example, we created two plots with differently scaled y-axes. This demonstrates one of the many possible uses of subplots. Another common use is for plotting data in a matrix where columns have a common `x` label and rows have a common `y` label, which is especially common in multivariate statistics when investigating the correlation between various sets of data. The `plt.subplots` routine for creating subplots accepts the `sharex` and `sharey` keyword parameters, which allows the axes to be shared among all the subplots or among a row or column. This setting affects the scale and ticks of the axes.

See also

Matplotlib supports more advanced layouts by providing the `gridspec_kw` keyword arguments to the `subplots` routine. See the documentation for `matplotlib.gridspec` for more information.

Saving Matplotlib figures

When you work in an interactive environment, such as an IPython console or a Jupyter notebook, displaying a figure at runtime is perfectly normal. However, there are plenty of situations where it would be more appropriate to store a figure directly to a file, rather than rendering it on screen. In this recipe, we will see how to save a figure directly to a file, rather than displaying it on screen.

Getting ready

You will need the data to be plotted and the path or file object in which you wish to store the output. We store the result in `savingfigs.png` in the current directory. In this example, we will plot the following data:

```
x = np.arange(1, 5, 0.1)
y = x*x
```

How to do it...

The following steps show how to save a Matplotlib plot directly to a file:

1. The first step is to create the figure, as usual, and add any labels, titles, and annotations that are necessary. The figure will be written to the file in its current state, so any changes to the figure should be made before saving:

```
fig, ax = plt.subplots()
ax.plot(x, y)
ax.set_title("Graph of $y = x^2$", usetex=True)
ax.set_xlabel("$x$", usetex=True)
ax.set_ylabel("$y$", usetex=True)
```

2. Then, we use the `savefig` method on `fig` to save this figure to a file. The only required argument is the path to output to or a file-like object that the figure can be written to. We can adjust various settings for the output format, such as the resolution, by providing the appropriate keyword arguments. We'll set the **Dots per Inch** (**DPI**) of the output figure to `300`, which is a reasonable resolution for most applications:

```
fig.savefig("savingfigs.png", dpi=300)
```

Matplotlib will infer that we wish to save the image in the **Portable Network Graphics** (**PNG**) format from the extension of the file given. Alternatively, a format can be explicitly provided as a keyword argument (by using the `format` keyword), or it will fall back to the default from the configuration file.

How it works...

The `savefig` method chooses the appropriate backend for the output format and then renders the current figure in that format. The resulting image data is written to the specified path or file-like object. If you have manually created a `Figure` instance, the same effect can be achieved by calling the `savefig` method on that instance.

There's more...

The `savefig` routine takes a number of additional optional keyword arguments to customize the output image. For example, the resolution of the image can be specified using the `dpi` keyword. The plots in this chapter have been produced by saving the Matplotlib figures to the file.

The output formats available include PNG, **Scalable Vector Graphics** (**SVG**), **PostScript** (**PS**), **Encapsulated PostScript** (**EPS**), and **Portable Document Format** (**PDF**). You can also save to JPEG format if the Pillow package is installed, but Matplotlib does not support this natively since version 3.1. There are additional customization keyword arguments for JPEG images, such as `quality` and `optimize`. A dictionary of image metadata can be passed to the `metadata` keyword, which will be written as image metadata when saving.

See also

The examples gallery on the Matplotlib website includes examples of embedding Matplotlib figures into a **Graphical User Interface** (**GUI**) application using several common Python GUI frameworks.

Surface and contour plots

Matplotlib can also plot three-dimensional data in a variety of ways. Two common choices for displaying data like this are by using **surface plots** or **contour plots** (think of contour lines on a map). In this recipe, we will see a method for plotting surfaces from three-dimensional data and how to plot contours of three-dimensional data.

Getting ready

To plot three-dimensional data, it needs to be arranged into two-dimensional arrays for the x, y, and z components, where both the x and y components must be of the same shape as the z component. For the sake of this demonstration, we will plot the surface corresponding to the $f(x, y) = x^2y^3$ function.

How to do it...

We want to plot the $f(x, y) = x^2y^3$ function on the $-2 \leq x \leq 2$ and $-1 \leq y \leq 1$ range. The first task is to create a suitable grid of (x, y) pairs on which to evaluate this function:

1. We first use `np.linspace` to generate a reasonable number of points in these ranges:

```
X = np.linspace(-2, 2)
Y = np.linspace(-1, 1)
```

2. Now, we need to create a grid on which to create our z values. For this, we use the `np.meshgrid` routine:

```
x, y = np.meshgrid(X, Y)
```

3. Now, we can create the z values to plot, which hold the value of the function at each of the grid points:

```
z = x**2 * y**3
```

4. To plot three-dimensional surfaces, we need to load a Matplotlib toolbox, `mplot3d`, which comes with the Matplotlib package. This won't be used explicitly in the code, but behind the scenes, it makes the three-dimensional plotting utilities available to Matplotlib:

```
from mpl_toolkits import mplot3d
```

5. Next, we create a new figure and a set of three-dimensional axes for the figure:

```
fig = plt.figure()
ax = fig.add_subplot(projection="3d")  # declare 3d plot
```

6. Now, we can call the `plot_surface` method on these axes to plot the data:

```
ax.plot_surface(x, y, z)
```

7. It is extra important to add axis labels to three-dimensional plots because it might not be clear which axis is which on the displayed plot:

```
ax.set_xlabel("$x$")
ax.set_ylabel("$y$")
ax.set_zlabel("$z$")
```

8. We should also set a title at this stage:

```
ax.set_title("Graph of the function $f(x) = x^2y^3$)
```

You can use the `plt.show` routine to display the figure in a new window (if you are using Python interactively and not in a Jupyter notebook or on an IPython console) or `plt.savefig` to save the figure to a file. The result of the preceding sequence is shown here:

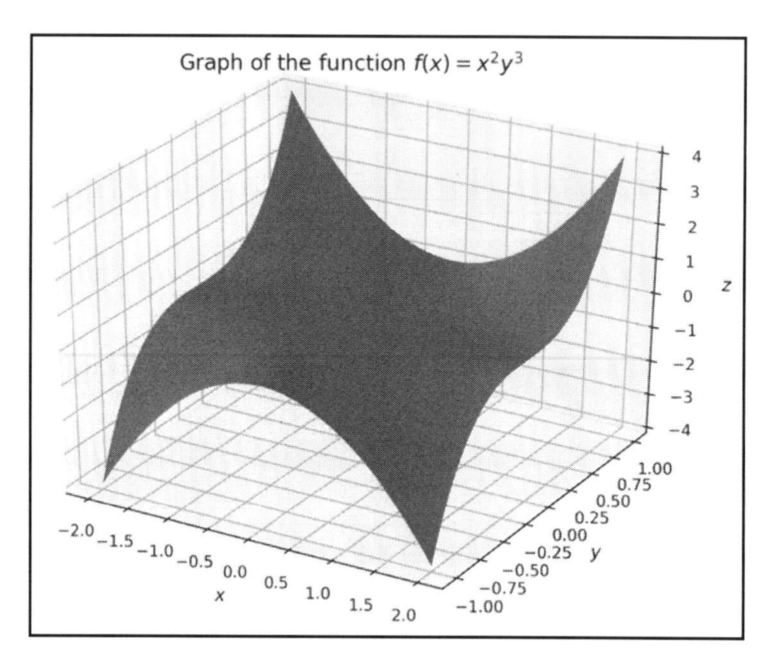

Figure 2.6: A three-dimensional surface plot produced with Matplotlib using the default settings

9. Contour plots do not require the `mplot3d` toolkit, and there is a `contour` routine in the `pyplot` interface that produces contour plots. However, unlike the usual (two-dimensional) plotting routines, the `contour` routine requires the same arguments as the `plot_surface` method. We use the following sequence to produce a plot:

```
fig = plt.figure()  # Force a new figure
plt.contour(x, y, z)
plt.title("Contours of $f(x) = x^2y^3$")
plt.xlabel("$x$")
plt.ylabel("$y$")
```

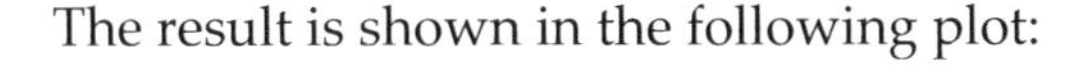

The result is shown in the following plot:

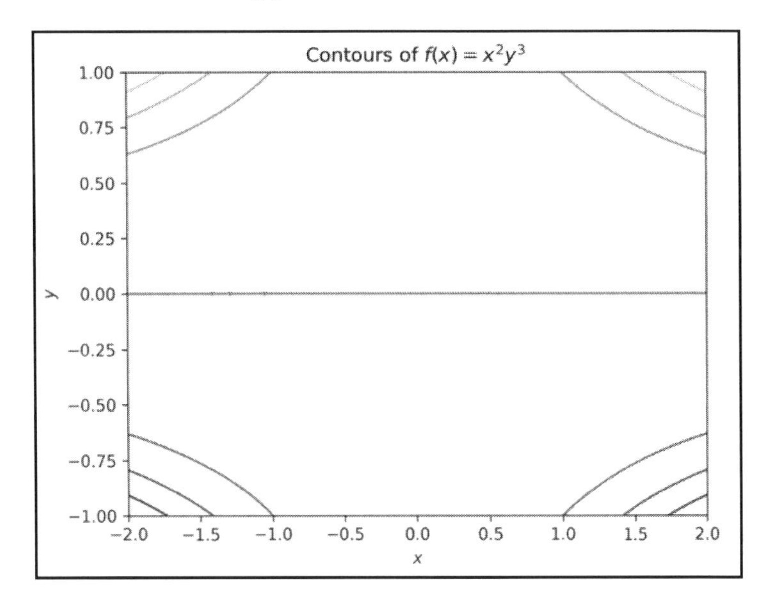

Figure 2.7: Contour plot produced using Matplotlib with the default settings

How it works...

The `mplot3d` toolkit provides an `Axes3D` object, which is a three-dimensional version of the `Axes` object in the core Matplotlib package. This is made available to the `axes` method on a `Figure` object when the `projection="3d"` keyword argument is given. A surface plot is obtained by drawing quadrilaterals, in the three-dimensional projection, between nearby points in the same way that a two-dimensional curve is approximated by straight lines joining adjacent points.

The `plot_surface` method needs the z values to be provided as a two-dimensional array that encodes the z values on a grid of (x, y) pairs. We created the range of x and y values that we are interested in, but if we simply evaluate our function on the pairs of corresponding values from these arrays, we will get the z values along a line and not over a grid. Instead, we use the `meshgrid` routine, which takes the two `X` and `Y` arrays and creates from them a grid consisting of all the possible combinations of values in `X` and `Y`. The output is a pair of two-dimensional arrays on which we can evaluate our function. We can then provide all three of these two-dimensional arrays to the `plot_surface` method.

There's more...

The routines described in the preceding section, `contour` and `plot_contour`, only work with highly structured data where the x, y, and z components are arranged into grids. Unfortunately, real-life data is rarely so structured. In this case, you need to perform some kind of interpolation between known points to approximate the value on a uniform grid, which can then be plotted. A common method for performing this interpolation is by triangulating the collection of (x, y) pairs and then using the values of the function on the vertices of each triangle to estimate the value on the grid points. Fortunately, Matplotlib has a method that does all of these steps and then plots the result, which is the `plot_trisurf` routine. We briefly explain how this can be used here:

1. To illustrate the use of `plot_trisurf`, we will plot a surface and contours from the following data:

```
x = np.array([ 0.19, -0.82, 0.8 , 0.95, 0.46, 0.71,
      -0.86, -0.55,   0.75,-0.98, 0.55, -0.17, -0.89,
          -0.4 , 0.48, -0.09, 1., -0.03, -0.87, -0.43])
y = np.array([-0.25, -0.71, -0.88, 0.55, -0.88, 0.23,
        0.18,-0.06, 0.95, 0.04, -0.59, -0.21, 0.14, 0.94,
            0.51, 0.47, 0.79, 0.33, -0.85, 0.19])
z = np.array([-0.04, 0.44, -0.53, 0.4, -0.31, 0.13,
        -0.12, 0.03, 0.53, -0.03, -0.25, 0.03, -0.1 ,
            -0.29, 0.19, -0.03, 0.58, -0.01, 0.55, -0.06])
```

2. This time, we will plot both the surface and contour (approximations) on the same figure as two separate subplots. For this, we supply the `projection="3d"` keyword argument to the subplot that will contain the surface. We use the `plot_trisurf` method on the three-dimensional axes to plot the approximated surface, and the `tricontour` method on the two-dimensional axes to plot the approximated contours:

```
fig = plt.figure(tight_layout=True)  # force new figure
ax1 = fig.add_subplot(1, 2, 1, projection="3d")  # 3d axes
ax1.plot_trisurf(x, y, z)
ax1.set_xlabel("$x$")
ax1.set_ylabel("$y$")
ax1.set_zlabel("$z$")
ax1.set_title("Approximate surface")
```

3. We can now plot the contours for the triangulated surface using the following command:

```
ax2 = fig.add_subplot(1, 2, 2)  # 2d axes
ax2.tricontour(x, y, z)
ax2.set_xlabel("$x$")
ax2.set_ylabel("$y$")
ax2.set_title("Approximate contours")
```

We include the `tight_layout=True` keyword argument with the figure to save a call to the `plt.tight_layout` routine later. The result is shown here:

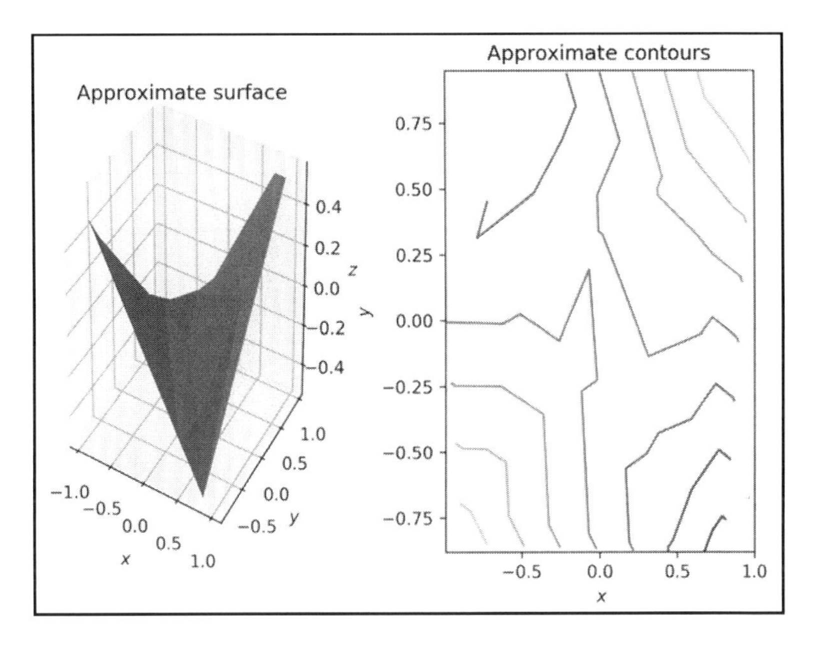

Figure 2.8: Approximate surface and contour plots generated from unstructured data using triangulation

In addition to surface plotting routines, the `Axes3D` object has a `plot` (or `plot3D`) routine for simple three-dimensional plotting, which works exactly as the usual `plot` routine but on the three-dimensional axes. This method can also be used to plot two-dimensional data on one of the axes.

Customizing three-dimensional plots

Contour plots can hide some detail of the surface that they represent since they only show where the "height" is similar and not what the value is, even in relation to the surrounding values. On a map, this is remedied by printing the height onto certain contours. Surface plots are more revealing, but the problem of projecting three-dimensional objects into 2D to be displayed on a screen can itself obscure some details. To address these issues, we can customize the appearance of a three-dimensional plot (or contour plot) to enhance the plot and make sure the detail that we wish to highlight is clear. The easiest way to do this is by changing the colormap of the plot.

In this recipe, we will use the reverse of the `binary` colormap.

Getting ready

We will generate surface plots for the following function:

$$f(x, y) = \cos(2\pi(x^2 + y^2))e^{-(x^2+y^2)}$$

We generate the points at which this should be plotted as in the previous recipe:

```
X = np.linspace(-2, 2)
Y = np.linspace(-2, 2)
x, y = np.meshgrid(X, Y)
t = x**2 + y**2  # small efficiency
z = np.cos(2*np.pi*t)*np.exp(-t)
```

How to do it...

Matplotlib has a number of built-in colormaps that can be applied to plots. By default, surface plots are plotted with a single color that is shaded according to a light source (see the *There's more...* section of this recipe). A colormap can dramatically improve the effect of a plot. The following steps show how to add a colormap to surface and contour plots:

1. To start, we simply apply one of the built-in colormaps, `binary_r`, which is done by providing the `cmap="binary_r"` keyword argument to the `plot_surface` routine:

```
fig = plt.figure()
ax = fig.add_subplot(projection="3d")
ax.plot_surface(x, y, z, cmap="binary_r")
```

```
ax.set_title("Surface with colormap")
ax.set_xlabel("$x$")
ax.set_ylabel("$y$")
ax.set_zlabel("$z$")
```

The result is a figure (*Figure* 2.9) where the surface is colored according to its value, with the most extreme values at either end of the colormap—in this case, the larger the z value, the lighter the shade of gray. Note that the jaggedness of the plot in the following diagram is due to the relatively small number of points in the mesh grid:

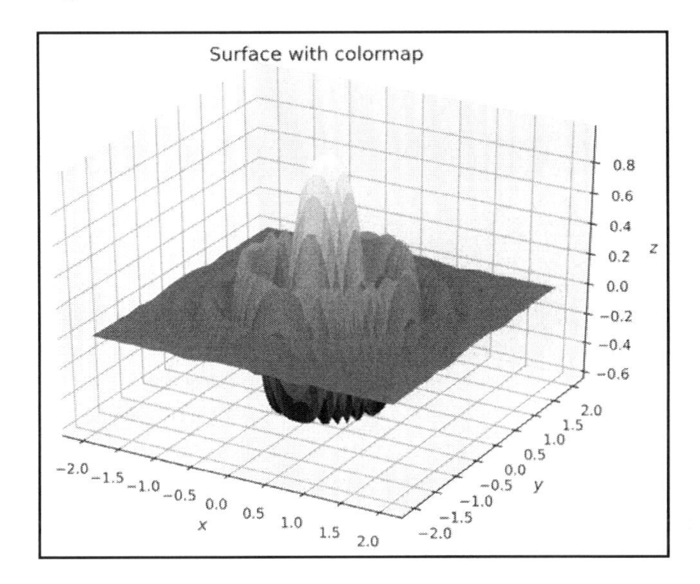

Figure 2.9: A surface plot with a grayscale colormap applied

Colormaps apply to other plot types in addition to surface plots. In particular, colormaps can be applied to contour plots, which can help to distinguish between the contours that represent higher values and those that represent lower values.

2. For the contour plot, the method for changing the colormap is the same; we simply specify a value for the `cmap` keyword argument:

```
fig = plt.figure()
plt.contour(x, y, z, cmap="binary_r")
plt.xlabel("$x$")
plt.ylabel("$y$")
plt.title("Contour plot with colormap set")
```

The result of the preceding code is shown here:

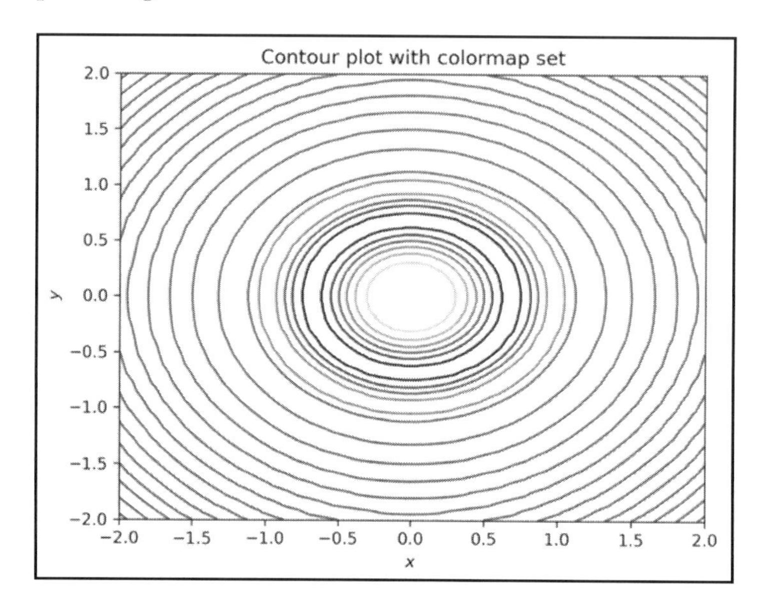

Figure 2.10: A contour plot with an alternative colormap set

The darker shades of gray in the diagram correspond to the lower values of z.

How it works...

Color mapping works by assigning an RGB value according to a scale—the **colormap**. First, the values are normalized so that they lie between `0` and `1`, which is typically done by a linear transformation that takes the minimum value to `0` and the maximum value to `1`. The appropriate color is then applied to each face of the surface plot (or line, in another kind of plot).

Matplotlib comes with a number of built-in colormaps that can be applied by simply passing the name to the `cmap` keyword argument. A list of these colormaps is given in the documentation (`https://matplotlib.org/tutorials/colors/colormaps.html`), and also comes with a reversed variant, which is obtained by adding the `_r` suffix to the name of the chosen colormap.

There's more...

The normalization step in applying a colormap is performed by an object derived from the `Normalize` class. Matplotlib provides a number of standard normalization routines, including `LogNorm` and `PowerNorm`. Of course, you can also create your own subclass of `Normalize` to perform the normalization. An alternative `Normalize` subclass can be added using the `norm` keyword of `plot_surface` or other plotting functions.

For more advanced uses, Matplotlib provides an interface for creating custom shading using light sources. This is done by importing the `LightSource` class from the `matplotlib.colors` package, and then using an instance of this class to shade the surface elements according to the *z* value. This is done using the `shade` method on the `LightSource` object:

```
from matplotlib.colors import LightSource
light_source = LightSource(0, 45)  # angles of lightsource
cmap = plt.get_cmap("binary_r")
vals = light_source.shade(z, cmap)
surf = ax.plot_surface(x, y, z, facecolors=vals)
```

Complete examples are shown in the Matplotlib gallery should you wish to learn more about how this works.

Further reading

The Matplotlib package is extensive and we can scarcely do it justice in such a short space. The documentation contains far more detail than is provided here. Moreover, there is a large gallery (`https://matplotlib.org/gallery/index.html#`) of examples covering many more of the capabilities of the package than in this book.

There are other packages that build on top of Matplotlib that offer high-level plotting methods for specific applications. For example, the Seaborn libraries provide routines for visualizing data (`https://seaborn.pydata.org/`).

3
Calculus and Differential Equations

In this chapter, we will discuss various topics related to calculus. Calculus is the branch of mathematics that concerns the processes of differentiation and integration. Geometrically, the derivative of a function represents the gradient of the curve of the function, and the integral of a function represents the area below the curve of the function. Of course, these characterizations only hold in certain circumstances, but they provide a reasonable foundation for this chapter.

We start by looking at calculus for a simple class of functions: the polynomials. In the first recipe, we create a class that represents a polynomial and define methods that differentiate and integrate the polynomial. Polynomials are convenient because the derivative or integral of a polynomial is again a polynomial. Then, we use the SymPy package to perform symbolic differentiation and integration on more general functions. After that, we see methods for solving equations using the SciPy package. Next, we turn our attention to numerical integration (quadrature) and solving differential equations. We use the SciPy package to solve ordinary differential equations and systems of ordinary differential equations, and then use a finite difference scheme to solve a simple partial differential equation. Finally, we use the fast Fourier transform to process a noisy signal and filter out the noise.

In this chapter, we will cover the following recipes:

- Working with polynomials and calculus
- Differentiating and integrating symbolically using SymPy
- Solving equations
- Integrating functions numerically using SciPy

- Solving simple differential equations numerically
- Solving systems of differential equations
- Solving partial differential equations numerically
- Using discrete Fourier transforms for signal processing

Technical requirements

In addition to the scientific Python packages NumPy and SciPy, we also need the SymPy package. This can be installed using your favorite package manager, such as `pip`:

```
python3.8 -m pip install sympy
```

The code for this chapter can be found in the `Chapter 03` folder of the GitHub repository at `https://github.com/PacktPublishing/Applying-Math-with-Python/tree/master/Chapter%2003`.

Check out the following video to see the Code in Action: `https://bit.ly/32HuH4X`.

Working with polynomials and calculus

Polynomials are among the simplest functions in mathematics and are defined as a sum:

$$p(x) = a_0 + a_1 x + \cdots + a_n x^n$$

x represents a placeholder to be substituted, and a_i is a number. Since polynomials are simple, they provide an excellent means for a brief introduction to calculus. Calculus concerns the *differentiation* and *integration* of functions. Integration is, roughly speaking, *anti-differentiation*, in the sense that first integrating and then differentiating yields the original function.

In this recipe, we will define a simple class that represents a polynomial and write methods for this class to perform differentiation and integration.

Getting ready

Geometrically, the *derivative*, obtained by *differentiating*, of a function is its *gradient*, and the *integral*, obtained by *integrating*, of a function is the area that lies between the curve of the function and the x axis, accounting for whether the curve lies above or below the axis. In practice, differentiating and integrating are done symbolically, using a set of rules and standard results that are particularly simple for polynomials.

There are no additional packages required for this recipe.

How to do it...

The following steps describe how to create a class representing a polynomial and implement differentiation and integration methods for this class:

1. Let's start by defining a simple class to represent a polynomial:

```
class Polynomial:
    """Basic polynomial class"""

    def __init__(self, coeffs):
        self.coeffs = coeffs

    def __repr__(self):
        return f"Polynomial({repr(self.coeffs)})"

    def __call__(self, x):
        return sum(coeff*x**i for i, coeff
                   in enumerate(self.coeffs))
```

2. Now that we have defined a basic class for a polynomial, we can move on to implement the differentiation and integration operations for this `Polynomial` class to illustrate how these operations change polynomials. We start with differentiation. We generate new coefficients by multiplying each element in the current list of coefficients without the first element. We use this new list of coefficients to create a new `Polynomial` instance that is returned:

```
    def differentiate(self):
        """Differentiate the polynomial and return the
derivative"""
        coeffs = [i*c for i, c in enumerate(self.coeffs[1:],
start=1)]
        return Polynomial(coeffs)
```

3. To implement the integration method, we need to create a new list of coefficients containing the new constant (converted to a float for consistency) given by the argument. We then add to this list of coefficients the old coefficients divided by their new position in the list:

```
def integrate(self, constant=0):
    """Integrate the polynomial, returning the integral"""
    coeffs = [float(constant)]
    coeffs += [c/i for i, c in enumerate(self.coeffs, start=1)]
    return Polynomial(coeffs)
```

4. Finally, to make sure these methods work as expected, we should test these two methods with a simple case. We can check this using a very simple polynomial, such as $x^2 - 2x + 1$:

```
p = Polynomial([1, -2, 1])
p.differentiate()
# Polynomial([-2, 2])
p.integrate(constant=1)
# Polynomial([1.0, 1.0, -1.0, 0.3333333333])
```

How it works...

Polynomials offer an easy introduction to the basic operations of calculus, but it isn't so easy to construct Python classes for other general classes of functions. That being said, polynomials are extremely useful because they are well understood and, perhaps more importantly, calculus for polynomials is very easy. For powers of a variable x, the rule for differentiation is to multiply by the power and reduce the power by 1, so that x^n becomes nx^{n-1}.

Integration is more complex, since the integral of a function is not unique. We can add any constant to an integral and obtain a second integral. For powers of a variable x, the rule for integration is to increase the power by 1 and divide by the new power, so that x^n becomes $x^{n+1}/(n+1)$, so to integrate a polynomial, we increase each power of x by 1 and divide the corresponding coefficient by the new power.

The `Polynomial` class that we defined in the recipe is rather simplistic, but represents the core idea. A polynomial is uniquely determined by its coefficients, which we can store as a list of numerical values. Differentiation and integration are operations that we can perform on this list of coefficients. We include a simple `__repr__` method to help with the display of `Polynomial` objects, and a `__call__` method to facilitate evaluation at specific numerical values. This is mostly to demonstrate the way that a polynomial is evaluated.

Polynomials are useful for solving certain problems that involve evaluating a computationally expensive function. For such problems, we can sometimes use some kind of polynomial interpolation, where we "fit" a polynomial to another function, and then use the properties of polynomials to help solve the original problem. Evaluating a polynomial is much "cheaper" than the original function, so this can lead to dramatic improvements in speed. This usually comes at the cost of some accuracy. For example, Simpson's rule for approximating the area under a curve approximates the curve by quadratic polynomials over intervals defined by three consecutive mesh points. The area below each quadratic polynomial can be calculated easily by integration.

There's more...

Polynomials have many more important roles in computational programming than simply demonstrating the effect of differentiation and integration. For this reason, a much richer `Polynomial` class is provided in the NumPy package, `numpy.polynomial`. The NumPy `Polynomial` class, and the various derived subclasses, are useful in all kinds of numerical problems, and support arithmetic operations as well as other methods. In particular, there are methods for fitting polynomials to collections of data.

NumPy also provides classes, derived from `Polynomial`, that represent various special kinds of polynomials. For example, the `Legendre` class represents a specific system of polynomials called the **Legendre** polynomials. The Legendre polynomials are defined for x satisfying $-1 \leq x \leq 1$ and form an orthogonal system, which is important for applications such as numerical integration and the **finite element method** for solving partial differential equations. The Legendre polynomials are defined using a recursive relation. We define

$$P_0(x) = 1 \quad \text{and} \quad P_1(x) = x$$

and for each $n \geq 2$, we define the nth Legendre polynomial to satisfy the recurrence relation,

$$nP_n(x) = (2n-1)xP_{n-1}(x) - (n-1)P_{n-2}(x)$$

There are several other so called *orthogonal (systems of) polynomials*, including *Laguerre polynomials*, *Chebyshev polynomials*, and *Hermite polynomials*.

See also

Calculus is certainly well documented in mathematical texts, and there are many textbooks that cover from the basic methods all the way to the deep theory. Orthogonal systems of polynomials are also well documented among numerical analysis texts.

Differentiating and integrating symbolically using SymPy

At some point, you may have to differentiate a function that is not a simple polynomial, and you may need to do this in some kind of automated fashion, for example, if you are writing software for education. The Python scientific stack includes a package called SymPy, which allows us to create and manipulate symbolic mathematical expressions within Python. In particular, SymPy can perform differentiation and integration of symbolic functions, just like a mathematician.

In this recipe, we will create a symbolic function, and then differentiate and integrate this function using the SymPy library.

Getting ready

Unlike some of the other scientific Python packages, there does not seem to be a standard alias under which SymPy is imported in the literature. Instead the documentation uses a star import at several points, which is not in line with the PEP8 style guide. This is possibly to make the mathematical expressions more natural. We will simply import the module under its name `sympy`, to avoid any confusion with the `scipy` package's standard abbreviation, `sp` (which is the natural choice for `sympy` too):

```
import sympy
```

In this recipe, we will define a symbolic expression that represents the function

$$f(x) = (x^2 - 2x)e^{3-x}$$

How to do it...

Differentiating and integrating symbolically (as you would do by hand) is very easy using the SymPy package. Follow these steps to see how it is done:

1. Once SymPy is imported, we define the symbols that will appear in our expressions. This is a Python object that has no particular value, just like a mathematical variable, but can be used in formulas and expressions to represent many different values simultaneously. For this recipe, we need only define a symbol for x, since we will only require constant (literal) symbols and functions in addition to this. We use the `symbols` routine from `sympy` to define a new symbol. To keep the notation simple, we will name this new symbol `x`:

   ```
   x = sympy.symbols('x')
   ```

2. The symbols defined using the `symbols` function support all of the arithmetic operations, so we can construct the expression directly using the symbol `x` we just defined:

   ```
   f = (x**2 - 2*x)*sympy.exp(3 - x)
   ```

3. Now we can use the symbolic calculus capabilities of SymPy to compute the derivative of `f`, that is, differentiate `f`. We do this using the `diff` routine in `sympy`, which differentiates a symbolic expression with respect to a specified symbol, and returns an expression for the derivative. This is often not expressed in its simplest form, so we use the `sympy.simplify` routine to simplify the result:

   ```
   fp = sympy.simplify(sympy.diff(f))  # (x*(2 - x) + 2*x - 2)
                                                           *exp(3 - x)
   ```

4. We can check whether the result of the symbolic differentiation using SymPy is correct, compared to the derivative computed by hand, defined as a SymPy expression, as follows:

   ```
   fp2 = (2*x - 2)*sympy.exp(3 - x) - (x**2 - 2*x)*sympy.exp(3 - x)
   ```

5. SymPy equality tests whether two expressions are equal, but not whether they are symbolically equivalent. Therefore, we must first simplify the difference of the two statements we wish to test and test for equality to `0`:

   ```
   sympy.simplify(fp2 - fp) == 0  # True
   ```

6. We can integrate the function `f` using SymPy by using the `integrate` function. It is a good idea to also provide the symbol with which the integration is to be performed by providing it as the second optional argument:

```
F = sympy.integrate(f, x)  # -x**2*exp(3 - x)
```

How it works...

SymPy defines various classes to represent certain kinds of expressions. For example, symbols, represented by the `Symbol` class, are examples of *atomic expressions*. Expressions are built up in a similar way to how Python builds an abstract syntax tree from source code. These expression objects can then be manipulated using methods and the standard arithmetic operations.

SymPy also defines standard mathematical functions that can operate on the `Symbol` objects to create symbolic expressions. The most important feature is the ability to perform symbolic calculus – rather than the numerical calculus that we explore in the remainder of this chapter – and give exact (sometimes called *analytic*) solutions to calculus problems.

The `diff` routine from the SymPy package performs differentiation on these symbolic expressions. The result of this routine is usually not in its simplest form, which is why we used the `simplify` routine to simplify the derivative in the recipe. The `integrate` routine symbolically integrates a `scipy` expression with respect to a given symbol. (The `diff` routine also accepts a symbol argument that specifies the symbol for differentiating against.) This returns an expression whose derivative is the original expression. This routine does not add a constant of integration, which is good practice when doing integrals by hand.

There's more...

SymPy can do much more than simple algebra and calculus. There are submodules for various areas of mathematics, such as number theory, geometry, and other discrete mathematics (such as combinatorics).

SymPy expressions (and functions) can be built into Python functions that can be applied to NumPy arrays. This is done using the `lambdify` routine from the `sympy.utilities` module. This converts a SymPy expression to a numerical expression that uses the NumPy equivalents of the SymPy standard functions to evaluate the expressions numerically. The result is similar to defining a Python Lambda, hence the name. For example, we could convert the function and derivative from this recipe into Python functions using this routine:

```
from sympy.utilities import lambdify
lam_f = lambdify(x, f)
lam_fp = lambdify(x, fp)
```

The `lambdify` routine takes two arguments. The first is the variables to be provided, `x` in the previous code block, and the second is the expression to be evaluated when this function is called. For example, we can evaluate the lambdified SymPy expressions defined previously as if they were ordinary Python functions:

```
lam_f(4)  # 2.9430355293715387
lam_fp(7)  # -0.4212596944408861
```

We can even evaluate these lambdified expressions on NumPy arrays:

```
lam_f(np.array([0, 1, 2]))  # array([ 0. , -7.3890561, 0. ])
```

The `lambdify` routine uses the Python `exec` routine to execute the code, so it should not be used with unsanitized input.

Solving equations

Many mathematical problems eventually reduce to solving an equation of the form $f(x) = 0$, where f is a function of a single variable. Here, we try to find a value of x for which the equation holds. The values of x for which the equation holds are sometimes called *roots* of the equation. There are numerous algorithms for finding solutions to equations of this form. In this recipe, we will use the Newton-Raphson and secant methods to solve an equation of the form $f(x) = 0$.

The Newton-Raphson method (Newton's method) and the secant method are good, standard root finding algorithms that can be applied in almost any situation. These are *iterative methods* that start with an approximation of the root and iteratively improve this approximation until it lies within a given tolerance.

To demonstrate these techniques, we will use the function from the *Symbolic calculus using SymPy* recipe defined by

$$f(x) = (x^2 - 2x)\exp(3 - x)$$

which is defined for all real values of x and has exactly two roots, one at $x = 0$ and one at $x = 2$.

Getting ready

The SciPy package contains routines for solving equations (among many other things). The root finding routines can be found in the `optimize` module from the `scipy` package.

If your equation is not in the form $f(x) = 0$, then you will need to rearrange it so that this is the case. This is usually not too difficult, and simply requires moving any terms on the right-hand side over to the left-hand side. For example, if you wish to find the fixed points of a function, that is, when $g(x) = x$, then we would apply the method to the related function given by $f(x) = g(x) - x$.

How to do it...

The `optimize` package provides routines for numerical root finding. The following instructions describe how to use the `newton` routine from this module:

1. The `optimize` module is not listed in the `scipy` namespace, so you must import it separately:

   ```
   from scipy import optimize
   ```

2. Then we must define this function and its derivative in Python:

   ```
   from math import exp

   def f(x):
       return x*(x - 2)*exp(3 - x)
   ```

3. The derivative of this function was computed in the previous recipe:

   ```
   def fp(x):
       return -(x**2 - 4*x + 2)*exp(3 - x)
   ```

4. For both the Newton-Raphson and secant methods, we use the `newton` routine from `optimize`. Both the secant method and the Newton-Raphson method require the function and the first argument and the first approximation, `x0`, as the second argument. To use the Newton-Raphson method, we must provide the derivative of *f*, using the `fprime` keyword argument:

```
optimize.newton(f, 1, fprime=fp) # Using the Newton-Raphson method
# 2.0
```

5. To use the secant method, only the function is needed, but we must provide the first two approximations for the root; the second is provided as the `x1` keyword argument:

```
optimize.newton(f, 1., x1=1.5) # Using x1 = 1.5 and the secant
method
# 1.9999999999999862
```

Neither the Newton-Raphson nor the secant method are guaranteed to converge to a root. It is perfectly possible that the iterates of the method will simply cycle through a number of points (periodicity) or fluctuate wildly (chaos).

How it works...

The Newton-Raphson method for a function $f(x)$ with derivative $f'(x)$ and initial approximation x_0 is defined iteratively using the formula

$$x_{i+1} = x_i - \frac{f(x_i)}{f'(x_i)}$$

for each integer $i \geq 0$. Geometrically, this formula arises by considering the direction in which the gradient is negative (so the function is decreasing) if $f(x_i) > 0$ or positive (so the function is increasing) if $f(x_i) < o$.

The secant method is based on the Newton-Raphson method, but replaces the first derivative by the approximation

$$f'(x_i) \approx \frac{f(x_i) - f(x_{i-1})}{x_i - x_{i-1}}$$

when x_i - x_{i-1} is sufficiently small, which occurs if the method is converging, then this is a good approximation. The price paid for not requiring the derivative of the function f is that we require an additional initial guess to start the method. The formula for the method is given by

$$x_{i+1} = x_i - f(x_i)\frac{x_i - x_{i-1}}{f(x_i) - f(x_{i-1})}$$

Generally speaking, if either method is given an initial guess (guesses for the secant method) that is sufficiently close to a root, then the method will converge to that root. The Newton-Raphson method can also fail if the derivative is zero at one of the iterations, in which case the formula is not well defined.

There's more...

The methods mentioned in this recipe are general purpose methods, but there are others that may be faster or more accurate in some circumstances. Broadly speaking, root finding algorithms fall into two categories: algorithms that use information about the function's gradient at each iterate (Newton-Raphson, secant, Halley) and algorithms that require bounds on the location of a root (bisection method, regula-falsi, Brent). The algorithms discussed so far are of the first kind, and while generally quite fast, they may fail to converge.

The second kind of algorithms are those for which a root is known to exist within a specified interval $a \leq x \leq b$. We can check whether a root lies within such an interval by checking that $f(a)$ and $f(b)$ have different signs, that is, one of $f(a) < 0 < f(b)$ or $f(b) < 0 < f(a)$ is true. (Provided, of course, that the function is *continuous,* which tends to be the case in practice.) The most basic algorithm of this kind is the bisection algorithm, which repeatedly bisects the interval until a sufficiently good approximation to the root is found. The basic premise is to split the interval between a and b at the mid-point and select the interval in which the function changes sign. The algorithm repeats until the interval is very small. The following is a rudimentary implementation of this algorithm in Python:

```
from math import copysign

def bisect(f, a, b, tol=1e-5):
    """Bisection method for root finding"""
    fa, fb = f(a), f(b)
    assert not copysign(fa, fb) == fa, "Function must change signs"
    while (b - a) > tol:
        m = (b - a)/2 # mid point of the interval
```

```
        fm = f(m)
        if fm == 0:
            return m
        if copysign(fm, fa) == fm: # fa and fm have the same sign
            a = m
            fa = fm
        else: # fb and fm have the same sign
            b = m
        return a
```

This method is guaranteed to converge, since at each step the distance *b-a* is halved. However, it is possible that the method will require more iterations than Newton-Raphson or the secant method. A version of the bisection method can also be found in `optimize`. This version is implemented in C and is considerably more efficient that the version presented here, but the bisection method is not the fastest method in most cases.

Brent's method is an improvement on the bisection method, and is available in the `optimize` module as `brentq`. It uses a combination of bisection and interpolation to quickly find the root of an equation:

```
optimize.brentq(f, 1.0, 3.0)   # 1.9999999999998792
```

It is important to note that the techniques that involve bracketing (bisection, regula-falsi, Brent) cannot be used to find the root functions of a complex variable, whereas those techniques that do not use bracketing (Newton, secant, Halley) can.

Integrating functions numerically using SciPy

Integration can be interpreted as the area that lies between a curve and the x axis, signed according to whether this area is above or below the axis. Some integrals cannot be computed directly, using symbolic means, and instead have to be approximated numerically. One classic example of this is the Gaussian error function, which was mentioned in the *Basic mathematical functions* section in `Chapter 1`, *Basic Packages, Functions, and Concepts*. This is defined by the formula

$$\operatorname{erf}(x) = \frac{1}{\sqrt{\pi}} \int_{-x}^{x} e^{-t^2} \, dt,$$

and the integral that appears here cannot be evaluated symbolically.

In this recipe, we will see how to use the numerical integration routines in the SciPy package to compute the integral of a function.

Getting ready

We use the `scipy.integrate` module, which contains several routines for computing numerical integrals. We import this module as follows:

```
from scipy import integrate
```

How to do it...

The following steps describe how to numerically integrate a function using SciPy:

1. We evaluate the integral that appears in the definition of the error function at the value $x = 1$. For this, we need to define the integrand (the function that appears inside the integral) in Python:

```
def erf_integrand(t):
    return np.exp(-t**2)
```

   There are two main routines in `scipy.integrate` for performing numerical integration (quadrature) that can be used. The first is the `quad` function, which uses QUADPACK to perform the integration, and the second is `quadrature`.

2. The `quad` routine is a general-purpose integration tool. It expects three arguments, which are the function to be integrated (`erf_integrand`), the lower limit (`-1.0`), and the upper limit (`1.0`):

```
val_quad, err_quad = integrate.quad(erf_integrand, -1.0, 1.0)
# (1.493648265624854, 1.6582826951881447e-14)
```

   The first returned value is the value of the integral and the second is an estimate for the error.

3. Repeating the computation with the `quadrature` routine, we get the following. The arguments are the same as for the `quad` routine:

```
val_quadr, err_quadr = integrate.quadrature(erf_integrand, -1.0,
    1.0)
# (1.4936482656450039, 7.459897144457273e-10)
```

The output is the same format as the code, with the value of the integral and then an estimate of the error. Notice that the error is larger for the `quadrature` routine. This is a result of the method terminating once the estimated error falls below a given tolerance, which can be modified when the routine is called.

How it works...

Most numerical integration techniques follow the same basic procedure. First, we choose points x_i for $i = 1, 2, \ldots, n$ in the region of integration, and then use these values and the values $f(x_i)$ to approximate the integral. For example, with the trapezium rule, we approximate the integral by

$$\int_a^b f(x)\,\mathrm{d}x \approx \frac{h}{2}\left(f(a) + f(b) + 2\sum_{j=1}^{n-1} f(x_i)\right)$$

where $a < x_1 < x_2 < \ldots < x_{n-1} < b$ and h is the (common) difference between adjacent x_i values, including the end points a and b. This can be implemented in Python as follows:

```
def trapezium(func, a, b, n_steps):
    """Estimate an integral using the trapezium rule"""
    h = (b - a) / n_steps
    x_vals = np.arange(a + h, b, h)
    y_vals = func(x_vals)
    return 0.5*h*(func(a) + func(b) + 2.*np.sum(y_vals))
```

The algorithms used by `quad` and `quadrature` are far more sophisticated than this. Using this function to approximate the integral of `erf_integrand` using `trapezium` yields a result of 1.4936463036001209, which agrees with the approximations from the `quad` and `quadrature` routines to 5 decimal places.

The `quadrature` routine uses a fixed tolerance Gaussian quadrature, whereas the `quad` routine uses an adaptive algorithm implemented in the Fortran library QUADPACK routines. Timing both routines, we find that the `quad` routine is approximately 5 times faster than the `quadrature` routine for the problem described in the recipe. The `quad` routine executes in approximately 27 µs, averaged over 1 million executions, while the `quadrature` routine executes in approximately 134 µs. (Your results may differ depending on your system.)

There's more...

The routines mentioned in this section require the integrand function to be known, which is not always the case. Instead, it might be the case that we know a number of pairs (x, y) with $y = f(x)$, but we don't know the function f to evaluate at additional points. In this case, we can use one of the sampling quadrature techniques from `scipy.integrate`. If the number of known points is very large and all points are equally spaced, we can use Romberg integration for a good approximation of the integral. For this, we use the `romb` routine. Otherwise, we can use a variant of the trapezium rule (as above) using the `trapz` routine, or Simpson's rule using the `simps` routine.

Solving simple differential equations numerically

Differential equations arise in situations where a quantity evolves, usually over time, according to a given relationship. They are extremely common in engineering and physics, and appear quite naturally. One of the classic examples of a (very simple) differential equation is the law of cooling devised by Newton. The temperature of a body cools at a rate proportional to the current temperature. Mathematically, this means that we can write the derivative of the temperature T of the body at time $t > 0$ using the differential equation

$$\frac{dT}{dt} = -kT$$

where k is a positive constant that determines the rate of cooling. This differential equation can be solved *analytically* by first "separating the variables" and then integrating and rearranging. After performing this procedure, we obtain the general solution

$$T(t) = T_0 e^{-kt}$$

where T_0 is the initial temperature.

In this recipe, we will solve a simple ordinary differential equation numerically using the `solve_ivp` routine from SciPy.

Getting ready

We will demonstrate the technique for solving a differential equation numerically in Python using the cooling equation described previously since we can compute the true solution in this case. We take the initial temperature to be $T_0 = 50$ and $k = 0.2$. Let's also find the solution for t values between 0 and 5.

A general (first order) differential equation has the form

$$\frac{dy}{dt} = f(t, y)$$

where f is some function of t (the independent variable) and y (the dependent variable). In this formula, T is the dependent variable and $f(t, T) = -kt$. The routines for solving differential equations in the SciPy package require the function f and an initial value y_0 and the range of t values where we need to compute the solution. To get started, we need to define our function f in Python and create the variables y_0 and t range ready to be supplied to the SciPy routine:

```
def f(t, y):
    return -0.2*y

t_range = (0, 5)
```

Next, we need to define the initial condition from which the solution should be found. For technical reasons, the initial y values must be specified as a one-dimensional NumPy array:

```
T0 = np.array([50.])
```

Since, in this case, we already know the true solution, we can also define this in Python ready to compare to the numerical solution that we will compute:

```
def true_solution(t):
    return 50.*np.exp(-0.2*t)
```

How to do it...

Follow these steps to solve a differential equation numerically and plot the solution along with the error:

1. We use the `solve_ivp` routine from the `integrate` module in SciPy to solve the differential equation numerically. We add a parameter for the maximum step size, with a value of `0.1`, so the solution is computed at a reasonable number of points:

```
sol = integrate.solve_ivp(f, t_range, T0, max_step=0.1)
```

2. Next, we extract the solution values from the `sol` object returned from the `solve_ivp` method:

```
t_vals = sol.t
T_vals = sol.y[0, :]
```

3. Next, we plot the solution on a set of axes as follows. Since we are also going to plot the approximation error on the same figure, we create two subplots using the `subplots` routine:

```
fig, (ax1, ax2) = plt.subplots(1, 2, tight_layout=True)
ax1.plot(t_vals, T_vals)
ax1.set_xlabel("$t$")
ax1.set_ylabel("$T$")
ax1.set_title("Solution of the cooling equation")
```

   This plots the solution on a set of axes displayed in the left-hand side of *Figure 3.1*.

4. To do this, we need to compute the true solution at the points that we obtained from the `solve_ivp` routine, and then calculate the absolute value of the difference between the true and approximated solutions:

```
err = np.abs(T_vals - true_solution(t_vals))
```

5. Finally, on the right-hand side of *Figure 3.1*, we plot the error in the approximation with a logarithmic scale on the y axis. We can then plot this on the right-hand side with a logarithmic scale y axis using the `semilogy` plot command as we saw in `Chapter 2`, *Mathematical Plotting with Matplotlib*:

```
ax2.semilogy(t_vals, err)
ax2.set_xlabel("$t$")
ax2.set_ylabel("Error")
ax2.set_title("Error in approximation")
```

The left-hand plot in *Figure 3.1* shows decreasing temperature over time, while the right-hand plot shows that the error increases as we move away from the known value given by the initial condition:

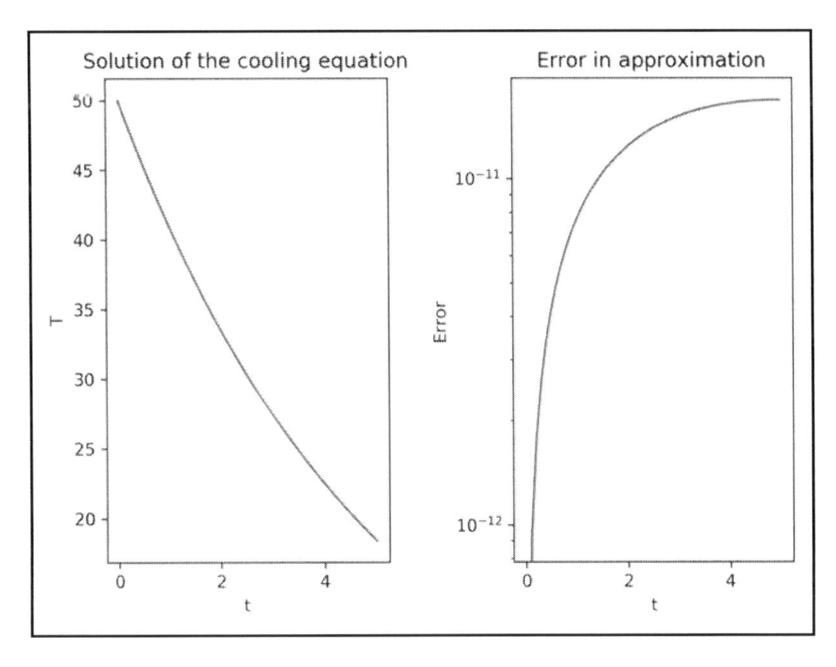

Figure 3.1: Plot of the numerical solution to the cooling equation obtained using the solve_ivp routine with default settings

How it works...

Most methods for solving differential equations are "time-stepping" methods. The pairs (t_i, y_i) are generated by taking small t steps and approximating the value of the function y. This is perhaps best illustrated by Euler's method, which is the most basic time-stepping method. Fixing a small step size $h > 0$, we form the approximation at the ith step using the formula

$$y_i = y_{i-1} + hf(t_{i-1}, y_{i-1})$$

starting from the known initial value y_0. We can easily write a Python routine that performs Euler's method as follows (there are, of course, many different ways to implement Euler's method; this is a very simple example):

1. First, we set up the method by creating lists that will store the t values and y values that we will return:

```
def euler(func, t_range, y0, step_size):
    """Solve a differential equation using Euler's method"""
    t = [t_range[0]]
    y = [y0]
    i = 0
```

2. Euler's method continues until we hit the end of the t range. Here, we use a `while` loop to accomplish this. The body of the loop is very simple; we first increment a counter `i`, and then append the new t and y values to their respective lists:

```
    while t[i] < t_range[1]:
        i += 1
        t.append(t[i-1] + step_size)  # step t
        y.append(y[i-1] + step_size*func(t[i-1], y[i-1]))  # step y
    return t, y
```

The method used by the `solve_ivp` routine, by default, is the Runge-Kutta-Fehlberg method (RK45), which has the ability to adapt the step size to ensure that the error in the approximation stays within a given tolerance. This routine expects three positional arguments: the function f, the t range on which the solution should be found, and the initial y value (T_0 in our example). Optional arguments can be provided to change the solver, the number of points to compute, and several other settings.

The function passed to the `solve_ivp` routine must have two arguments as in the general differential equation described in *Getting ready* section. The function can have additional arguments, which can be provided using the `args` keyword for the `solve_ivp` routine, but these must be positioned after the two necessary arguments. Comparing the `euler` routine we defined earlier to the `solve_ivp` routine, both with a step size of 0.1, we find that the maximum true error between the `solve_ivp` solution is in the order of 10^{-6}, whereas the `euler` solution only manages an error of 31. The `euler` routine is working, but the step size is much too large to overcome the accumulating error.

The `solve_ivp` routine returns a solution object that stores information about the solution that has been computed. Most important here are the `t` and `y` attributes, which contain the t values on which the solution y is computed and the solution y itself. We used these values to plot the solution we computed. The y values are stored in a NumPy array of shape `(n, N)`, where `n` is the number of components of the equation (here, 1), and `N` is the number of points computed. The y values held in `sol` are stored in a two-dimensional array, which in this case has 1 row and many columns. We use the slice `y[0, :]` to extract this first row as a one-dimensional array that can be used to plot the solution in *step 4*.

We use a logarithmically scaled y axis to plot the error because what is interesting there is the order of magnitude. Plotting it on a non-scaled y axis would give a line that is very close to the x axis, which doesn't show the increase in the error as we move through the t values. The logarithmically scaled y axis shows this increase clearly.

There's more...

The `solve_ivp` routine is a convenient interface for a number of solvers for differential equations, the default being the Runge-Kutta-Fehlberg (RK45) method. The different solvers have different strengths, but the RK45 method is a good general-purpose solver.

See also

For more detailed instructions on how to add subplots to a figure in Matplotlib, see the *Adding subplots* recipe from `Chapter 2`, *Mathematical Plotting with Matplotlib*.

Solving systems of differential equations

Differential equations sometimes occur in systems consisting of two or more interlinked differential equations. A classical example is a simple model of the populations of competing species. This is a simple model of competing species labeled P (the prey) and W (the predators) given by the following equations:

$$\frac{dP}{dt} = 5P - 0.1WP$$
$$\frac{dW}{dt} = 0.1PW - 6W$$

The first equation dictates the growth of the prey species P, which, without any predators, would be exponential growth. The second equation dictates the growth of the predator species W, which, without any prey, would be exponential decay. Of course, these two equations are *coupled*; each population change depends on both populations. The predators consume the prey at a rate proportional to the product of their two populations, and the predators grow at a rate proportional to the relative abundance of prey (again the product of the two populations).

In this recipe, we will will analyze a simple system of differential equations and use the SciPy `integrate` module to obtain approximate solutions.

Getting ready

The tools for solving a system of differential equations using Python are the same as those for solving a single equation. We again use the `solve_ivp` routine from the `integrate` module in SciPy. However, this will only give us a predicted evolution over time with given starting populations. For this reason, we will also employ some plotting tools from Matplotlib to better understand the evolution.

How to do it...

The following steps walk through how to analyze a simple system of differential equations:

1. Our first task is to define a function that holds the system of equations. This function needs to take two arguments as for a single equation, except the dependent variable y (in the notation from the *Solving simple differential equations numerically* recipe) will now be an array with as many elements as there are equations. Here, there will be two elements. The function we need for the example system in this recipe is as follows:

```
def predator_prey_system(t, y):
    return np.array([5*y[0] - 0.1*y[0]*y[1], 0.1*y[1]*y[0] -
       6*y[1]])
```

2. Now we have defined the system in Python, we can use the `quiver` routine from Matplotlib to produce a plot that will describe how the populations will evolve—given by the equations—at numerous starting populations. We first set up a grid of points on which we will plot this evolution. It is a good idea to choose a relatively small number of points for the `quiver` routine, otherwise it becomes difficult to see details in the plot. For this example, we plot the population values between 0 and 100:

```
p = np.linspace(0, 100, 25)
w = np.linspace(0, 100, 25)
P, W = np.meshgrid(p, w)
```

3. Now, we compute the values of the system at each of these pairs. Notice that neither equation in the system is time-dependent (they are autonomous); the time variable t is unimportant in the calculation. We supply the value `0` for the t argument:

```
dp, dw = predator_prey_system(0, np.array([P, W]))
```

4. The variables `dp` and `dw` now hold the "direction" in which the population of P and W will evolve, respectively, if we started at each point in our grid. We can plot these directions together using the `quiver` routine from `matplotlib.pyplot`:

```
fig, ax = plt.subplots()
ax.quiver(P, W, dp, dw)
ax.set_title("Population dynamics for two competing species")
ax.set_xlabel("P")
ax.set_ylabel("W")
```

Plotting the result of these commands now gives us *Figure 3.2*, which gives a "global" picture of how solutions evolve:

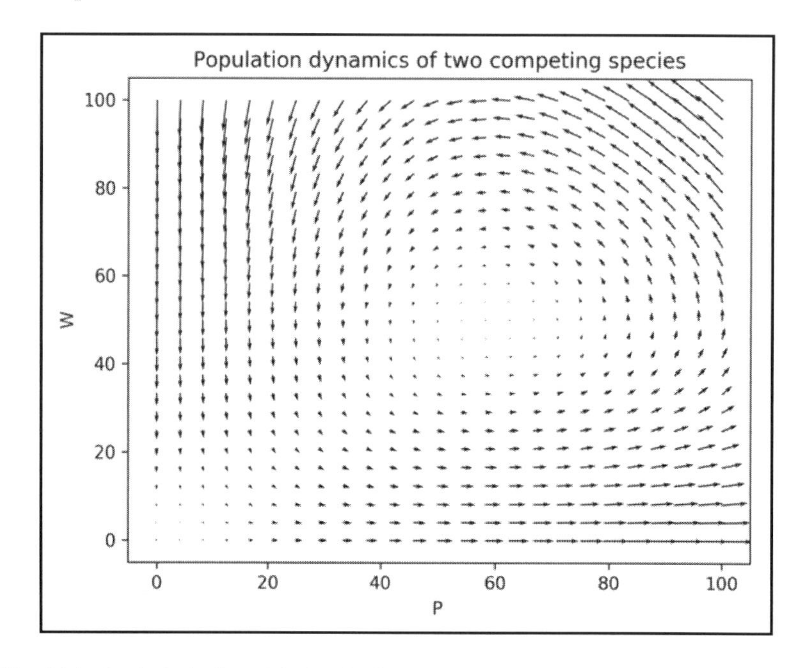

Figure 3.2: A quiver plot showing the population dynamics of two competing species modeled by a system of differential equations

To understand a solution more specifically, we need some initial conditions so we can use the `solve_ivp` routine described in the previous recipe.

5. Since we have two equations, our initial conditions will have two values. (Recall in the *Solving simple differential equations numerically* recipe, we saw that the initial condition provided to `solve_ivp` needs to be a NumPy array.) Let's consider the the initial values $P(0) = 85$ and $W(0) = 40$. We define these in a NumPy array, being careful to place them in the correct order:

```
initial_conditions = np.array([85, 40])
```

6. Now we can use `solve_ivp` from the `scipy.integrate` module. We need to provide the `max_step` keyword argument to make sure that we have enough points in the solution to give a smooth solution curve:

```
from scipy import integrate
sol = integrate.solve_ivp(predator_prey_system, (0., 5.),
   initial_conditions, max_step=0.01)
```

7. Let's plot this solution on our existing figure to show how this specific solution relates to the direction plot we have already produced. We also plot the initial condition at the same time:

```
ax.plot(initial_conditions[0], initial_conditions[1], "ko")
ax.plot(sol.y[0, :], sol.y[1, :], "k", linewidth=0.5)
```

The result of this is shown in *Figure 3.3*:

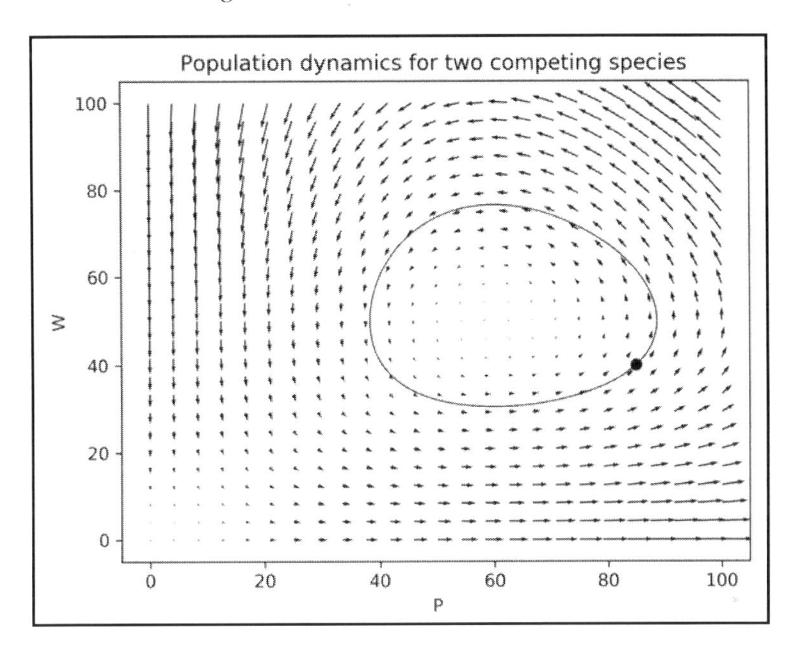

Figure 3.3: Solution trajectory plotted over a quiver plot showing the general behavior

How it works...

The method used for a system of ordinary differential equations is exactly the same as for a single ordinary differential equation. We start by writing the system of equations as a single vector differential equation,

$$\frac{d\mathbf{y}}{dt} = \mathbf{f}(t, \mathbf{y})$$

that can then be solved using a time-stepping method as though $\mathbf{y}$ were a simple scalar value.

The technique of plotting the directional arrows on a plane using the `quiver` routine is a quick and easy way of learning how a system might evolve from a given state. The derivative of a function represents the gradient of the curve $(x, u(x))$, and so a differential equation describes the gradient of the solution function at position y and time t. A system of equations describes the gradient of separate solution functions at a given position $\mathbf{y}$ and time t. Of course, the position is now a two-dimensional point, so when we plot the gradient at a point, we represent this as an arrow that starts at the point, in the direction of the gradient. The length of the arrow represents the size of the gradient; the longer the arrow, the "faster" the solution curve will move in that direction.

When we plot the solution trajectory on top of this direction field, we can see that the curve (starting at the point) follows the direction indicated by the arrows. The behavior shown by the solution trajectory is a *limit cycle*, where the solution for each variable is periodic as the two species populations grow or decline. This description of the behavior is perhaps more clear if we plot each population against time, as seen in *Figure 3.4*. What is not immediately obvious from *Figure 3.3* is that the solution trajectory loops around several times, but this is clearly shown in *Figure 3.4*:

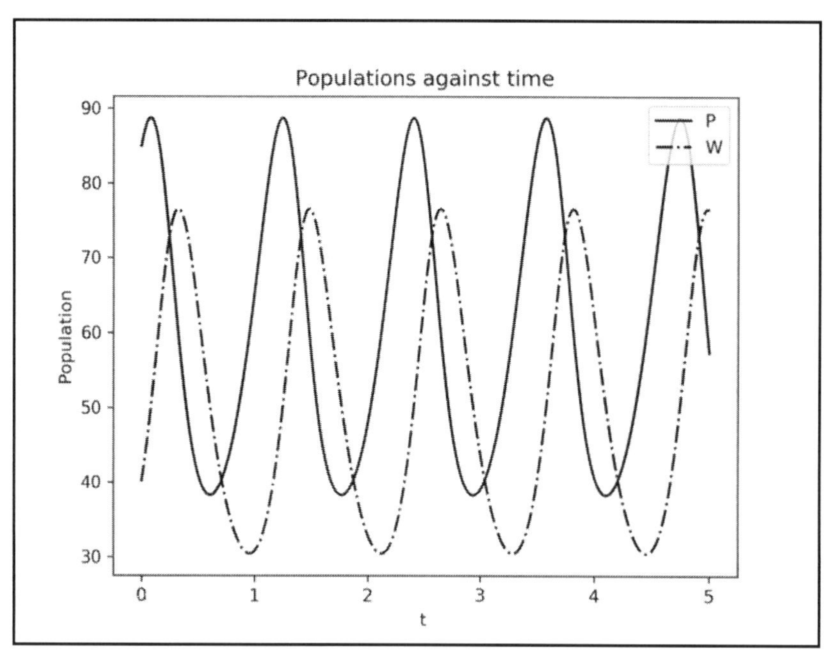

Figure 3.4: Plots of populations P and W against time. Both populations exhibit periodic behavior

There's more...

The technique of analyzing a system of ordinary differential equations by plotting the variables against one another, starting at various initial conditions, is called *phase space (plane) analysis*. In this recipe, we used the `quiver` plotting routine to quickly generate an approximation of the phase plane for the system of differential equations. By analyzing the phase plane of a system of differential equations, we can identify different local and global characteristics of the solution, such as limit cycles.

Solving partial differential equations numerically

Partial differential equations are differential equations that involve *partial derivatives* of functions in two or more variables, as opposed to *ordinary derivatives* in only a single variable. Partial differential equations is a vast topic, and could easily fill a series of books. A typical example of a partial differential equation is the (one-dimensional) *heat equation*

$$\frac{\partial u}{\partial t} = \alpha \frac{\partial^2 u}{\partial x^2} + f(t, x)$$

where α is a positive constant and $f(t, x)$ is a function. The solution to this partial differential equation is a function $u(t, x)$, which represents the temperature of a rod, occupying the x range $0 \leq x \leq L$, at a given time $t > 0$. To keep things simple, we will take $f(t, x) = 0$, which amounts to saying that no heating/cooling is applied to the system, $\alpha = 1$, and $L = 2$. In practice, we can rescale the problem to fix the constant α, so this is not a restrictive problem. In this example, we will use the boundary conditions

$$u(t, 0) = u(t, L) = 0 \qquad (t > 0)$$

which are equivalent to saying that the ends of the rod are held at the constant temperature 0. We will also use the initial temperature profile

$$u(0, x) = 3 \sin\left(\frac{\pi}{2} x\right) \qquad (0 \leq x \leq 2)$$

This initial temperature profile describes a smooth curve between the values of 0 and 2, that peaks at a value of 3, which might be the result of heating the rod at the center to a temperature of 3.

We're going to use a method called *finite differences*, where we divide the rod into a number of equal segments and the time range into a number of discrete steps. We then compute approximations for the solution at each of the segments and each time step.

In this recipe, we will use finite differences to solve a simple partial differential equation.

Getting ready

For this recipe, we will need the NumPy package and Matplotlib package, imported as `np` and `plt` as usual. We also need to import the `mplot3d` module from `mpl_toolkits` since we will be producing a 3D plot:

```
from mpl_toolkits import mplot3d
```

We will also need some modules from the SciPy package.

How to do it...

In the following steps, we work through solving the heat equation using finite differences:

1. Let's first create variables that represent the physical constraints of the system: the extent of the bar and the value of α:

```
alpha = 1
x0 = 0 # Left hand x limit
xL = 2 # Right hand x limit
```

2. We first divide the x range into N equal intervals—we take $N = 10$ for this example—using $N+1$ points. We can use the `linspace` routine from NumPy to generate these points. We also need the common length of each interval h:

```
N = 10
x = np.linspace(x0, xL, N+1)
h = (xL - x0) / N
```

3. Next, we need to set up the steps in the time direction. We take a slightly different approach here; we set the time step size k and the number of steps (implicitly making the assumption that we start at time 0):

```
k = 0.01
steps = 100
t = np.array([i*k for i in range(steps+1)])
```

4. In order for the method to behave properly, we must have

$$\frac{\alpha k}{h^2} < \frac{1}{2}$$

otherwise the system can become unstable. We store the left-hand side of this in a variable for use in *Step 4*, and use an assertion to check that this inequality holds:

```
r = alpha*k / h**2
assert r < 0.5, f"Must have r < 0.5, currently r={r}"
```

5. Now we can construct a matrix that holds the coefficients from the finite difference scheme. To do this, we use the `diags` routine from the `scipy.sparse` module to create a sparse, tridiagonal matrix:

```
from scipy import sparse
diag = [1, *(1-2*r for _ in range(N-1)), 1]
abv_diag = [0, *(r for _ in range(N-1))]
blw_diag = [*(r for _ in range(N-1)), 0]

A = sparse.diags([blw_diag, diag, abv_diag], (-1, 0, 1),
shape=(N+1,
       N+1), dtype=np.float64, format="csr")
```

6. Next, we create a blank matrix that will hold the solution:

```
u = np.zeros((steps+1, N+1), dtype=np.float64)
```

7. We need to add the initial profile to the first row. The best way to do this is to create a function that holds the initial profile and store the result of evaluating this function on the `x` array in the matrix `u` that we just created:

```
def initial_profile(x):
    return 3*np.sin(np.pi*x/2)

u[0, :] = initial_profile(x)
```

8. Now we can simply loop through each step, computing the next row of the matrix `u` by multiplying `A` and the previous row:

```
for i in range(steps):
    u[i+1, :] = A @ u[i, :]
```

9. Finally, to visualize the solution we have just computed, we can plot the solution as a surface using Matplotlib:

```
X, T = np.meshgrid(x, t)
fig = plt.figure()
ax = fig.add_subplot(projection="3d")

ax.plot_surface(T, X, u, cmap="hot")
ax.set_title("Solution of the heat equation")
ax.set_xlabel("t")
ax.set_ylabel("x")
ax.set_zlabel("u")
```

The result of this is the surface plot shown in *Figure 3.5*:

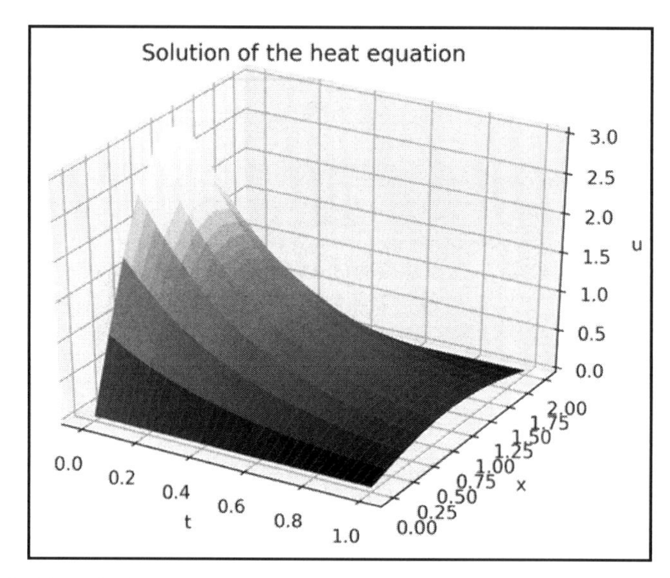

Figure 3.5: Surface plot of the solution of the heat equation over the range $0 \le x \le 2$ computed using the finite difference method with 10 mesh points

How it works...

The finite difference method works by replacing each of the derivatives with a simple fraction that involves only the value of the function, which we can estimate. To implement this method, we first break down the spatial range and time range into a number of discrete intervals, separated by mesh points. This process is called *discretization*. Then we use the differential equation and the initial conditions and boundary conditions to form successive approximations, in a manner very similar to the time-stepping methods used by the `solve_ivp` routine in the *Solving differential equations numerically* recipe.

In order to solve a partial differential equation such as the heat equation, we need at least three pieces of information. Usually, for the heat equation, this will come in the form of *boundary conditions* for the spatial dimension, which tell us what the behavior is at either end of the rod, and *initial conditions* for the time dimension, which is the initial temperature profile over the rod.

The finite difference scheme described previously is usually referred to as the **forward time central spatial** (**FTCS**) scheme, since we use the *forward finite difference* to estimate the time derivative and the *central finite difference* to estimate the (second order) spatial derivative. The formulas for these finite differences are given by

$$\frac{\partial u}{\partial t} \approx \frac{u(t+k, x) - u(t, x)}{k}$$

and

$$\frac{\partial^2 u}{\partial x^2} \approx \frac{u(t, x+h) - 2u(t, x) + u(t, x-h)}{h^2}$$

Substituting these approximations into the heat equation, and using the approximation u_i^j for the value of $u(t_j, x_i)$ after j time steps at the i spatial point, we get

$$\frac{u_i^{j+1} - u_i^j}{k} = \alpha \frac{u_{i+1}^j - 2u_i^j + u_{i-1}^j}{h^2}$$

which can be rearranged to obtain the formula

$$u_i^{j+1} = \frac{\alpha k}{h^2} u_{i+1}^j + \left(1 - 2\frac{\alpha k}{h^2}\right) u_i^j + \frac{\alpha k}{h^2} u_{i-1}^j$$

Roughly speaking, this equation says that the next temperature at a given point depends on the surrounding temperatures at the previous time. This also shows why the condition on the `r` value is necessary; if the condition does not hold, the middle term on the right-hand side will be negative.

We can write this system of equations in matrix form,

$$\mathbf{u}^{j+1} = A\mathbf{u}^j$$

where $\mathbf{u}^j$ is a vector containing the approximation u_i^j and matrix A, which was defined in *step 4*. This matrix is tridiagonal, which means the non-zero entries appear on, or adjacent to, the leading diagonal. We use the `diag` routine from the SciPy `sparse` module, which is a utility for defining these kinds of matrices. This is very similar to the process described in the *Solving equations* recipe of this chapter. The first and last row of this matrix have zeros, except in the top left and bottom right, respectively, that represent the (non-changing) boundary conditions. The other rows have coefficients that are given by the finite difference approximations for the derivatives on either side of differential equation. We first create the diagonal entries and the entries above and below the diagonal, and then we use the `diags` routine to create the sparse matrix. The matrix should have *N+1* rows and columns, to match the number of mesh points, and we set the data type as double-precision floats and CSR format.

The initial profile gives us the vector $\mathbf{u}^0$, and from this first point, we can compute each subsequent time step by simply performing a matrix multiplication, as we saw in *step 7*.

There's more...

The method we describe here is rather crude since the approximation can become unstable, as we mentioned, if the relative sizes of time steps and spatial steps are not carefully controlled. This method is *explicit* since each time step is computed explicitly using only information from the previous time step. There are also *implicit* methods, which give a system of equations that can be solved to obtain the next time step. Different schemes have different characteristics in terms of the stability of the solution.

When the function $f(t, x)$ is not 0, we can easily accommodate this change by instead using the assignment

$$\mathbf{u}^{j+1} = A\mathbf{u}^j + f(t_j, \mathbf{x})$$

where the function is suitably vectorized to make this formula valid. In terms of the code used to solve the problem, we need only include the definition of the function and then change the loop of the solution as follows:

```
for i in range(steps):
    u[i+1, :] = A @ u[i, :] + f(t[i], x)
```

Physically, this function represents an external heat source (or sink) at each point along the rod. This may change over time, which is why, in general, the function should have both t and x as arguments (though they need not both be used).

The boundary conditions we gave in this example represent the ends of the rod being kept at a constant temperature of 0. These kinds of boundary conditions are sometimes called *Dirichlet* boundary conditions. There are also *Neumann* boundary conditions, where the derivative of the function u is given at the boundary. For example, we might have been given the boundary conditions

$$\frac{\partial u}{\partial x}(t,0) = \frac{\partial u}{\partial x}(t,L) = 0$$

which could be interpreted physically as the ends of the rod being insulated so that heat cannot escape through the end points. For such boundary conditions we need to modify the matrix A slightly, but otherwise the method remains the same. Indeed, inserting an imaginary x value to the left of the boundary and using the backward finite difference at the left-hand boundary ($x = 0$), we obtain

$$0 = \frac{\partial u}{\partial x}(t_j, 0) = \frac{u^j_{-1} - u^j_0}{h} \implies u^j_{-1} = u^j_0$$

Using this in the second order finite difference approximation, we get

$$\frac{\partial^2 u}{\partial x^2}(t_j, 0) \approx \frac{u^j_1 - 2u^j_0 + u^j_{-1}}{h^2} = \frac{u^j_1 - u^j_0}{h^2}$$

which means that the first row of our matrix should contain $1-r$, then r, followed by 0. Using a similar computation for the right-hand limit gives a similar final row of the matrix:

```
diag = [1-r, *(1-2*r for _ in range(N-1)), 1-r]
abv_diag = [*(r for _ in range(N))]
blw_diag = [*(r for _ in range(N))]

A = sparse.diags([blw_diag, diag, abv_diag], (-1, 0, 1), shape=(N+1, N+1),
dtype=np.float64, format="csr")
```

For more complex problems involving partial differential equations, it is probably more appropriate to use a *finite elements* solver. Finite element methods use a more sophisticated approach for computing solutions than partial differential equations, which are generally more flexible than the finite difference method we saw in this recipe. However, this comes at the cost of requiring more setup that relies on more advanced mathematical theory. On the other hand, there is a Python package for solving partial differential equations using finite element methods such as FEniCS (`fenicsproject.org`). The advantage of using a package such as FEniCS is that they are usually tuned for performance, which is important when solving with complex problems to high accuracy.

See also

The FEniCS documentation gives a good introduction to the finite element method and a number of examples of using the package to solve various classic partial differential equations. A more comprehensive introduction to the method and the theory is given in the following book:

- *Johnson, C. (2009). Numerical solution of partial differential equations by the finite element method. Mineola, N.Y.: Dover Publications.*

For more details on how to produce three-dimensional surface plots using Matplotlib, see the *Surface and contour plots* recipe from `Chapter 2`, *Mathematical Plotting with Matplotlib.*

Using discrete Fourier transforms for signal processing

One of the most useful tools coming from calculus is the *Fourier transform*. Roughly speaking, the Fourier transform changes the representation, in a reversible way, of certain functions. This change of representation is particularly useful in dealing with signals represented as a function of time. In this instance, the Fourier transform takes the signal and represents it as a function of frequency; we might describe this as transforming from signal space to frequency space. This can be used to identify the frequencies present in a signal for identification and other processing. In practice, we will usually have a discrete sample of a signal, so we have to use the *discrete Fourier transform* to perform this kind of analysis. Fortunately, there is a computationally efficient algorithm, called the **fast Fourier transform** (**FFT**), for applying the discrete Fourier transform to a sample.

We will follow a common process for filtering a noisy signal using FFT. The first step is to apply the FFT and use the data to compute the power spectral density of the signal. Then we identify the peaks and filter out the frequencies that do no contribute a sufficiently large amount to the signal. Then we apply the inverse FFT to obtain the filtered signal.

In this recipe, we use the FFT to analyze a sample of a signal and identify the frequencies present and clean the noise from the signal.

Getting ready

For this recipe, we will only need the NumPy and Matplotlib packages imported as `np` and `plt`, as usual.

How to do it...

Follow these instructions to use the FFT to process a noisy signal:

1. We define a function that will generate our underlying signal:

```
def signal(t, freq_1=4.0, freq_2=7.0):
    return np.sin(freq_1 * 2 * np.pi * t) + np.sin(freq_2 * 2 *
        np.pi * t)
```

2. Next, we create our sample signal by adding some Gaussian noise to the underlying signal. We also create an array that holds the true signal at the sample *t* values for convenience later:

```
state = np.random.RandomState(12345)
sample_size = 2**7 # 128
sample_t = np.linspace(0, 4, sample_size)
sample_y = signal(sample_t) + state.standard_normal(sample_size)
sample_d = 4./(sample_size - 1) # Spacing for linspace array
true_signal = signal(sample_t)
```

3. We use the `fft` module from NumPy to compute discrete Fourier transforms. We import this from NumPy before we start our analysis:

```
from numpy import fft
```

4. To see what the noisy signal looks like, we can plot the sample signal points with the true signal superimposed:

```
fig1, ax1 = plt.subplots()
ax1.plot(sample_t, sample_y, "k.", label="Noisy signal")
ax1.plot(sample_t, signal(sample_t), "k--", label="True signal")

ax1.set_title("Sample signal with noise")
ax1.set_xlabel("Time")
ax1.set_ylabel("Amplitude")
ax1.legend()
```

The plot created here is shown in *Figure 3.6*. As we can see, the noisy signal does not bear much resemblance to the true signal (shown with the dashed line):

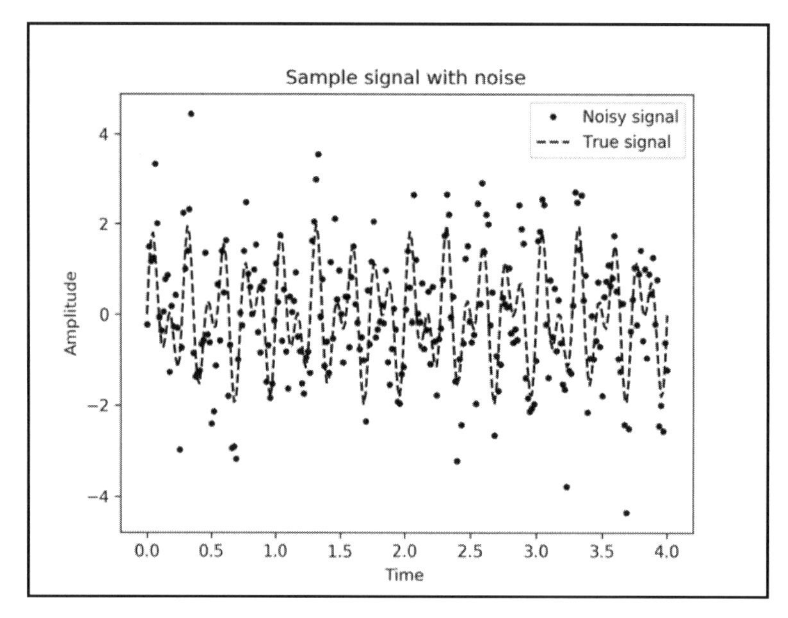

Figure 3.6: Noisy signal sample with true signal superimposed

5. Now, we will use the discrete Fourier transform to extract the frequencies that are present in the sample signal. The `fft` routine in the `fft` module performs the FFT (discrete Fourier transform):

```
spectrum = fft.fft(sample_y)
```

6. The `fft` module provides a routine for constructing the appropriate frequency values called `fftfreq`. For convenience, we also generate an array containing the integers at which the positive frequencies occur:

```
freq = fft.fftfreq(sample_size, sample_d)
pos_freq_i = np.arange(1, sample_size//2, dtype=int)
```

7. Next, compute the **power spectral density** (**PSD**) of the signal as follows:

```
psd = np.abs(spectrum[pos_freq_i])**2 + np.abs(spectrum[-
        pos_freq_i])**2
```

8. Now, we can plot the PSD of the signal for the positive frequencies and use this plot to identify the frequencies:

```
fig2, ax2 = plt.subplots()
ax2.plot(freq[pos_freq_i], psd)
ax2.set_title("PSD of the noisy signal")
ax2.set_xlabel("Frequency")
ax2.set_ylabel("Density")
```

The result can be seen in *Figure 3.7*. We can see in this diagram that there are spikes at roughly 4 and 7, which are the frequencies of the signal that we defined earlier:

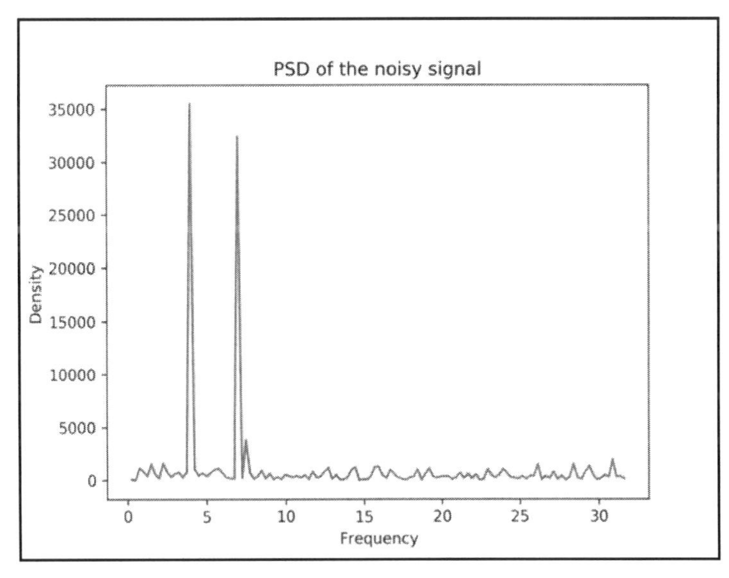

Figure 3.7: Power spectral density of a signal generated using the FFT

9. We can identify these two frequencies to try and reconstruct the true signal from the noisy sample. All of the minor peaks that appear are not larger than 10,000, so we can use this as a cut-off value for the filter. Let's now extract from the list of all positive frequency indices the (hopefully 2) indices that correspond to the peaks above 10,000 in the PSD:

```
filtered = pos_freq_i[psd > 1e4]
```

10. Next, we create a new, clean spectrum that contains only the frequencies that we have extracted from the noisy signal. We do this by creating an array that contains only 0, and then copying the value of `spectrum` from those indices that correspond to the filtered frequencies and the negatives thereof:

```
new_spec = np.zeros_like(spectrum)
new_spec[filtered] = spectrum[filtered]
new_spec[-filtered] = spectrum[-filtered]
```

11. Now, we use the inverse FFT (using the `ifft` routine) to transform this clean spectrum back to the time domain of the original sample. We take the real part using the `real` routine from NumPy to eliminate the erroneous imaginary parts:

```
new_sample = np.real(fft.ifft(new_spec))
```

12. Finally, we plot this filtered signal over the true signal and compare the results:

```
fig3, ax3 = plt.subplots()
ax3.plot(sample_t, true_signal, color="#8c8c8c", linewidth=1.5,
label="True signal")
ax3.plot(sample_t, new_sample, "k--", label="Filtered signal")
ax3.legend()
ax3.set_title("Plot comparing filtered signal and true signal")
ax3.set_xlabel("Time")
ax3.set_ylabel("Amplitude")
```

The result of *step 12* is shown in *Figure 3.8*. We can see that the filtered signal closely matches the true signal, except for some small discrepancies:

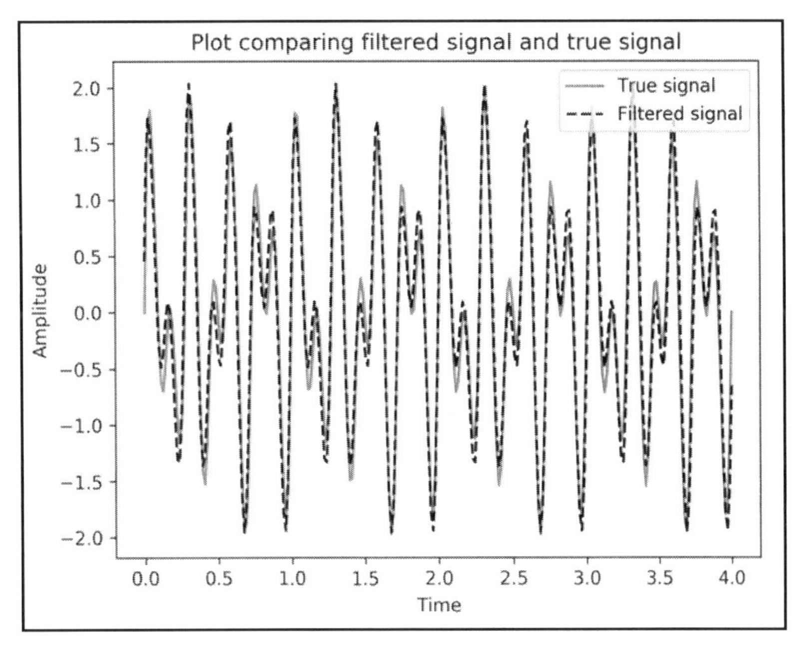

Figure 3.8: Plot comparing the filtered signal generated using FFTs and filtering to the true signal

How it works...

The *Fourier transform* of a function $f(t)$ is given by the integral

$$\widehat{f}(x) = \int_{-\infty}^{\infty} f(t)e^{-2\pi ixt}\,\mathrm{d}t$$

and the discrete Fourier transform is given by

$$\widehat{f}_n = \sum_{k=0}^{N-1} f_k e^{-2\pi ikn/N} \qquad \text{for } n = 0, 1, \dots, N-1$$

Here, the f_k values are the sample values as complex numbers. The discrete Fourier transform can be computed using the preceding formula, but in practice this is not efficient. Computing using this formula is $O(N^2)$. The FFT algorithm improves the complexity to $O(N \log N)$, which is significantly better. The book *Numerical Recipes* (full bibliographic details given in the *Further reading* section) gives a very good description of the FFT algorithm and the discrete Fourier transform.

We will apply the discrete Fourier transform to a sample generated from a known signal (with known frequency modes) so we can see the connection between the results we obtain and the original signal. To keep this signal simple, we created a signal that has only two frequency components with values 4 and 7. From this signal, we generated the sample that we analyzed. Because of the way the FFT works, it is best if the sample has a size that is a power of 2; if this isn't the case, we can pad the sample with zero elements to make this the case. We add some Gaussian noise to the sample signal, which takes the form of a normally distributed random number.

The array returned by the `fft` routine contains $N+1$ elements, where N is the sample size. The element that index 0 corresponds to is the 0 frequency, or DC shift. The next $N/2$ elements are the values corresponding to the positive frequencies, and the final $N/2$ elements are the values corresponding to the negative frequencies. The actual values of the frequencies are determined by the number of sampled points N and the sample spacing, which, in this example, is stored in `sample_d`.

The power spectral density at the frequency ω is given by the formula

$$\mathrm{PSD}(\omega) = |H(\omega)|^2 + |H(-\omega)|^2$$

where $H(\omega)$ represents the Fourier transform of the signal at frequency ω. The power spectral density measures the contribution of each frequency to the overall signal, which is why we see peaks at approximately 4 and 7. Since Python indexing allows us to use negative indices for elements starting from the end of the sequence, we can use the positive index array to get both the positive and negative frequency elements from `spectrum`.

In *step 9*, we extracted the indices of the two frequencies that peak above 10,000 on the plot. The frequencies that correspond to these indices are 3.984375 and 6.97265625, which are not exactly equal to 4 and 7, but are very close. The reason for this discrepancy is the fact that we have sampled a continuous signal using a finite number of points. (Using more points will, of course, yield better approximations.)

In *step 11*, we took the real part of the data returned from the inverse FFT. This is because, technically speaking, the FFT works with complex data. Since our data contained only real data, we expect that this new signal should also contain only real data. However, there will be some small errors made, meaning that the results are not totally real. We can remedy this by taking the real part of the inverse FFT. This is appropriate because we can see that the imaginary parts are very small.

We can see in *Figure 3.8* that the filtered signal very closely matches the true signal, but not exactly. This is because, as mentioned previously, we are approximating a continuous signal with a relatively small sample.

There's more...

Signal processing in a production setting would probably make use of a specialized package, such as the `signal` module from `scipy`, or some lower-level code or hardware to perform filtering or cleaning of a signal. This recipe should be taken as more of a demonstration of the use of FFT as a tool for working with data sampled from some kind of underlying periodic structure (the signal). FFTs are useful for solving partial differential equations, such as the heat equation seen in the *Solving partial differential equations numerically* recipe.

See also

More information about random numbers and the normal distribution (Gaussian) can be found in `Chapter 4`, *Working with Randomness and Probability.*

Further reading

Calculus is a very important part of every undergraduate mathematics course. There are a number of excellent textbooks on calculus, including the classic textbook by Spivak and the more comprehensive course by Adams and Essex:

- *Spivak, M. (2006). Calculus. 3rd ed. Cambridge: Cambridge University Press*
- *Adams, R. and Essex, C. (2018). Calculus: A Complete Course. 9th ed. Don Mills, Ont: Pearson.Guassian*

A good source for numerical differentiation and integration is the classic *Numerical Recipes* book, which gives a comprehensive description of how to solve many computational problems in C++, including a summary of the theory:

- *Press, W., Teukolsky, S., Vetterling, W. and Flannery, B. (2007). Numerical recipes: The Art of Scientific Computing. 3rd ed. Cambridge: Cambridge University Press*

4
Working with Randomness and Probability

In this chapter, we will discuss randomness and probability. We will start by briefly exploring the fundamentals of probability by selecting elements from a set of data. Then, we will learn how to generate (pseudo) random numbers using Python and NumPy, and how to generate samples according to a specific probability distribution. We will conclude the chapter by looking at a number of advanced topics covering random processes and Bayesian techniques, and using Markov chain Monte Carlo methods to estimate parameters on a simple model.

Probability is a quantification of the likelihood of a specific event occurring. We use probabilities intuitively all of the time, although sometimes the formal theory can be quite counterintuitive. Probability theory aims to describe the behavior of *random variables*, whose value is not known, but where the probabilities of the value of this random variable taking some (range of) values is known. These probabilities are usually in the form of one of several probability distributions. Arguably, the most famous such probability distribution is normal distribution which, for example, can describe the spread of a certain characteristic over a large population.

We will see probability again in a more applied setting in `Chapter 6`, *Working with Data and Statistics*, where we discuss statistics. Here, we will put probability theory to use to quantify errors and build a systematic theory of analyzing data.

In this chapter, we will cover the following recipes:

- Selecting items at random
- Generating random data
- Changing the random number generator
- Generating normally distributed random numbers

- Working with random processes
- Analyzing conversion rates with Bayesian techniques
- Estimating parameters with Monte Carlo simulations

Technical requirements

For this chapter, we require the standard scientific Python packages, NumPy, Matplotlib, and SciPy. We will also require the PyMC3 package for the final recipe. You can install this using your favorite package manager, such as `pip`:

```
python3.8 -m pip install pymc3
```

This command will install the most recent version of PyMC3, which, at the time of writing, was 3.9.2. This package provides facilities for probabilistic programming, which involves performing many calculations driven by randomly generated data to understand the likely distribution of a solution to a problem.

The code for this chapter can be found in the `Chapter 04` folder of the GitHub repository at `https://github.com/PacktPublishing/Applying-Math-with-Python/tree/master/Chapter%2004`.

Check out the following video to see the Code in Action: `https://bit.ly/2OP3FAo`.

Selecting items at random

At the core of probability and randomness is the idea of selecting an item from some kind of collection. As we know, the probability of selecting an item from a collection quantifies the likelihood of that item being selected. Randomness describes the selection of items from a collection according to the probabilities without any additional bias. The opposite of a random selection might be described as a *deterministic* selection. In general, it is very difficult to replicate a purely random process using a computer, because computers and their processing are inherently deterministic. However, we can generate sequences of pseudo-random numbers that, when properly constructed, demonstrate a reasonable approximation of randomness.

In this recipe, we will select items from a collection and learn some of the key terminology associated with probability and randomness that we will need throughout this chapter.

Getting ready

The Python Standard Library contains a module for generating (pseudo) random numbers called `random`, but in this recipe, and throughout this chapter, we will instead use the NumPy `random` module. The routines in the NumPy `random` module can be used to generate arrays of random numbers and are slightly more flexible than their standard library counterparts. As usual, we import NumPy under the alias `np`.

Before we can proceed, we need to fix some terminology. A *sample space* is a set (a collection with no repeated elements), and an *event* is a subset of the sample space. The *probability* that an event A occurs is denoted as $P(A)$, and is a number between 0 and 1. A probability of 0 indicates that the event can never occur, while a probability of 1 indicates that an event will certainly occur. The probability of the whole sample space must be 1.

When the sample space is discrete, then probabilities are just numbers between 0 and 1 associated with each of the elements, where the sum of all these numbers is 1. This gives meaning to the probability of selecting a single item (an event consisting of a single element) from a collection. We will consider methods for selecting items from a discrete collection here and deal with the *continuous* case in the *Generating normally distributed random numbers* recipe.

How to do it...

Perform the following steps to select items at random from a container:

1. The first step is to set up the random number generator. For the moment, we will use the default random number generator for NumPy, which is recommended in most cases. We can do this by calling the `default_rng` routine from the NumPy `random` module, which will return an instance of a random number generator. We will usually call this function without a seed, but for this recipe, we will add the seed `12345` so that our results are repeatable:

```
rng = np.random.default_rng(12345)
# changing seed for repeatability
```

2. Next, we need to create the data and probabilities that we will select from. This step can be skipped if you already have the data stored or if you want to select elements with equal probabilities:

```
data = np.arange(15)
probabilities = np.array(
    [0.3, 0.2, 0.1, 0.05, 0.05, 0.05, 0.05, 0.025,
    0.025, 0.025, 0.025, 0.025, 0.025, 0.025, 0.025]
)
```

As a quick sanity test, we can use an assertion to check that these probabilities do indeed sum to 1:

```
assert round(sum(probabilities), 10) == 1.0, \
    "Probabilities must sum to 1"
```

3. Now, we can use the `choice` method on the random number generator, `rng`, to select the samples from `data` according to the probabilities just created. For this selection, we want to turn the replacement on, so calling the method multiple times can select from the whole of `data`:

```
selected = rng.choice(data, p=probabilities, replace=True)
# 0
```

4. To select multiple items from `data`, we can also supply the `size` argument, which specifies the shape of the array to be selected. This plays the same role as the `shape` keyword argument to many of the other NumPy array creation routines. The argument given to `size` can be either an integer or a tuple of integers:

```
selected_array = rng.choice(data, p=probabilities, replace=True,
size=(5, 5))
#array([[ 1, 6, 4, 1, 1],
#       [ 2, 0, 4, 12, 0],
#       [12, 4, 0, 1, 10],
#       [ 4, 1, 5, 0, 0],
#       [ 0, 1, 1, 0, 7]])
```

How it works...

The `default_rng` routine creates a new **pseudo random number generator** (**PRNG**) instance (with or without a seed) that can be used to generate random numbers or, as we saw in the recipe, select items at random from predefined data. NumPy also has an **implicit state**-based interface for generating random numbers using routines directly from the `random` module. However, it is generally advisable to create the generator explicitly, using `default_rng` or create a `Generator` instance yourself. Being more explicit in this way is more Pythonic, and should lead to more reproducible results (in some sense).

A **seed** is a value that is passed to a random number generator in order to generate the values. The generator generates a sequence of numbers in a completely deterministic way based only on the seed. This means that two instances of the same PRNGs provided with the same seed will generate the same sequence of random numbers. If no seed is provided, the generators typically produce a seed that depends on the user's system.

The `Generator` class from NumPy is a wrapper around a low-level pseudo random bit generator, which is where the random numbers are actually generated. In recent versions of NumPy, the default PRNG algorithm is the 128-bit *permuted congruential generator.* By contrast, Python's built-in `random` module uses a Mersenne Twister PRNG. More information about the different options for PRNG algorithms is given in the *Changing the random number generator* recipe.

The `choice` method on a `Generator` instance performs selections according to random numbers generated by the underlying `BitGenerator`. The optional `p` keyword argument specifies the probability associated with each item from the data provided. If this argument isn't provided, then a *uniform probability* is assumed, where each item has equal probability of being selected. The `replace` keyword argument specifies whether selections should be made with or without a replacement. We turned replacement on so that the same element can be selected more than once. The `choice` method uses the random numbers given by the generator to make the selections, which means that two PRNGs of the same type using the same seed will select the same items when using the `choice` method.

There's more...

The `choice` method can also be used to create random samples of a given size by passing `replace=False` as an argument. This guarantees the selection of distinct items from the data, which is good for generating a random sample. This might be used, for example, to select users to test a new version of an interface from the whole group of users; most sample statistical techniques rely on randomly selected samples.

Generating random data

Many tasks involve generating large quantities of random numbers, which, in their most basic form, are either integers or floating-point numbers (double precision) lying in the range $0 \leq x < 1$. Ideally, these numbers should be selected uniformly, so that if we draw a large quantity of such numbers, they should be distributed roughly evenly across the range $0 \leq x < 1$.

In this recipe, we will see how to generate large quantities of random integers and floating-point numbers using NumPy, and show the distribution of these numbers using a histogram.

Getting ready

Before we start, we need to import the `default_rng` routine from the NumPy `random` module and create an instance of the default random number generator to use in the recipe:

```
from numpy.random import default_rng
rng = default_rng(12345) # changing seed for reproducibility
```

We have discussed this process in the *Selecting items at random* recipe.

We also import the Matplotlib `pyplot` module under the alias `plt`.

How to do it...

Perform the following steps to generate uniform random data and plot a histogram to understand its distribution:

1. To generate random floating-point numbers between 0 and 1, including 0 but not 1, we use the `random` method on the `rng` object:

```
random_floats = rng.random(size=(5, 5))
# array([[0.22733602, 0.31675834, 0.79736546, 0.67625467,
0.39110955],
#        [0.33281393, 0.59830875, 0.18673419, 0.67275604,
0.94180287],
#        [0.24824571, 0.94888115, 0.66723745, 0.09589794,
0.44183967],
#        [0.88647992, 0.6974535 , 0.32647286, 0.73392816,
0.22013496],
#        [0.08159457, 0.1598956 , 0.34010018, 0.46519315,
0.26642103]])
```

2. To generate random integers, we use the `integers` method on the `rng` object. This will return integers in the specified range:

```
random_ints = rng.integers(1, 20, endpoint=True, size=10)
# array([12, 17, 10, 4, 1, 3, 2, 2, 3, 12])
```

3. To examine the distribution of the random floating-point numbers, we first need to generate a large array of random numbers, just as we did in *Step 1*. While this is not strictly necessary, a larger sample will be able to show the distribution more clearly. We generate these numbers as follows:

```
dist = rng.random(size=1000)
```

4. To show the distribution of the numbers we have generated, we plot a *histogram* of the data:

```
fig, ax = plt.subplots()
ax.hist(dist)
ax.set_title("Histogram of random numbers")
ax.set_xlabel("Value")
ax.set_ylabel("Density")
```

The resulting plot is shown in *Figure 4.1*. As we can see, the data is roughly evenly distributed across the whole range:

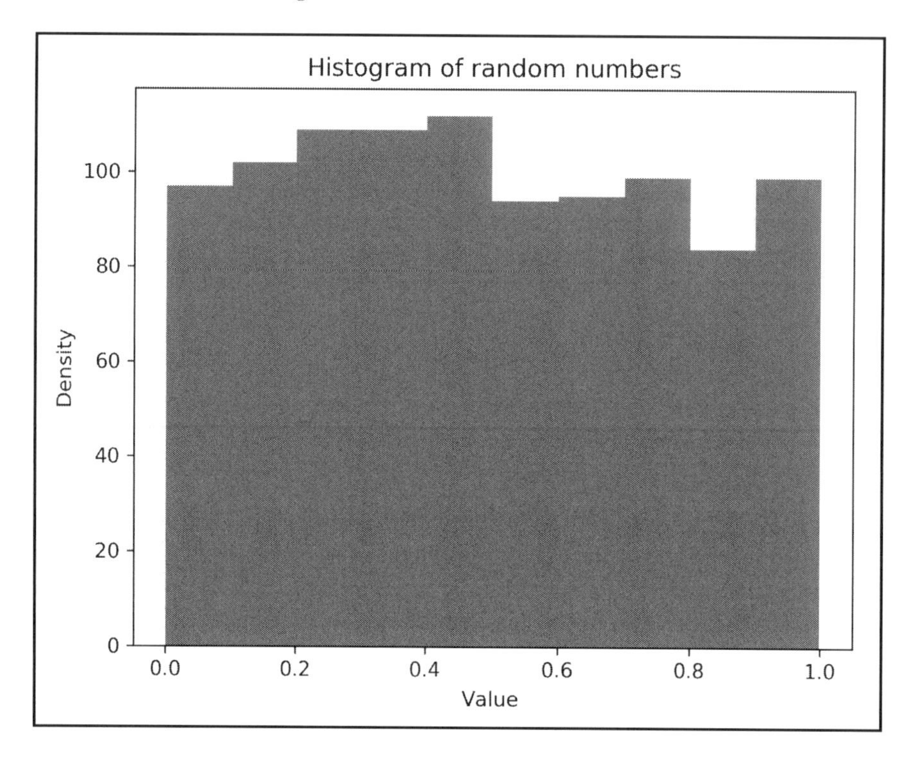

Figure 4.1: Histogram of randomly generated random numbers between 0 and 1

How it works...

The `Generator` interface provides three simple methods for generating basic random numbers, not including the `choice` method that we discussed in the *Selecting items at random* recipe. In addition to the `random` method, for generating random floating-point numbers, and the `integers` method, for generating random integers, there is also a `bytes` method for generating raw random bytes. Each of these methods calls a relevant method on the underlying `BitGenerator` instance. Each of these methods also enables the data type of the generated numbers to be changed, for example, from double to single precision floating-point numbers.

There's more...

The `integers` method on the `Generator` class combines the functionality of the `randint` and `random_integers` methods on the old `RandomState` interface through the addition of the `endpoint` optional argument. (In the old interface, the `randint` method excluded the upper end point, whereas the `random_integers` method included the upper end point.) All of the random data generating methods on `Generator` allow the data type of the data they generate to be customized, which was not possible using the old interface. (This interface was introduced in NumPy 1.17.)

In *Figure 4.1*, we can see that the histogram of the data that we generated is approximately uniform over the range $0 \leq x < 1$. That is, all of the bars are approximately level. (They are not completely level due to the random nature of the data.) This is what we expect from uniformly distributed random numbers, such as those generated by the `random` method. We will explain distributions of random numbers in greater detail in the *Generating normally distributed random numbers* recipe.

Changing the random number generator

The `random` module in NumPy provides several alternatives to the default PRNG, which uses a 128-bit permutation congruential generator. While this is a good general-purpose random number generator, it might not be sufficient for your particular needs. For example, this algorithm is very different from the one used in Python's internal random number generator. We will follow the guidelines for best practice set out in the NumPy documentation for running repeatable, but suitably random, simulations.

In this recipe, we will show you how to change to an alternative pseudo random number generator, and how to use seeds effectively in your programs.

Getting ready

As usual, we import NumPy under the alias `np`. Since we will be using multiple items from the `random` package, we import that module from NumPy, too, using the following code:

```
from numpy import random
```

You will need to select one of the alternative random number generators that are provided by NumPy (or define your own; refer to the *There's more...* section in this recipe). For this recipe, we will use the MT19937 random number generator, which uses a Mersenne Twister-based algorithm like the one used in Python's internal random number generator.

How to do it...

The following steps show how to generate seeds and different random number generators in a reproducible way:

1. We will generate a `SeedSequence` object that can reproducibly generate new seeds from a given source of entropy. We can either provide our own entropy as an integer, very much like how we provide the seed to `default_rng`, or we can let Python gather entropy from the operating system. We will use the latter case here, to demonstrate its use. For this, we do not provide any additional arguments to create the `SeedSequence` object:

```
seed_seq = random.SeedSequence()
```

2. Now that we have a means to generate the seeds for random number generators for the rest of the session, we next log the entropy so that we can reproduce this session later, if necessary. The following is an example of what the entropy should look like; your results will inevitably differ somewhat:

```
print(seed_seq.entropy)
# 9219863422733683567749127389169034574
```

3. Now, we can create the underlying `BitGenerator` instance that will provide the random numbers for the wrapping `Generator` object:

```
bit_gen = random.MT19937(seed_seq)
```

4. Next, we create the wrapping `Generator` object around this `BitGenerator` instance to create a usable random number generator:

```
rng = random.Generator(bit_gen)
```

How it works...

As mentioned in the *Selecting items at random* recipe, the `Generator` class is a wrapper around an underlying `BitGenerator` that implements a given pseudo random number algorithm. NumPy provides several implementations of pseudo random number algorithms through the various subclasses of the `BitGenerator` class: `PCG64` (default); `MT19937` (as seen in this recipe); `Philox`; and `SFC64`. These bit generators are implemented in Cython.

The `PCG64` generator should provide high-performance random number generation with good statistical quality. (This might not be the case on 32 bit systems.)
The `MT19937` generator is slower than more modern PRNGs and does not produce random numbers with good statistical properties. However, this is the random number generator algorithm that is used by the Python Standard Library `random` module. The `Philox` generator is relatively slow, but produces random numbers of very high quality, and the `SFC64` generator is fast and of good quality, but lacks some features available in other generators.

The `SeedSequence` object created in this recipe is a means to create seeds for random number generators in an independent and reproducible manner. In particular, this is useful if you need to create independent random number generators for several parallel processes, but still need to be able to reconstruct each session later to debug or inspect results. The entropy stored on this object is a 128-bit integer that was gathered from the operating system, and serves as a source of random seeds.

The `SeedSequence` object allows us to create a separate random number generator for each process/thread that are independent of one another, which eliminates any data race problems that might make results unpredictable. It also generates seed values that are very different from one another, which can help avoid problems with some PRNGs (such as MT19937, which can produce very similar streams with two similar 32-bit integer seed values). Obviously having two independent random number generators producing the same or very similar values will be problematic when we are depending on the independence of these values.

There's more...

The `BitGenerator` class serves as a common interface for generators of raw random integers. The classes mentioned previously are those that are implemented in NumPy with the `BitGenerator` interface. You can also create your own `BitGenerator` subclasses, although this needs to be implemented in Cython.

Refer to the NumPy documentation at `https://numpy.org/devdocs/reference/random/extending.html#new-bit-generators` for more information.

Generating normally distributed random numbers

In the *Generating random data* recipe, we generated random floating-point numbers following a uniform distribution between 0 and 1, but not including 1. However, in most cases where we require random data, we need to instead follow one of several different **distributions**. Roughly speaking, a **distribution function** is a function $f(x)$ that describes the probability that a random variable has a value that is below x. In practical terms, the distribution describes the spread of the random data over a range. In particular, if we create a histogram of data that follows a particular distribution, then it should roughly resemble the graph of the distribution function. This is best seen by example.

One of the most common distributions is **normal distribution**, which appears frequently in statistics and forms the basis for many statistical methods that we will see in `Chapter 6`, *Working with Data and Statistics*. In this recipe, we will demonstrate how to generate data following the normal distribution, and plot a histogram of this data to see the shape of the distribution.

Getting ready

As in the *Generating random data* recipe, we import the `default_rng` routine from the NumPy `random` module and create a `Generator` instance with a seeded generator for demonstration purposes:

```
from numpy.random import default_rng
rng = default_rng(12345)
```

As usual, we have the Matplotlib `pyplot` module imported as `plt`, and NumPy imported as `np`.

How to do it...

In the following steps, we generate random data that follows a normal distribution:

1. We use the `normal` method on our `Generator` instance to generate the random data according to the `normal` distribution. The normal distribution has two *parameters, location* and *scale*. There is also an optional `size` argument that specifies the shape of the generated data. (See the *Generating random data* recipe for more information on the `size` argument.) We generate an array of 10,000 values to get a reasonably sized sample:

```
mu = 5.0 # mean value
sigma = 3.0 # standard deviation
rands = rng.normal(loc=mu, scale=sigma, size=10000)
```

2. Next, we plot a histogram of this data. We have increased the number of `bins` in the histogram. This isn't strictly necessary as the default number (10) is perfectly adequate, but it does show the distribution slightly better:

```
fig, ax = plt.subplots()
ax.hist(rands, bins=20)
ax.set_title("Histogram of normally distributed data")
ax.set_xlabel("Value")
ax.set_ylabel("Density")
```

3. Next, we create a function that will generate the expected density for a range of values. This is given by multiplying the probability density function for normal distribution by the number of samples (10,000):

```
def normal_dist_curve(x):
    return 10000*np.exp(-0.5*((x-
        mu)/sigma)**2)/(sigma*np.sqrt(2*np.pi))
```

4. Finally, we plot our expected distribution over the histogram of our data:

```
x_range = np.linspace(-5, 15)
y = normal_dist_curve(x_range)
ax.plot(x_range, y, "k--")
```

The result is shown in *Figure 4.2*. We can see here that the distribution of our sampled data closely follows the expected distribution from the normal distribution curve:

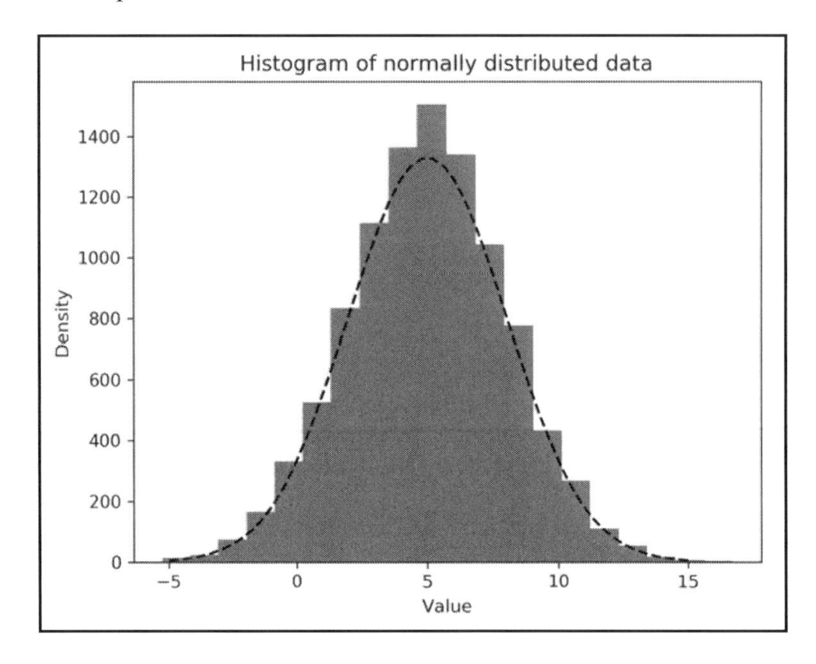

Figure 4.2: Histogram of data drawn from a normal distribution centered at 5 with a scale of 3, with the expected density overlaid

How it works...

Normal distribution has a probability density function defined by the following formula:

$$f(x) = \frac{1}{\sigma\sqrt{2\pi}} e^{-\frac{1}{2}\left(\frac{x-\mu}{\sigma}\right)^2}$$

This is related to the normal distribution function $F(x)$ according to the following formula:

$$F(x) = \int_{-\infty}^{x} f(t)\,\mathrm{d}t$$

This probability density function peaks at the mean value, which coincides with the location parameter, and the width of the "bell shape" is determined by the scale parameter. We can see in *Figure 4.2* that the histogram of the data generated by the `normal` method on the `Generator` object fits the expected distribution very closely.

The `Generator` class uses a 256-step Ziggurat method to generate normally distributed random data, which is fast compared to the Box-Muller or inverse CDF implementations that are also available in NumPy.

There's more...

The normal distribution is one example of a *continuous* probability distribution, in that it is defined for real numbers and the distribution function is defined by an integral (rather than a sum). An interesting feature of normal distribution (and other continuous probability distributions) is that the probability of selecting any given real number is 0. This is reasonable, because it only makes sense to measure the probability that a value selected in this distribution lies within a given range. (It shouldn't make sense that the probability of selecting a specific value should be not zero.)

The normal distribution is important in statistics, mostly due to the *central limit theorem*. Roughly speaking, this theorem states that sums of **independent and identically distributed** (**IID**) random variables, with a common mean and variance, are eventually like normal distribution with the common mean and variance. This holds, regardless of the actual distribution of these random variables. This allows us to use statistical tests based on normal distribution in many cases even if the actual distribution of the variables is not necessarily normal. (We do, however, need to be extremely cautious when appealing to the central limit theorem.)

There are many other continuous probability distributions aside from normal distribution. We have already encountered *uniform* distribution over the range 0 to 1. More generally, uniform distribution over the range $a \leq x \leq b$ has a probability density function given by the following equation:

$$f(x) = \frac{1}{b - a}$$

Other common examples of continuous probability density functions include *exponential* distribution, *beta* distribution, and *gamma* distribution. Each of these distributions has a corresponding method on the `Generator` class that generates random data from that distribution. These are typically named according to the name of the distribution, all in lowercase letters. So, for the aforementioned distributions, the corresponding methods are `exponential`, `beta`, and `gamma`. These distributions each have one or more *parameters*, like location and scale for normal distribution, that determine the final shape of the distribution. You may need to consult the NumPy documentation (`https://numpy.org/doc/1.18/reference/random/generator.html#numpy.random.Generator`) or other sources to see what parameters are required for each distribution. The NumPy documentation also lists the probability distributions from which random data can be generated.

Working with random processes

Random processes exist everywhere. Roughly speaking, a random process is a system of related random variables, usually indexed with respect to time $t \geq 0$, for a continuous random process, or by natural numbers $n = 1, 2, \ldots$, for a discrete random process. Many (discrete) random processes satisfy the **Markov property**, which makes them a **Markov chain**. The Markov property is the statement that the process is *memoryless*, in that only the current value is important for the probabilities of the next value.

In this recipe, we will examine a simple example of a random process that models the number of bus arrivals at a stop over time. This process is called a **Poisson process**. A Poisson process $N(t)$ has a single parameter, λ, which is usually called the *intensity* or *rate*, and the probability that $N(t)$ takes the value n at a given time t is given by the following formula:

$$P(N(t) = n) = \frac{(\lambda t)^n}{n!} e^{-\lambda t}$$

This equation describes the probability that n buses have arrived by time t. Mathematically, this equation means that $N(t)$ has a Poisson distribution with the parameter λt. There is, however, an easy way to construct a Poisson process by taking sums of inter-arrival times that follow an exponential distribution. For instance, let X_i be the time between the $(i-1)$-st arrival and the i-th arrival, which are exponentially distributed with parameter λ. Now, we take the following equation:

$$T_n = X_1 + X_2 + \cdots + X_n$$

Here, the number $N(t)$ is the maximum n such that $T_n <= t$. This is the construction that we will work through in this recipe. We will also estimate the intensity of the process by taking the mean of the inter-arrival times.

Getting ready

Before we start, we import the `default_rng` routine from NumPy's `random` module and create a new random number generator with a seed for the purpose of demonstration:

```
from numpy.random import default_rng
rng = default_rng(12345)
```

In addition to the random number generator, we also import NumPy as `np` and the Matplotlib `pyplot` module as `plt`. We also need to have the SciPy package available.

How to do it...

The following steps show how to model the arrival of buses using a Poisson process:

1. Our first task is to create the sample inter-arrival times by sampling data from an exponential distribution. The `exponential` method on the NumPy `Generator` class requires a `scale` parameter, which is $1/\lambda$, where λ is the rate. We choose a rate of 4, and create 50 sample inter-arrival times:

```
rate = 4.0
inter_arrival_times = rng.exponential(scale=1./rate, size=50)
```

2. Next, we compute the actual arrival times by using the `accumulate` method of the NumPy `add` universal function. We also create an array containing the integers 0 to 49, representing the number of arrivals at each point:

```
arrivals = np.add.accumulate(inter_arrival_times)
count = np.arange(50)
```

3. Next, we plot the arrivals over time using the `step` plotting method:

```
fig1, ax1 = plt.subplots()
ax1.step(arrivals, count, where="post")
ax1.set_xlabel("Time")
ax1.set_ylabel("Number of arrivals")
ax1.set_title("Arrivals over time")
```

The result is shown in *Figure 4.3*, where the length of each horizontal line represents the inter-arrival times:

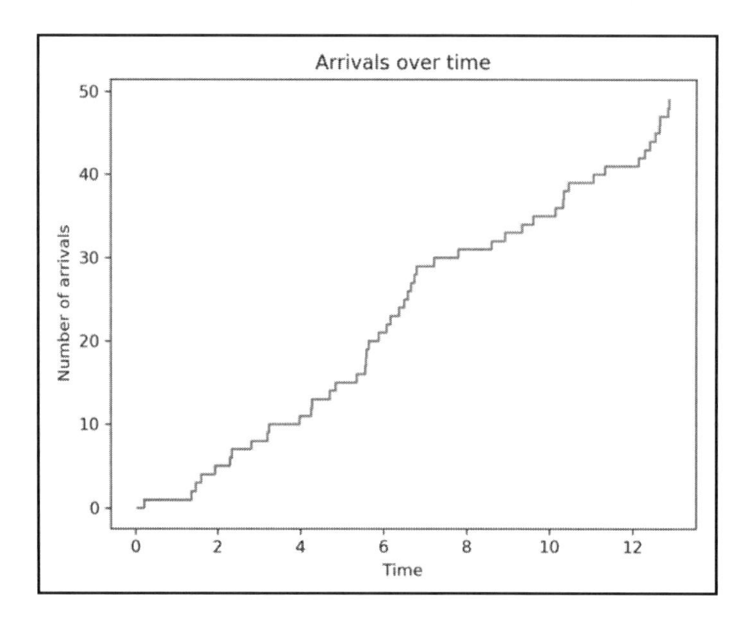

Figure 4.3: Arrivals over time, where inter-arrival times are exponentially distributed, which makes the number of arrivals at a time a Poisson process

4. Next, we define a function that will evaluate the probability distribution of the counts at a time, which we will take as `1` here. This uses the formula for the Poisson distribution that we gave in the introduction to this recipe:

```
from scipy.special import factorial
N = np.arange(15)
def probability(events, time=1, param=rate):
    return ((param*time)**events/factorial(events))*np.exp(-
       param*time)
```

5. Now, we plot the probability distribution over the count per unit of time, since we chose `time=1` in the previous step. We will add to this plot later:

```
fig2, ax2 = plt.subplots()
ax2.plot(N, probability(N), "k", label="True distribution")
ax2.set_xlabel("Number of arrivals in 1 time unit")
ax2.set_ylabel("Probability")
ax2.set_title("Probability distribution")
```

6. Now, we move on to estimate the rate from our sample data. We do this by computing the mean of the inter-arrival times, which, for exponential distribution, is an estimator of the scale *1/λ*:

```
estimated_scale = np.mean(inter_arrival_times)
estimated_rate = 1.0/estimated_scale
```

7. Finally, we plot the probability distribution with this estimated rate for the counts per unit of time. We plot this on top of the true probability distribution that we produced in *Step 5:*

```
ax2.plot(N, probability(N, param=estimated_rate), "k--",
label="Estimated distribution")
ax2.legend()
```

The resulting plot is given in *Figure 4.4,* where we can see that, apart from a small discrepancy, the estimated distribution is very close to the true distribution:

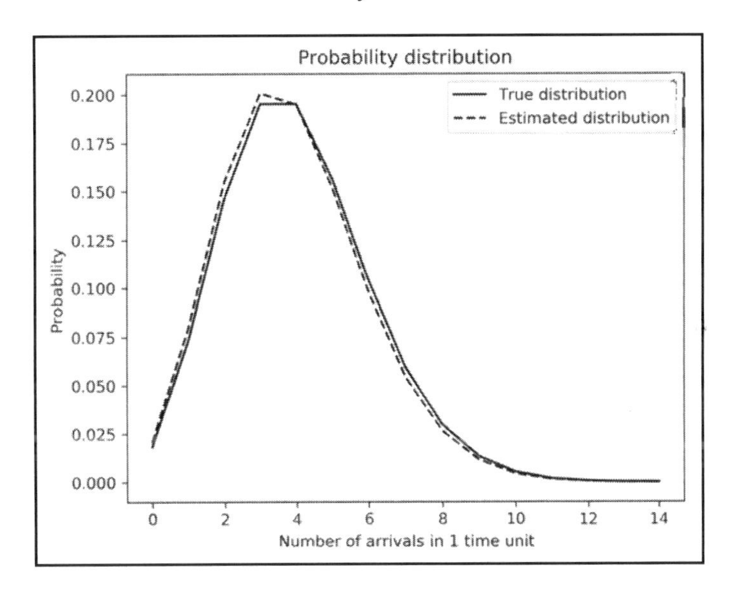

Figure 4.4: Poisson distribution of the number of arrivals per time unit, the true distribution, and the distribution estimated from the sampled data

How it works...

A Poisson process is a counting process that counts the number of events (bus arrivals) that occur in an amount of time if the events are randomly spaced (in time) with an exponential distribution with a fixed parameter. We constructed the Poisson process by sampling inter-arrival times from exponential distribution, following the construction we described in the introduction. However, it turns out that this fact (that the inter-arrival times are exponentially distributed) is a property of all Poisson processes when they are given their formal definition in terms of probabilities.

In this recipe, we sampled 50 points from an exponential distribution with a given `rate` parameter. We had to do a small conversion because the NumPy `Generator` method for sampling from an exponential distribution uses a related `scale` parameter, which is `1` over the `rate`. Once we have these points, we create an array that contains cumulative sums of these exponentially distributed numbers. This creates our arrival times. The actual Poisson process is that displayed in *Figure 4.3*, and is a combination of the arrival times with the corresponding number of events that had occurred at that time.

The mean (expected value) of an exponential distribution coincides with the scale parameter, so the mean of a sample drawn from an exponential distribution is one way to estimate the scale (rate) parameter. This estimate will not be perfect, since our sample is relatively small. This is why there is a small discrepancy between the two plots in *Figure 4.4*.

There's more...

There are many types of random processes describing a wide variety of real-world scenarios. In this recipe, we modeled arrival times using a Poisson process. A Poisson process is a continuous random process, meaning that it is parameterized by a continuous variable, $t \geq 0$, rather than a discrete variable, $n=1,2,\ldots$. Poisson processes are actually Markov chains, under a suitably generalized definition of a Markov chain, and also an example of a *renewal process*. A renewal process is a process that describes the number of events that occur within a period of time. The Poisson process described here is an example of a renewal process.

Many Markov chains also satisfy some properties in addition to their defining Markov property. For example, a Markov chain is *homogeneous* if the following equality holds for all n, i, and j values:

$$P(X_{n+1} = j \mid x_n = i) = P(X_1 = j \mid X_0 = i)$$

In simple terms, this means that the probabilities of moving from one state to another over a single step does not change as we increase the number of steps. This is extremely useful for examining the long-term behavior of a Markov chain.

It is very easy to construct simple examples of homogeneous Markov chains. Suppose that we have two states, A and B. At any given step, we could be either at state A or at state B. We move between states according to a probability. For instance, let's say that the probability of transitioning from state A to state A is 0.4, and that the probability of transitioning from A to B is 0.6. Similarly, let's say that the probability of transitioning from B to B is 0.2, and transitioning from B to A is 0.8. Notice that both the probability of switching plus the probability of staying the same sum to 1 in both cases. We can represent the probability of transitioning from each state in matrix form given, in this case, by the following equation:

$$T = \begin{pmatrix} 0.4 & 0.8 \\ 0.6 & 0.2 \end{pmatrix}$$

This matrix is called the *transition matrix*. The idea here is that the probability of being in a particular state after a step is given by multiplying the vector containing the probability of being in state A and B (position 0 and 1, respectively). For example, if we start in state A then the probability vector will contain a 1 at index 0 and 0 at index 1. Then, the probability of being in state A after 1 step is given by 0.4, and the probability of being in state B is 0.6. This is what we expect, given the probabilities we outlined previously. However, we could also write this calculation using the matrix formula:

$$\begin{pmatrix} 0.4 & 0.8 \\ 0.6 & 0.2 \end{pmatrix} \begin{pmatrix} 1 \\ 0 \end{pmatrix} = \begin{pmatrix} 0.4 \\ 0.6 \end{pmatrix}$$

To get the probability of being in either state after two steps, we multiply the right-hand side vector again by the transition matrix, T, to obtain the following:

$$\begin{pmatrix} 0.4 & 0.8 \\ 0.6 & 0.2 \end{pmatrix} \begin{pmatrix} 0.4 \\ 0.6 \end{pmatrix} = \begin{pmatrix} 0.64 \\ 0.36 \end{pmatrix}$$

We can continue this process *ad infinitum* to obtain a sequence of state vectors, which constitute our Markov chain. This construction can be applied, with more states if necessary, to model many simple, real-world problems.

Analyzing conversion rates with Bayesian techniques

Bayesian probability allows us to systematically update our understanding (in a probabilistic sense) of a situation by considering data. In more technical language, we update the *prior* distribution (our current understanding) using data to obtain a *posterior* distribution. This is particularly useful, for example, when examining the proportion of users who go on to buy a product after viewing a website. We start with our prior belief distribution. For this we will use the *beta* distribution, which models the probability of success given numbers of successes (completed purchases) against failures (no purchases). For this recipe, we will assume that our prior belief is that we expect 25 successes from 100 views (75 fails). This means that our prior belief follows a beta (25, 75) distribution. Let's say that we wish to calculate the probability that the true rate of success is at least 33%.

Our method is roughly divided into three steps. We first need to understand our prior belief for the conversion rate, which we have decided follows a beta (25, 75) distribution. We compute the probability that the conversion rate is at least 33% by integrating (numerically) the probability density function for the prior distribution from 0.33 to 1. The next step is to apply the Bayesian reasoning to update our prior belief with new information. Then, we can perform the same integration with the posterior belief to examine the probability that the conversion rate is at least 33% given this new information.

In this recipe, we will see how to use Bayesian techniques to update a prior belief based on new information for our hypothetical website.

Getting ready

As usual, we will need the NumPy and Matplotlib packages imported as `np` and `plt`, respectively. We will also require the SciPy package, imported as `sp`.

How to do it...

The following steps show how to estimate and update conversion rate estimations using Bayesian reasoning:

1. The first step is to set up the prior distribution. For this we use the `beta` distribution object from the SciPy `stats` module, which has various methods for working with the beta distribution. We import the `beta` distribution from the `stats` module under the alias `beta_dist` and then create a convenience function for the probability density function:

```
from scipy.stats import beta as beta_dist
beta_pdf = beta_dist.pdf
```

2. Next, we need to compute the probability, under the prior belief distribution, that the success rate is at least 33%. To do this, we use the `quad` routine from the SciPy `integrate` module, which performs numerical integration of a function. We use this to integrate the probability density function for the beta distribution, imported in *Step 1*, with our prior parameters. We print the probability according to our prior distribution to the console:

```
prior_alpha = 25
prior_beta = 75
args = (prior_alpha, prior_beta)
prior_over_33, err = sp.integrate.quad(beta_pdf, 0.33, 1,
args=args)
print("Prior probability", prior_over_33)
# 0.037830787030165056
```

3. Now, suppose we have received some information about successes and failures over a new period of time. For example, we observed 122 successes and 257 failures over this period. We create new variables to reflect these values:

```
observed_successes = 122
observed_failures = 257
```

4. To obtain the parameter values for the posterior distribution with a beta distribution, we simply add the observed successes and failures to the `prior_alpha` and `prior_beta` parameters, respectively:

```
posterior_alpha = prior_alpha + observed_successes
posterior_beta = prior_beta + observed_failures
```

5. Now, we repeat our numerical integration to compute the probability that the success rate is now above 33% using the posterior distribution (with our new parameters computed earlier). Again, we print this probability in the terminal:

```
args = (posterior_alpha, posterior_beta)
posterior_over_33, err2 = sp.integrate.quad(beta_pdf, 0.33, 1,
    args=args)
print("Posterior probability", posterior_over_33)
# 0.13686193416281017
```

6. We can see here that the new probability, given the updated posterior distribution, is 13% as opposed to the prior 3%. This is a significant difference, although we are still not confident that the conversion rate is above 33% given these values. Now, we plot the prior and posterior distribution to visualize this increase in probability. To start with, we create an array of values and evaluate our probability density function based on these values:

```
p = np.linspace(0, 1, 500)
prior_dist = beta_pdf(p, prior_alpha, prior_beta)
posterior_dist = beta_pdf(p, posterior_alpha, posterior_beta)
```

7. Finally, we plot the two probability density functions computed in *Step 6* onto a new plot:

```
fig, ax = plt.subplots()
ax.plot(p, prior_dist, "k--", label="Prior")
ax.plot(p, posterior_dist, "k", label="Posterior")
ax.legend()
ax.set_xlabel("Success rate")
ax.set_ylabel("Density")
ax.set_title("Prior and posterior distributions for success rate")
```

The resulting plot is shown in *Figure 4.5*, where we can see that the posterior distribution is much more narrow and centered to the right of the prior:

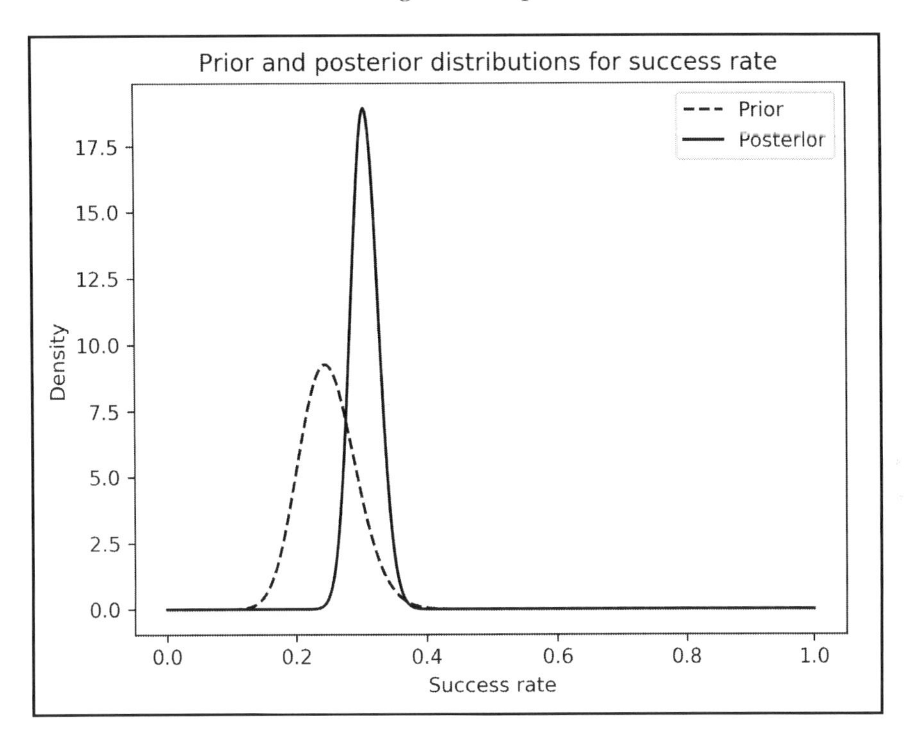

Figure 4.5: Prior and posterior distributions of a success rate following a beta distribution

How it works...

Bayesian techniques work by taking a prior belief (probability distribution) and using *Bayes' theorem* to combine the prior belief with the likelihood of our data given this prior belief to form a posterior belief. This is actually similar to how we might understand things in real life. For example, when you wake up on a given day, you might have the belief (from a forecast or otherwise) that there is a 40% chance of rain outside. Upon opening the blinds, you see that it is very cloudy outside, which might indicate that rain is more likely, so we update our belief according to this new data, to say a 70% chance of rain.

To understand how this works, we need to understand *conditional probability*. Conditional probability deals with the probability that one event will occur *given that* another event has already occurred. In symbols, the probability of event A given that event B has occurred is written as follows:

$$P(A \mid B)$$

Bayes' theorem is a powerful tool that can be written (symbolically) as follows:

$$P(A \mid B) = \frac{P(A)P(B \mid A)}{P(B)}$$

The probability $P(A)$ represents our prior belief. The event B represents the data that we have gathered, so that $P(B \mid A)$ is the likelihood that our data arose given our prior belief. The probability $P(B)$ represents the probability that our data arose, and $P(A \mid B)$ represents our posterior belief given the data. In practice, the probability $P(B)$ can be difficult to calculate or otherwise estimate, so it is quite common to replace the strong equality above with a proportional version of Bayes' theorem:

$$P(A \mid B) \propto P(B \mid A)P(A)$$

In the recipe, we assumed that our prior was beta distributed. The beta distribution has a probability density function given by the following equation:

$$\mathrm{Beta}(p; \alpha, \beta) = \frac{\Gamma(\alpha + \beta)}{\Gamma(\alpha)\Gamma(\beta)} p^{\alpha - 1}(1 - p)^{\beta - 1}$$

Here, $\Gamma(\alpha)$ is the gamma function. The likelihood is binomially distributed, which has a probability density function given by the following equation:

$$B(p; k, j) = \binom{k}{j} p^j (1 - p)^{k-j}$$

Here, k is the number of observations, and j is one of those that was successful. In the recipe, we observed $m = 122$ successes and $n = 257$ failures, which gives $k = m + n = 379$ and $j = m = 122$. To calculate the posterior distribution, we can use the fact that the beta distribution is a conjugate prior for the binomial distribution to see that the right-hand side of the proportional form of Bayes' theorem is beta distributed with parameters $\alpha + m$ and $\beta + n$. This is what we used in the recipe. The fact that the beta distribution is a conjugate prior for binomial random variables makes them useful in Bayesian statistics.

The method we demonstrated in this recipe is a rather basic example of using a Bayesian method, but it is still useful for updating our prior beliefs given new data in a systematic way.

There's more...

Bayesian methods can be used for a wide variety of tasks, making it a powerful tool. In this recipe, we used a Bayesian approach to model the success rate of a website based on our prior belief of how it performs and additional data gathered from users. This is a rather complex example since we modeled our prior belief on a beta distribution. Here is another example of using Bayes' theorem to examine two competing hypotheses using only simple probabilities (numbers between 0 and 1).

Suppose you place your keys in the same place every day when you return home, but one morning you wake up to find that they are not in this place. After searching for a short time, you cannot find them and so conclude that they must have vanished from existence. Let's call this hypothesis H_1. Now, H_1 certainly explains the data, D, that you cannot find your keys, hence the likelihood $P(D \mid H_1) = 1$. (If your keys vanished from existence, then you could not possibly find them.) An alternative hypothesis is that you simply placed them somewhere else when you got home the night before. Let's call this hypothesis H_2. Now this hypothesis also explains the data, so $P(D \mid H_2) = 1$, but in reality, H_2 is far more plausible than H_1. Let's say that the probability that your keys completely vanished from existence is 1 in 1 million – this is a huge overestimation, but we need to keep the numbers reasonable – while you estimate that the probability that you placed them elsewhere the night before is 1 in 100. Computing the posterior probabilities, we have the following:

$$P(H_1 \mid D) \propto P(D \mid H_1)P(H_1) \propto \frac{1}{100}, \quad P(H_2 \mid D) = \frac{1}{1000000}$$

This highlights the reality that it is 10,000 times more likely that you simply misplaced your keys as opposed to the fact that they simply vanished. Sure enough, you soon find your keys already in your pocket, because you had picked them up earlier that morning.

Estimating parameters with Monte Carlo simulations

Monte Carlo methods broadly describe techniques that use random sampling to solve problems. These techniques are especially powerful when the underlying problem involves some kind of uncertainty. The general method involves performing large numbers of simulations, each sampling different inputs according to a given probability distribution, and then aggregating the results to give a better approximation of the true solution than any individual sample solution.

Markov Chain Monte Carlo (**MCMC**) is a specific kind of Monte Carlo simulation in which we construct a Markov chain of successively better approximations of the true distribution that we seek. This works by accepting or rejecting a proposed state, sampled at random, based on carefully selected *acceptance probabilities* at each stage, with the aim of constructing a Markov chain whose unique stationary distribution is precisely the unknown distribution that we wish to find.

In this recipe, we will use the PyMC3 package and MCMC methods to estimate the parameters of a simple model. The package will deal with most of the technical details of running simulations, so we don't need to go any further into the details of how the different MCMC algorithms actually work.

Getting ready

As usual, we import the NumPy package and Matplotlib `pyplot` module as `np` and `plt`, respectively. We also import and create a default random number generator, with a seed for the purpose of demonstration, as follows:

```
from numpy.random import default_rng
rng = default_rng(12345)
```

We will also need a module from the SciPy package for this recipe as well as the PyMC3 package, which is a package for probabilistic programming.

How to do it...

Perform the following steps to use Markov chain Monte Carlo simulations to estimate the parameters of a simple model using sample data:

1. Our first task is to create a function that represents the underlying structure that we wish to identify. In this case, we will be estimating the coefficients of a quadratic (a polynomial of degree 2). This function takes two arguments, which are the points in the range, which is fixed, and the variable parameters that we wish to estimate:

```
def underlying(x, params):
    return params[0]*x**2 + params[1]*x + params[2]
```

2. Next, we set up the `true` parameters and a `size` parameter that will determine how many points are in the sample that we generate:

```
size = 100
true_params = [2, -7, 6]
```

3. We generate the sample that we will use to estimate the parameters. This will consist of the underlying data, generated by the `underlying` function we defined in *Step 1*, plus some random noise that follows a normal distribution. We first generate a range of x values, which will stay constant throughout the recipe, and then use the `underlying` function and the `normal` method on our random number generator to generate the sample data:

```
x_vals = np.linspace(-5, 5, size)
raw_model = underlying(x_vals, true_params)
noise = rng.normal(loc=0.0, scale=10.0, size=size)
sample = raw_model + noise
```

4. It is a good idea to plot the sample data, with the underlying data overlaid, before we begin the analysis. We use the `scatter` plotting method to plot only the data points (without connecting lines), and then plot the underlying quadratic structure using a dashed line:

```
fig1, ax1 = plt.subplots()
ax1.scatter(x_vals, sample, label="Sampled data")
ax1.plot(x_vals, raw_model, "k--", label="Underlying model")
ax1.set_title("Sampled data")
ax1.set_xlabel("x")
ax1.set_ylabel("y")
```

The result is *Figure 4.6*, where we can see that the shape of the underlying model is still visible even with the noise, although the exact parameters of this model are no longer obvious:

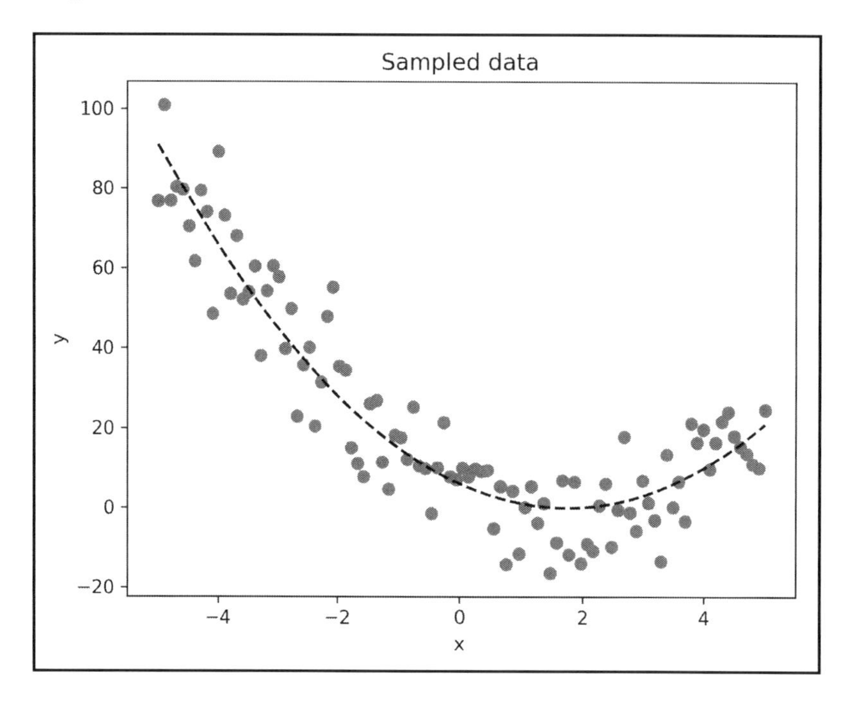

Figure 4.6: Sampled data with the underlying model overlaid

5. We are ready to start our analysis, so we now import the PyMC3 package under the alias `pm` as follows:

```
import pymc3 as pm
```

6. The basic object of PyMC3 programming is the `Model` class, which is usually created using the context manager interface. We also create our prior distributions for the parameters. In this case, we will assume that our prior parameters are normally distributed with a mean of 1 and a standard deviation of 1. We need 3 parameters, so we provide the `shape` argument. The `Normal` class creates random variables that will be used in the Monte Carlo simulations:

```
with pm.Model() as model:
    params = pm.Normal("params", mu=1, sigma=1, shape=3)
```

7. We create a model for the underlying data, which can be done by passing the random variable, `param`, that we created in *Step 6* into the `underlying` function that we defined in *Step 1*. We also create a variable that handles our observations. For this we use the `Normal` class, since we know that our noise is normally distributed around the underlying data, `y`. We set a standard deviation of `2`, and pass our observed `sample` data into the `observed` keyword argument (this is also inside the `Model` context):

```
y = underlying(x_vals, params)
y_obs = pm.Normal("y_obs", mu=y, sigma=2, observed=sample)
```

8. To run the simulations, we need only call the `sample` routine inside the `Model` context. We pass the `cores` argument to speed up the calculations, but leave all of the other arguments at the default values:

```
trace = pm.sample(cores=4)
```

   These simulations should take a short time to execute.

9. Next, we plot the posterior distributions that use the `plot_posterior` routine from PyMC3. This routine takes the `trace` result from the sampling step that performed the simulations. We create our own figure and axes using the `plt.subplots` routine in advance, but this isn't strictly necessary. We are using three subplots on a single figure, and we pass the `axs2` tuple of `Axes` to the plotting routing under the `ax` keyword argument:

```
fig2, axs2 = plt.subplots(1, 3, tight_layout=True)
pm.plot_posterior(trace, ax=axs2)
```

The resulting plot is shown in *Figure 4.7*, where you can see that each of these distributions is approximately normal, with a mean that is similar to the true parameter values:

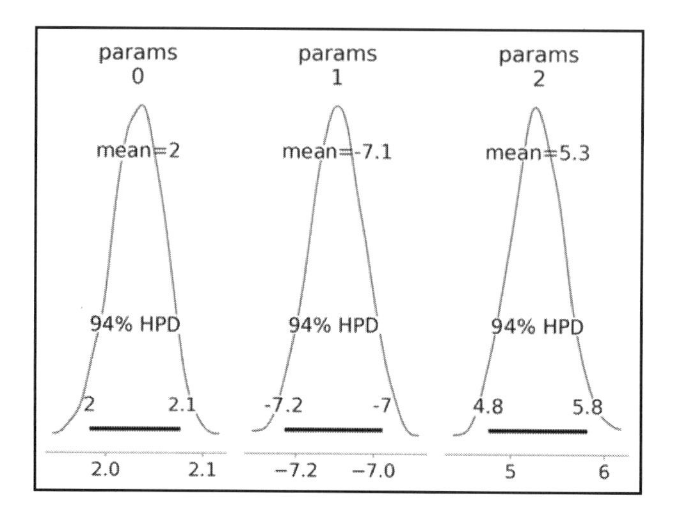

Figure 4.7: Posterior distributions of estimated parameters

10. Now retrieve the mean of each of the estimated parameters from the trace by using the `mean` method on the `params` item from the trace, which is simply a NumPy array. We pass the `axis=0` argument because we want the mean of each of the rows of the matrix of parameter estimates. We print these estimated parameters in the terminal:

```
estimated_params = trace["params"].mean(axis=0)
print("Estimated parameters", estimated_params)
# Estimated parameters [ 2.03213559 -7.0957161 5.27045299]
```

11. Finally, we use our estimated parameters to generate our estimated underlying data by passing the x values and the estimated parameters to the `underlying` function defined in *Step 1*. We then plot this estimated underlying data together with the true underlying data on the same axes:

```
estimated = underlying(x_vals, estimated_params)
fig3, ax3 = plt.subplots()
ax3.plot(x_vals, raw_model, "k", label="True model")
ax3.plot(x_vals, estimated, "k--", label="Estimated model")
ax3.set_title("Plot of true and estimated models")
ax3.set_xlabel("x")
ax3.set_ylabel("y")
ax3.legend()
```

The resulting plot is in *Figure 4.8*, where there is only a small difference between these two models on this range:

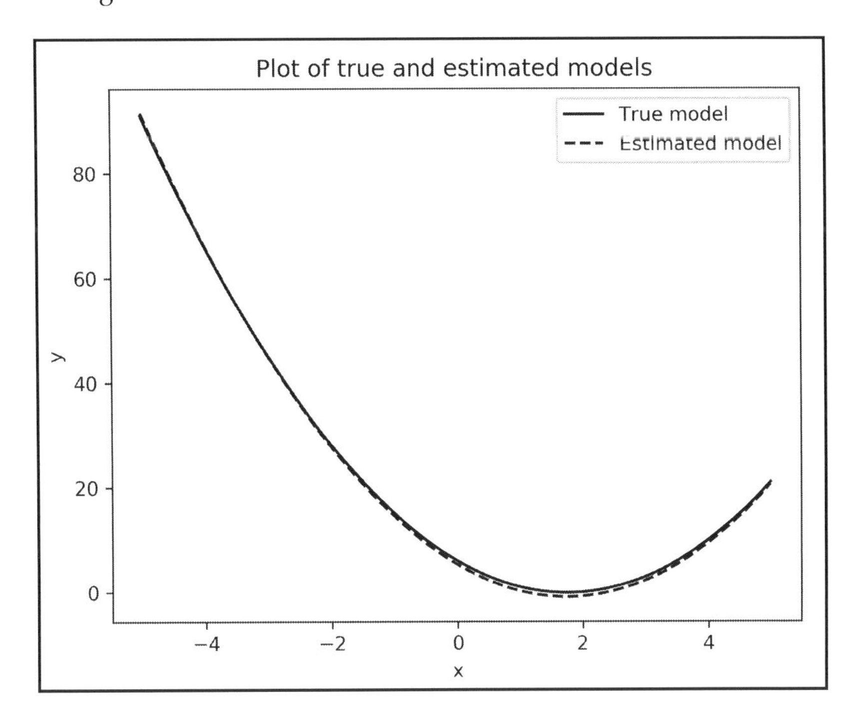

Figure 4.8: True model and estimated model plotted on the same axes. There is a small discrepancy between the estimated parameters and the true parameters

How it works...

The interesting part of the code in this recipe can be found in the `Model` context manager. This object keeps track of the random variables, orchestrates the simulations, and keeps track of the state. The context manager gives us a convenient way to separate the probabilistic variables from the surrounding code.

We start by proposing a prior distribution for the distribution of the random variables representing our parameters, of which there are three. We proposed a normal distribution since we know that the parameters cannot stray too far from the value 1. (We can tell this by looking at the plot that we generated in *Step 4*, for example.) Using a normal distribution will give a higher probability to the values that are close to the current values. Next, we add the details relating to the observed data, which is used to calculate the acceptance probabilities that are used to either accept or reject a state. Finally, we start the sampler using the `sample` routine. This constructs the Markov chain and generates all of the step data.

The `sample` routine sets up the sampler based on the types of variables that will be simulated. Since the normal distribution is a continuous variable, the `sample` routine selected the **No U-turn sampler** (**NUTS**). This is a reasonable general-purpose sampler for continuous variables. A common alternative to NUTS is the Metropolis sampler, which is less reliable but faster than NUTS in some cases. The PyMC3 documentation recommends using NUTS whenever possible.

Once the sampling is complete, we plotted the posterior distribution of the trace (the states given by the Markov chain) to see the final shape of the approximations we generated. We can see here that all three of our random variables (parameters) are normally distributed around approximately the correct value.

Under the hood, PyMC3 uses Theano to speed up its calculations. This makes it possible for PyMC3 to perform computations on a **Graphics Processing Unit** (**GPU**) rather than on the **Central Processing Unit** (**CPU**) for a considerable boost to computation speed. Theano also supports the dynamic generation of C code to improve computation speeds further.

There's more...

The Monte Carlo method is very flexible, and the example we gave here is one particular case where it can be used. A more typical basic example of where the Monte Carlo method is applied is in estimating the value of integrals, commonly, Monte Carlo integration. A really interesting case of Monte Carlo integration is estimating the value of $\pi \approx 3.1415$. Let's briefly look at how this works.

First, we take the unit disk, whose radius is 1 and therefore has an area, π. We can enclose this disk inside a square with vertices at the points (1, 1), (-1, 1), (1, -1), and (-1, -1). This square has an area 4, since the edge length is 2. Now we can generate random points uniformly over this square. When we do this, the probability that any one of these random points lies inside a given region is proportional to the area of that region. Thus, the area of a region can be estimated by multiplying the proportion of randomly generated points that lie within the region by the total area of the square. In particular, we can estimate the area of the disk by simply multiplying the number of randomly generate points that lie within the disk by 4, and dividing by the total number of points we generated.

We can easily write a function in Python that performs this calculation, which might be the following:

```
import numpy as np
from numpy.random import default_rng

def estimate_pi(n_points=10000):
    rng = default_rng()
    points = rng.uniform(-1, 1, size=(2, n_points))
    inside = np.less(points[0, :]**2 + points[1, :]**2, 1)
    return 4.0*inside.sum() / n_points
```

Running this function just once will give a reasonable approximation of π:

```
estimate_pi()  # 3.14224
```

We can improve the accuracy of our estimation by using more points, but we could also run this a number of times and average the results. Let's run this simulation 100 times and average the results (we'll use concurrent futures to parallelize this so that we can run larger numbers of samples if we want):

```
from concurrent.futures import ProcessPoolExecutor, as_completed
from statistics import mean

with ProcessPoolExecutor() as pool:
    fts = [pool.submit(estimate_pi) for _ in range(100)]
    results = list(ft.result() for ft in as_completed(fts))

print(mean(results))
```

Running this code once prints the estimated value of π as 3.1415752, which is an even better estimate of the true value.

See also

The PyMC3 package has many features that are documented by numerous examples (`https://docs.pymc.io/`). There is also another probabilistic programming library based on TensorFlow (`https://www.tensorflow.org/probability`).

Further reading

A good, comprehensive reference for probability and random processes is the following book:

- *Grimmett, G. and Stirzaker, D. (2009). Probability and random processes. 3rd ed. Oxford: Oxford Univ. Press.*

An easy introduction to Bayes' theorem and Bayesian statistics is the following:

- *Kurt, W. (2019). Bayesian statistics the fun way. San Francisco, CA: No Starch Press, Inc.*

5
Working with Trees and Networks

Networks are objects that contain *nodes* and *edges* between pairs of nodes. They can be used to represent a wide variety of real-world situations, such as distribution and scheduling. Mathematically, networks are useful for visualizing combinatorial problems and make for a rich and fascinating theory.

There are, of course, several different kinds of networks. We will mostly deal with simple networks, where edges connect two distinct nodes (so there are no self-loops), there is, at most, one edge between any two nodes, and all the edges are bidirectional. A *tree* is a special kind of network in which there are no cycles; that is, there are no lists of nodes in which each node is connected to the following node by an edge, and the final node is connected to the first. Trees are especially simple in terms of their theory because they connect a number of nodes with the fewest possible edges. A *complete network* is a network in which every node is connected to every other node by an edge.

Networks can be directed, where each edge has a source and a destination node or can carry additional attributes such as weights. Weighted networks are especially useful in certain applications. There are also networks in which we allow multiple edges between two given nodes.

In this chapter, we will learn how to create, manipulate, and analyze networks, and then apply network algorithms to solve various problems.

In the literature, especially in mathematical texts, networks are more commonly called *graphs*. Nodes are sometimes called *vertices*. We favor the term network to avoid confusion with the more common usage of graph to mean a plot of a function.

We will cover the following recipes in this chapter:

- Creating networks in Python
- Visualizing networks
- Getting the basic characteristics of networks
- Generating the adjacency matrix for a network
- Creating directed and weighted networks
- Finding the shortest paths in a network
- Quantifying clustering in a network
- Coloring a network
- Finding minimal spanning trees and dominating sets

Let's get started!

Technical requirements

In this chapter, we will primarily use the NetworkX package for working with trees and networks. This package can be installed using your favorite package manager, such as `pip`:

```
python3.8 -m pip install networkx
```

We usually import this under the alias `nx`, following the conventions established in the official NetworkX documentation, using the following `import` statement:

```
import networkx as nx
```

The code for this chapter can be found in the `Chapter 05` folder of the GitHub repository at `https://github.com/PacktPublishing/Applying-Math-with-Python/tree/master/Chapter%2005`.

Check out the following video to see the Code in Action: `https://bit.ly/2WJQt4p`.

Creating networks in Python

In order to solve the multitude of problems that can be expressed as network problems, we first need a way of creating networks in Python. For this, we will make use of the NetworkX package and the routines and classes it provides to create, manipulate, and analyze networks.

In this recipe, we'll create an object in Python that represents a network and add nodes and edges to this object.

Getting ready

As we mentioned in the *Technical requirements* section, we need the NetworkX package to be imported under the alias `nx` by using the following `import` statement:

```
import networkx as nx
```

How to do it...

Follow these steps to create a Python representation of a simple graph:

1. We need to create a new `Graph` object that will store the nodes and edges that constitute the graph:

   ```
   G = nx.Graph()
   ```

2. Next, we need to add the nodes for the network using the `add_node` method:

   ```
   G.add_node(1)
   G.add_node(2)
   ```

3. To avoid calling this method repetitively, we can use the `add_nodes_from` method to add nodes from an iterable such as a list:

   ```
   G.add_nodes_from([3, 4, 5, 6])
   ```

4. Next, we need to add edges between the nodes that we've added using either the `add_edge` method or the `add_edges_from` method, which add either a single edge or a list of edges (as tuples), respectively:

   ```
   G.add_edge(1, 2)  # edge from 1 to 2
   G.add_edges_from([(2, 3), (3, 4), (3, 5), (3, 6), (4, 5), (5, 6)])
   ```

5. Finally, we retrieve a view of the current nodes and edges in a graph by accessing the `nodes` and `edges` attributes, respectively:

   ```
   print(G.nodes)
   print(G.edges)
   # [1, 2, 3, 4, 5, 6]
   # [(1, 2), (2, 3), (3, 4), (3, 5), (3, 6), (4, 5), (5, 6)]
   ```

How it works...

The NetworkX package adds several classes and routines for creating, manipulating, and analyzing networks using Python. The `Graph` class is the most basic class for representing networks that do not contain multiple edges between any given nodes and where their edges are undirected (bidirectional).

Once a blank `Graph` object has been created, we can add new nodes and edges using the methods described in this recipe. In this recipe, we created nodes that hold integer values. However, a node can hold any hashable Python object except `None`. Moreover, associated data can be added to a node via keyword arguments passed to the `add_node` method. Attributes can also be added when using the `add_nodes_from` method by supplying a list of tuples containing the node object and a dictionary of attributes. The `add_nodes_from` method is useful for adding nodes in bulk, while `add_node` is useful for attaching individual nodes to an existing network.

An edge in a network is a tuple containing two (distinct) nodes. In a simple network, such as the one represented by the basic `Graph` class, there can be, at most, one edge between any two given nodes. The edges are added via the `add_edge` or `add_edges_from` methods, which add either a single edge or a list of edges to the network, respectively. As for the nodes, edges can hold arbitrary associated data via an attributes dictionary. In particular, weights can be added by supplying the `weight` attribute when adding edges. We will provide more details about weighted graphs in the *Creating directed and weighted networks* recipe.

The `nodes` and `edges` attributes hold the nodes and edges that constitute the network, respectively. The `nodes` attribute returns a `NodesView` object, which is a dictionary-like interface to the nodes and their associated data. Similarly, the `edges` attribute returns an `EdgeView` object. This can be used to inspect individual edges and their associated data.

There's more...

The `Graph` class represents *simple networks*, which are networks in which nodes are joined by, at most, one edge, and the edges are not directed. We will discuss directed networks in the *Creating directed and weighted networks* recipe. There is a separate class for representing networks in which there can be multiple edges between a pair of nodes called `MultiGraph`. All of the network types allow self-loops, which are sometimes not allowed in a "simple network" in the literature, where a simple network typically refers to an undirected network with no self-loops.

All network types offer various methods for adding nodes and edges, as well as inspecting the current nodes and edges. There are also methods for copying networks into some other kind of network or extracting subnetworks. There are also several utility routines in the NetworkX package for generating standard networks and adding subnetworks to an existing network.

NetworkX also provides various routines for reading and writing networks to different file formats, such as GraphML, JSON, and YAML. For example, we can write a network to a GraphML file using the `nx.write_graphml` routine and read it using the `nx.read_graphml` routine.

Visualizing networks

A common first step in analyzing a network is to draw the network, which can help us identify some of the prominent features of a network. (Of course, drawings can be misleading, so we should not rely on them too heavily in our analysis.)

In this recipe, we'll describe how to use the network drawing facilities in the NetworkX package to visualize a network.

Getting ready

For this recipe, we will need to import the NetworkX package under the name `nx`, as described in the *Technical requirements* section. We will also need the Matplotlib package. For this, as usual, we import the `pyplot` module as `plt` using the following `import` statement:

```
import matplotlib.pyplot as plt
```

How to do it...

The following steps outline how to draw a simple network object using the drawing routines from NetworkX:

1. First, we create a simple example network to draw:

```
G = nx.Graph()

G.add_nodes_from(range(1, 7))
G.add_edges_from([
```

```
        (1, 2), (2, 3), (3, 4), (3, 5),
        (3, 6), (4, 5), (5, 6)
    ])
```

2. Next, we create new Matplotlib `Figure` and `Axes` objects for it, ready to plot the network using the `subplots` routine from `plt`:

```
fig, ax = plt.subplots()
```

3. Now, we can create a layout that will be used to position the nodes on the figure. For this figure, we shall use a shell layout using the `shell_layout` routine:

```
layout = nx.shell_layout(G)
```

4. We can use the `draw` routine to draw the network on the figure. Since we have already created a Matplotlib `Figure` and `Axes`, we will supply the `ax` keyword argument. We will also add labels to the nodes using the `with_labels` keyword argument and specify the layout that we just created using the `pos` argument:

```
nx.draw(G, ax=ax, pos=layout, with_labels=True)
ax.set_title("Simple network drawing")
```

The resulting drawing can be seen in the following figure:

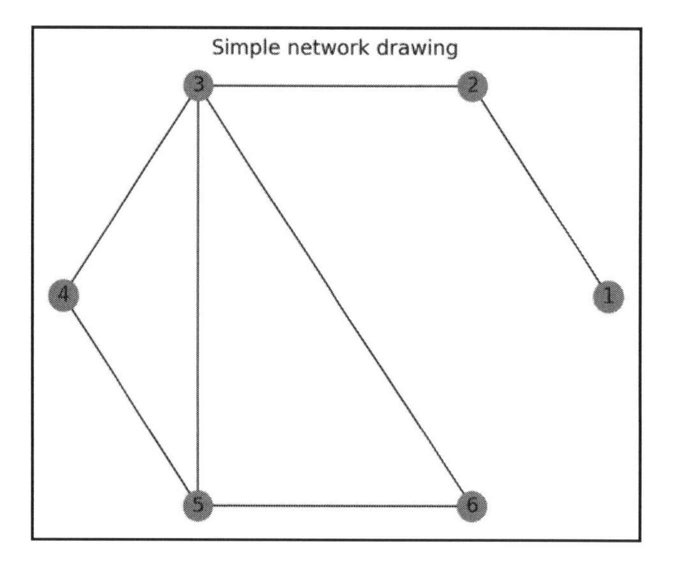

Figure 5.1: A drawing of a simple network arranged using a shell layout

How it works...

The `draw` routine is a specialized plotting routine specifically for drawing networks. The layout we created specifies the coordinates at which each of the nodes will be placed. We used a *shell layout*, which arranges the nodes in a concentric circle arrangement, which is determined by the nodes and edges of the network. By default, the `draw` routine creates a randomized layout.

The `draw` routine has numerous keyword arguments for customizing the appearance of the plotted network. In this recipe, we added the `with_labels` keyword argument to label the nodes in the figure according to the objects they hold. The nodes hold integers, which is why the nodes in the preceding figure are labeled by integers.

We also created a set of axes separately using the `plt.subplots` routine. This isn't strictly necessary since the `draw` routine will automatically create a new figure and axes if they're not provided.

There's more...

The NetworkX package provides several layout-generating routines, similar to the `shell_layout` routine that we used in this recipe. The layout is simply a dictionary, indexed by the nodes, whose elements are the x and y coordinates of the position where the node should be plotted. The NetworkX routines for creating layouts represent common arrangements that will be useful for most cases, but you can also create custom layouts, should you need them. A full list of the different layout creation routines is provided in the NetworkX documentation. There are also shortcut drawing routines that will use a specific layout with the need to create the layout separately; for example, the `draw_shell` routine will draw the network with the shell layout that is equivalent to the `draw` call given in this recipe.

The `draw` routine takes a number of keyword arguments to customize the appearance of the figure. For example, there are keyword arguments to control the node's size, color, shape, and transparency. We can also add arrows (for directed edges) and/or only draw a specific set of nodes and edges from the network.

Getting the basic characteristics of networks

Networks have various basic characteristics beyond the number of nodes and edges that are useful for analyzing a graph. For example, the *degree* of a node is the number of edges that start (or end) at that node. A higher degree indicates that the node is better connected to the rest of the network.

In this recipe, we will learn how to access the basic attributes and compute various basic measures associated with a network.

Getting ready

As usual, we need to import the NetworkX package under the name `nx`. We also need to import the Matplotlib `pyplot` module under the name `plt`.

How to do it...

Follow these steps to access the various basic characteristics of a network:

1. Create a sample network that we will analyze in this recipe, like so:

```
G = nx.Graph()
G.add_nodes_from(range(10))
G.add_edges_from([
    (0, 1), (1, 2), (2, 3), (2, 4),
    (2, 5), (3, 4), (4, 5), (6, 7),
    (6, 8), (6, 9), (7, 8), (8, 9)
])
```

2. Next, it is good practice to draw the network and arrange the nodes in a circular layout:

```
fig, ax = plt.subplots()
nx.draw_circular(G, ax=ax, with_labels=True)
ax.set_title("Simple network")
```

The resulting plot can be seen in the following figure. As we can see, the network is split into two distinct parts:

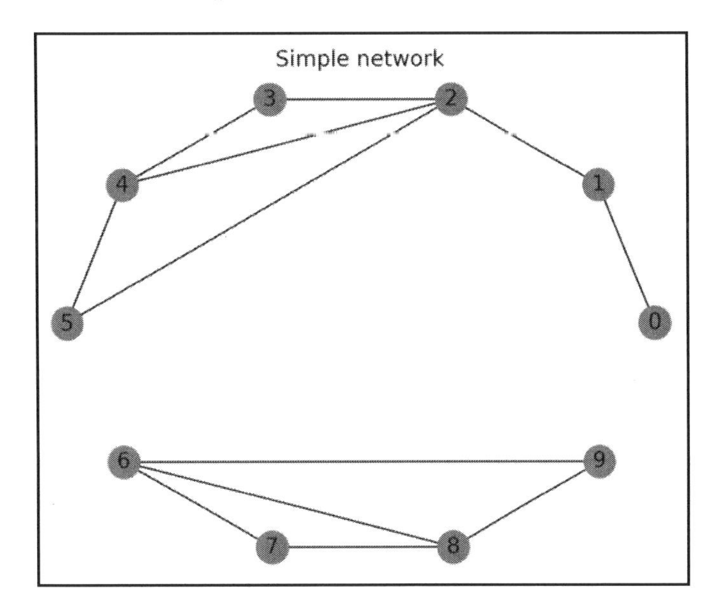

Figure 5.2: Simple network drawn in a circular arrangement. There are two distinct components visible in this network

3. Next, we use the `nx.info` routine to display some basic information about the network:

```
print(nx.info(G))
# Name:
# Type: Graph
# Number of nodes: 10
# Number of edges: 12
# Average degree: 2.4000
```

4. Now, we use the `degree` property of the `Graph` object to retrieve the degree of a specific node:

```
for i in [0, 2, 7]:
    degree = G.degree[i]
    print(f"Degree of {i}: {degree}")
# Degree of 0: 1
# Degree of 2: 4
# Degree of 7: 2
```

5. We can get the connected components of the network using the `connected_components` routine, which returns a generator that we make into a list:

```
components = list(nx.connected_components(G))
print(components)
# [{0, 1, 2, 3, 4, 5}, {8, 9, 6, 7}]
```

6. We compute the *density* of a network using the `density` routine, which returns a float between 0 and 1. This represents the proportion of edges meeting the node to the total number of possible edges at the node:

```
density = nx.density(G)
print("Density", density)
# Density 0.26666666666666666
```

7. Finally, we can determine whether a network is *planar* – meaning that no two edges need to be drawn crossing one another – by using the `check_planarity` routine:

```
is_planar, _ = nx.check_planarity(G)
print("Is planar", is_planar)
# Is planar True
```

How it works...

The `info` routine generates a small summary of the network, including the type of the network (which is a simple `Graph` type in this recipe), the number of nodes and edges, and the average degrees of the nodes in the network. The actual degree of a node in the network can be accessed using the `degree` property, which offers a dictionary-like interface for finding the degree of each node.

A set of nodes is said to be connected if every node in the set is joined to the others by an edge or sequence of edges. The *connected components* of a network are the largest sets of nodes that are connected. Any two distinct connected components are obviously disjointed. Every network can be decomposed into one or more connected components. The network we defined in this recipe has two connected components, `{0, 1, 2, 3, 4, 5}` and `{8, 9, 6, 7}`. These are clearly visible in the preceding figure, where the first connected component is drawn above the second connected component. In this figure, we can trace a path along the edges of the network from any node in a component to any other; for example, from 0 to 5.

The *density* of a network measures the ratio of the number of edges in the network to the total possible number of edges given by the number of nodes in a network. The density of a complete network is 1, but in general, the density will be less than 1.

A network is *planar* if it can be drawn on a flat surface without crossing edges. The easiest example of a non-planar network is a complete network with five nodes. Complete networks with, at most, four nodes are planar. A little experimentation with the way you draw these networks on paper will reveal a drawing that doesn't contain crossing edges. In addition, any network that contains a complete graph with at least five nodes is not planar. Planar networks are important in theory due to their relative simplicity, but they are less common in networks that arise in applications.

There's more...

In addition to the methods on the network classes, there are a number of other routines in the NetworkX package that can be used to access the attributes of the nodes and edges in a network. For example, `nx.get_node_attributes` gets a named attribute from each node in the network.

Generating the adjacency matrix for a network

One potent tool in the analysis of graphs is the adjacency matrix, which has entries $a_{ij} = 1$ if there is an edge from node i to node j, and 0 otherwise. For most networks, the adjacency matrix will be sparse (most of the entries are 0). For networks that are not directed, the matrix will also be symmetric ($a_{ij} = a_{ji}$). There are numerous other matrices that can be associated with a network. We will briefly discuss these in the *There's more...* section of this recipe.

In this recipe, we will generate the adjacency matrix for a network and learn how to get some basic properties of the network from this matrix.

Getting ready

For this recipe, we will need the NetworkX package imported under the name `nx`, and the NumPy module imported under the name `np`.

How to do it...

The following steps outline how to generate the adjacency matrix for a network and derive some simple properties of the network from this matrix:

1. First, we will generate a network to work with throughout this recipe. We'll generate a random network with five nodes and five edges while using a seed for reproducibility:

```
G = nx.dense_gnm_random_graph(5, 5, seed=12345)
```

2. To generate the adjacency matrix, we use the `adjacency_matrix` routine from NetworkX. This returns a sparse matrix by default, so we will also convert this into a full NumPy array for this demonstration using the `todense` method:

```
matrix = nx.adjacency_matrix(G).todense()
print(matrix)
# [[0 0 1 0 0]
#  [0 0 1 1 0]
#  [1 1 0 0 1]
#  [0 1 0 0 1]
#  [0 0 1 1 0]]
```

3. Taking the *n*th power of the adjacency matrix gives us the number of paths of length *n* from one node to another:

```
paths_len_4 = np.linalg.matrix_power(matrix, 4)
print(paths_len_4)
# [[ 3 5  0  0 5]
#  [ 5 9  0  0 9]
#  [ 0 0 13 10 0]
#  [ 0 0 10  8 0]
#  [ 5 9  0  0 9]]
```

How it works...

The `dense_gnm_random_graph` routine generates a (dense) random network, chosen uniformly from the family of all networks with n nodes and m edges. In the recipe, $n=5$ and $m=5$. The dense prefix indicates that this routine uses an algorithm that should be faster than the alternative `gnm_random_graph` for dense networks with a relatively large number of edges compared to nodes.

The adjacency matrix of a network is easy to generate, especially in sparse form, when the graph is relatively small. For larger networks, this can be an expensive operation, so it might not be practical, particularly if you convert it into a full matrix, as we saw in this recipe. You don't need to do this in general, since we can simply use the sparse matrix generated by the `adjacency_matrix` routine and the sparse linear algebra tools in the SciPy `sparse` module instead.

The matrix powers provide information about the number of paths of a given length. This can easily be seen by tracing through the definitions of matrix multiplication. Remember that the entries of the adjacency matrix are 1 when there is an edge (path of length 1) between two given nodes.

There's more...

The Eigenvalues of the adjacency matrix for a network provide some additional information about the structure of the network, such as the bounds for the chromatic number of the network. (See the *Coloring a network* recipe for more information about coloring a network.) There is a separate routine for computing the Eigenvalues of the adjacency matrix. For example, we can use the `adjacency_spectrum` routine to generate the Eigenvalues of the adjacency matrix of a network. Methods involving the Eigenvalues of a matrix associated with a network are usually called *spectral methods*.

There are other matrices associated with networks, such as the *incidence matrix* and the *Laplacian matrix*. The incidence matrix of a network is an $M \times N$ matrix, where M is the number of nodes and N is the number of edges. This has an i-jth entry of 1 if node i appears in edge j and 0 otherwise. The Laplacian matrix of a network is defined to be the $L = D - A$ matrix, where D is the diagonal matrix containing the degrees of the nodes in the network and A is the adjacency matrix of the network. Both of these matrices are useful for analyzing networks.

Creating directed and weighted networks

Simple networks, such as those described in the previous recipes, are useful for describing networks where the direction of an edge is unimportant and where the edges carry equal weight. In practice, most networks carry additional information, such as weights or direction.

In this recipe, we will create a directed and weighted network and explore some of the basic properties of such networks.

Getting ready

For this recipe, we will need the NetworkX package, imported under the name `nx` (as usual), the Matplotlib `pyplot` module imported as `plt`, and the NumPy package imported as `np`.

How to do it...

The following steps outline how to create a directed network with weights, as well as how to explore some of the properties and techniques we discussed in the previous recipes:

1. To create a directed network, we use the `DiGraph` class from NetworkX rather than the simple `Graph` class:

   ```
   G = nx.DiGraph()
   ```

2. As usual, we add nodes to the network using the `add_node` or `add_nodes_from` methods:

   ```
   G.add_nodes_from(range(5))
   ```

3. To add weighted edges, we can use either the `add_edge` method and provide the `weight` keyword argument, or use the `add_weighted_edges_from` method:

   ```
   G.add_edge(0, 1, weight=1.0)
   G.add_weighted_edges_from([
       (1, 2, 0.5), (1, 3, 2.0), (2, 3, 0.3), (3, 2, 0.3),
       (2, 4, 1.2), (3, 4, 0.8)
   ])
   ```

4. Next, we draw the network with arrows to indicate the direction of each edge. We also provide our own positions for this plot:

   ```
   fig, ax = plt.subplots()
   pos = {0: (-1, 0), 1: (0, 0), 2: (1, 1), 3: (1, -1), 4: (2, 0)}
   nx.draw(G, ax=ax, pos=pos, with_labels=True)
   ax.set_title("Weighted, directed network")
   ```

The resulting plot can be seen in the following figure:

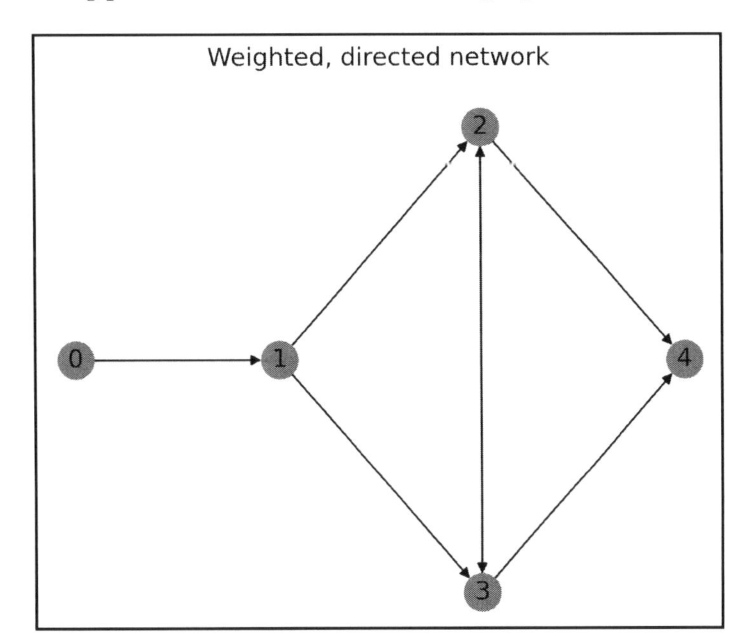

Figure 5.3: A weighted, directed network

5. The adjacency matrix of a directed matrix is created in the same way as a simple network, but the resulting matrix will not be symmetric:

```
adj_mat = nx.adjacency_matrix(G).todense()
print(adj_mat)
# [[0. 1. 0. 0. 0. ]
# [0. 0. 0.5 2. 0. ]
# [0. 0. 0. 0.3 1.2]
# [0. 0. 0.3 0. 0.8]
# [0. 0. 0. 0. 0. ]]
```

How it works...

The `DiGraph` class represents a directed network, where the order of the nodes when adding an edge is important. In this recipe, we added two edges for connecting nodes 2 and 3, one in each direction. In a simple network (the `Graph` class), the addition of the second edge would not add an additional edge. However, for a directed network (the `DiGraph` class), the order that the nodes are given in when adding the edge determines the direction.

There is nothing special about weighted edges except for the addition of the `weight` attribute that's attached to the edge. (Arbitrary data can be attached to an edge or node in a network via keyword arguments.) The `add_weighted_edges_from` method simply adds the corresponding weight value (the third value in the tuple) to the edge in question. Weights can be added to any edge in any network, not just the directed networks shown in this recipe.

The `draw` routine automatically adds arrows to edges when drawing a directed network. This behavior can be turned off by passing the `arrows=False` keyword argument. The adjacency matrix for a directed or weighted network also differs from that of a simple network. In a directed network, the matrix is not generally symmetrical, because edges may exist in one direction but not the other. For a weighted network, the entries can be different from 1 or 0, and will instead be the weight of the corresponding edge.

There's more...

Weighted networks appear in lots of applications, such as when describing transportation networks with distances or speeds. You can also use networks to examine flow through a network by providing a "capacity" for edges in the network (as a weight or as another attribute). NetworkX has several tools for analyzing flow through a network, such as finding the maximum flow through a network via the `nx.maximum_flow` routine.

Directed networks add directional information to a network. Many real-world applications give rise to networks that have unidirectional edges, such as those in industrial processes or supply chain networks. This additional directional information has consequences for many of the algorithms for working with networks, as we'll see throughout this chapter.

Finding the shortest paths in a network

A common problem where networks make an appearance is in the problem of finding the shortest – or perhaps more precisely, the highest reward – route between two nodes in a network. For instance, this could be the shortest distance between two cities, where the nodes represent the cities and the edges are roads connecting pairs of cities. In this case, the weights of the edges would be their lengths.

In this recipe, we will find the shortest path between two nodes in a network with weights.

Getting ready

For this recipe, we will need the NetworkX package imported, as usual, under the name `nx`, the Matplotlib `pyplot` module imported as `plt`, and a random number generator object from NumPy:

```
from numpy.random import default_rng
rng = default_rng(12345) # seed for reproducibility
```

How to do it...

Follow these steps to find the shortest path between two nodes in a network:

1. First, we will create a random network using `gnm_random_graph` and a `seed` for this demonstration:

   ```
   G = nx.gnm_random_graph(10, 17, seed=12345)
   ```

2. Next, we'll draw the network with a circular arrangement to see how the nodes connect to each other:

   ```
   fig, ax = plt.subplots()
   nx.draw_circular(G, ax=ax, with_labels=True)
   ax.set_title("Random network for shortest path finding")
   ```

   The resulting plot can be seen in the following image. Here, we can see that there is no direct edge from node 7 to node 9:

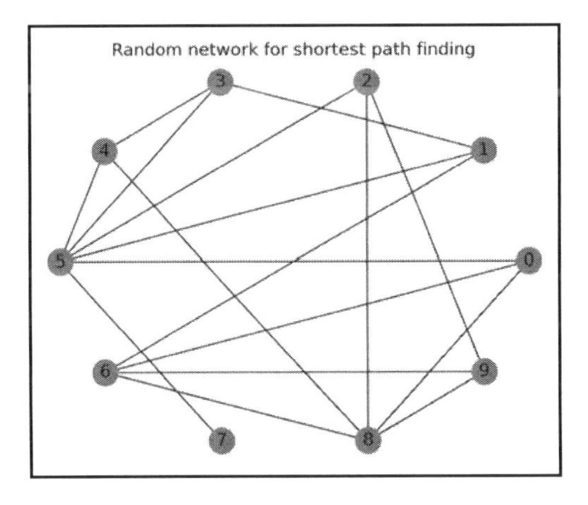

Figure 5.4: A randomly generated network with 10 nodes and 17 edges

3. Now, we need to add a weight to each of the edges so that some routes are preferable to others in terms of the shortest path:

   ```
   for u, v in G.edges:
       G.edges[u, v]["weight"] = rng.integers(5, 15)
   ```

4. Next, we will compute the shortest path from node 7 to node 9 using the `nx.shortest_path` routine:

   ```
   path = nx.shortest_path(G, 7, 9, weight="weight")
   print(path)
   # [7, 5, 2, 9]
   ```

5. We can find the length of this shortest path using the `nx.shortest_path_length` routine:

   ```
   length = nx.shortest_path_length(G, 7, 9, weight="weight")
   print("Length", length)
   # Length 32
   ```

How it works...

The `shortest_path` routine computes the shortest path between each pair of nodes. Alternatively, when supplied with the source and destination node, which is what we did in this recipe, it computes the shortest path between the two specified nodes. We supplied the optional `weight` keyword argument, which makes the algorithm find the shortest path according to the "weight" attribute of the edge. This argument changes the meaning of "shortest", with the default being "fewest edges".

The default algorithm for finding the shortest path between two nodes is Dijkstra's algorithm, which is a staple of computer science and mathematics courses. It is a good general-purpose algorithm but is not particularly efficient. Other route-finding algorithms include the A* algorithm. Greater efficiency can be obtained by using the A* algorithm with additional heuristic information to guide node selection.

There's more...

There are many algorithms for finding the shortest path between two nodes in a network. There are also variants for finding the maximum weighted path.

There are several related problems regarding finding the paths in a network, such as the *traveling salesperson problem* and the *route inspection problem*. In the traveling salesperson problem, we find a cycle (a path starting and ending at the same node) that visits every node in the network, with the smallest (or largest) total weight. In the route inspection problem, we seek the shortest cycle (by weight) that traverses every edge in the network and returns to the starting point. The traveling salesperson problem is known to be NP-hard, but the route inspection problem can be solved in polynomial time.

A famous problem in graph theory is the bridges at Königsberg, which asks to find a path in a network that traverses every edge in the network exactly once. It turns out, as proved by Euler, that finding such a path in the Königsberg bridges problem is impossible. A path that traverses every edge exactly once is called an *Eulerian circuit*. A network that admits an Eulerian circuit is called *Eulerian*. In fact, a network is Eulerian if and only if every node has an even degree. The network representation of the Königsberg bridge problem can be seen in the following image. The edges in this represent the different bridges over the rivers, while the nodes represent the different landmasses. We can see that all four of the nodes have an odd degree, which means that there cannot be a path that crosses every edge exactly once:

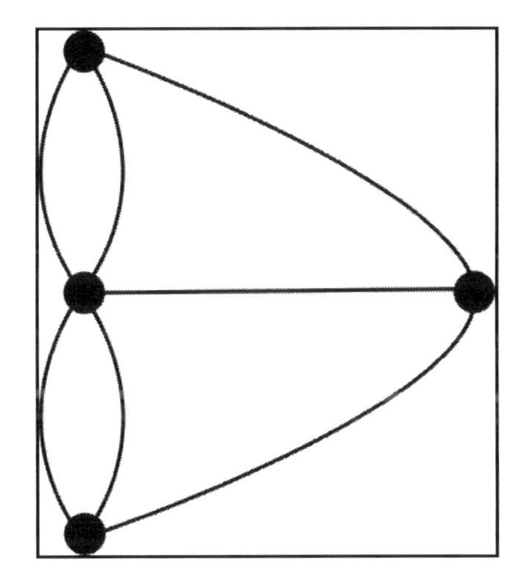

Figure 5.5: A network representing the Königsberg bridge problem

The edges represent the bridges between the different landmasses represented by the nodes.

Quantifying clustering in a network

There are various quantities associated with networks that measure the characteristics of the network. For example, the clustering coefficient of a node measures the interconnectivity between the nodes nearby (here, nearby means connected by an edge). In effect, it measures how close the neighboring nodes are to forming a complete network or *clique*.

The clustering coefficient of a node measures the proportion of the adjacent nodes that are connected by an edge; that is, two adjacent nodes form a triangle with the given node. We count the number of triangles and divide this by the total number of possible triangles that could be formed, given the degree of the node. Numerically, the clustering coefficient at a node, u, in a simple unweighted network is given by the following equation:

$$c_u = \frac{2T_u}{\deg(u)(\deg(u) - 1)}$$

Here, T_u is the number of triangles at u and the denominator is the total possible number of triangles at u. If the degree of u (the number of edges from u) is 0 or 1, then we set c_u to 0.

In this recipe, we will learn how to compute the clustering coefficient of a node in a network.

Getting ready

For this recipe, we will need the NetworkX package imported as `nx` and the Matplotlib `pyplot` module imported as `plt`.

How to do it...

The following steps show you how to compute the clustering coefficient of a node in a network:

1. First, we need to create a sample network to work with:

```
G = nx.Graph()
complete_part = nx.complete_graph(4)
cycle_part = nx.cycle_graph(range(4, 9))
G.update(complete_part)
G.update(cycle_part)
G.add_edges_from([(0, 8), (3, 4)])
```

2. Next, we will draw the network so that we can compare the clustering coefficients that we'll be calculating. This will allow us to see how these nodes appear in the network:

```
fig, ax = plt.subplots()
nx.draw_circular(G, ax=ax, with_labels=True)
ax.set_title("Network with different clustering behavior")
```

The resulting plot can be seen in the following figure:

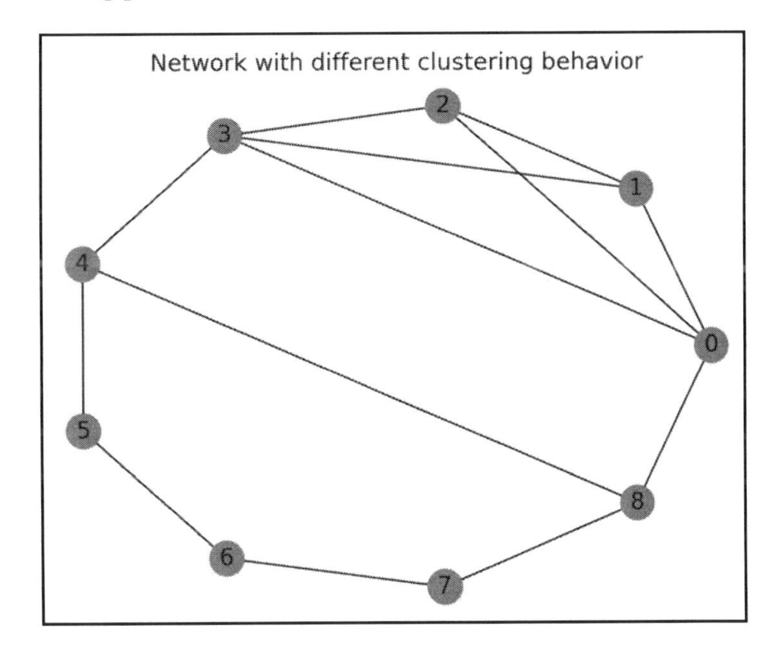

Figure 5.6: Sample network for testing clustering

3. Now, we can compute the clustering coefficients of the nodes in the network using the `nx.clustering` routine:

```
cluster_coeffs = nx.clustering(G)
```

4. The output of the `nx.clustering` routine is a dictionary over the nodes in the network. So, we can print some selected nodes as follows:

```
for i in [0, 2, 6]:
    print(f"Node {i}, clustering {cluster_coeffs[i]}")
# Node 0, clustering 0.5
# Node 2, clustering 1.0
# Node 6, clustering 0
```

5. The average clustering coefficient for all the nodes in the network can be computed using the `nx.average_clustering` routine:

```
av_clustering = nx.average_clustering(G)
print(av_clustering)
# 0.3333333333333333
```

How it works...

The clustering coefficient of a node measures how close the neighborhood of that node is to being a complete network (all the nodes are connected to one another). In this recipe, we can see that we have three different computed values: 0 has a clustering coefficient of 0.5, 2 has a clustering coefficient of 1.0, and 6 has a clustering coefficient of 0. This means that the nodes connected to node 2 form a complete network, which is because we designed our network in this way. (Nodes 0-4 form a complete network by design.) The neighborhood of node 6 is very far from being complete since there are no interconnecting edges between either of its neighbors.

The average clustering value is a simple average of the clustering coefficients over all the nodes in the network. It is not quite the same as the global clustering coefficient (computed using the `nx.transitivity` routine in NetworkX), but it does give us an idea of how close the network as a whole is to being a complete network. The global clustering coefficient measures the ratio of the number of triangles to the number of triplets – a collection of three nodes that are connected by at least two edges – over the whole network.

The difference between average clustering is quite subtle. The global clustering coefficient measures the clustering of the network as a whole, but the average clustering coefficient measures how much, on average, the network is locally clustered. The difference is best seen in a windmill network, which consists of a single node surrounded by a circle of an even number of nodes. All the nodes are connected to the center, but the nodes on the circle are only connected in an alternating pattern. The outer nodes have a local clustering coefficient of 1, while the center node has a local clustering coefficient of $1/(2N - 1)$, where N denotes the number of triangles joining to the center node. However, the global clustering coefficient is $3/(2N - 1)$.

There's more...

Clustering coefficients are related to *cliques* in a network. A clique is a subnetwork that is complete (all the nodes are connected by an edge). An important problem in network theory is finding the maximal cliques in a network, which is a very difficult problem in general (here, maximal means "cannot be made larger").

Coloring a network

Networks are also useful in scheduling problems, where you need to arrange activities into different slots so that there are no conflicts. For example, we could use networks to schedule classes to make sure that students who are taking different options do not have to be in two classes at once. In this scenario, the nodes will represent the different classes and the edges will indicate that there are students taking both classes. The process we use to solve these kinds of problems is called *network coloring*. This process involves assigning the fewest possible colors to the nodes in a network so that no two adjacent nodes have the same color.

In this recipe, we will learn how to color a network to solve a simple scheduling problem.

Getting ready

For this recipe, we need the NetworkX package imported as `nx` and the Matplotlib `pyplot` module imported as `plt`.

How to do it...

Follow these steps to solve a network coloring problem:

1. First, we will create a sample network to use in this recipe:

```
G = nx.complete_graph(3)
G.add_nodes_from(range(3, 7))
G.add_edges_from([
    (2, 3), (2, 4), (2, 6), (0, 3), (0, 6), (1, 6),
    (1, 5), (2, 5), (4, 5)
])
```

2. Next, we will draw the network so that we can understand the coloring when it is generated. For this, we will use the `draw_circular` routine:

```
fig, ax = plt.subplots()
nx.draw_circular(G, ax=ax, with_labels=True)
ax.set_title("Scheduling network")
```

The resulting plot can be seen in the following figure:

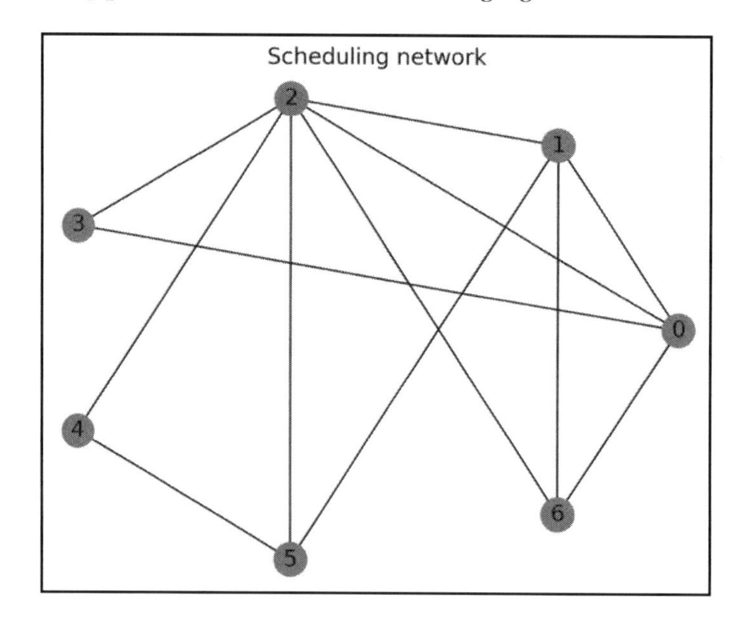

Figure 5.7: Example network for a simple scheduling problem

3. We will generate the coloring using the `nx.greedy_color` routine:

```
coloring = nx.greedy_color(G)
print("Coloring", coloring)
# Coloring {2: 0, 0: 1, 1: 2, 5: 1, 6: 3, 3: 2, 4: 2}
```

4. To see the actual colors that were used in this coloring, we will generate a set of values from the `coloring` dictionary:

```
different_colors = set(coloring.values())
print("Different colors", different_colors)
# Different colors {0, 1, 2, 3}
```

How it works...

The `nx.greedy_color` routine colors the network using one of a number of possible strategies. By default, it works in order of degree from largest to smallest. In our case, it started by assigning color 0 to node 2, which has a degree of 6, then color 1 to node 0, which has a degree of 4, and so on. The first available color is chosen for each node in this sequence. This is not necessarily the most efficient algorithm for coloring a network.

Obviously, any network can be colored by assigning every node a different color, but in most cases, fewer colors are necessary. In the recipe, the network has seven nodes, but only four colors are required. The smallest number of colors necessary is called the *chromatic number* of the network.

There's more...

There are several variations of the coloring problem for networks. One such variation is the *list coloring problem*, in which we seek a coloring for a network where each node is given a color from a predefined list of possible colors. This problem is obviously more difficult than the general coloring problem.

The general coloring problem has surprising results. For example, every planar network can be colored by, at most, four different colors. This is a famous theorem from graph theory called the *four-color theorem*, and was proved by Appel and Haken in 1977.

Finding minimal spanning trees and dominating sets

Networks have applications for a wide variety of problems. Two obvious areas that see many applications are communication and distribution. For example, we might wish to find a way of distributing goods to a number of cities (nodes) in a road network that covers the smallest distance from a particular point. For problems like this, we need to look at minimal spanning trees and dominating sets.

In this recipe, we will find a minimal spanning tree and a dominating set in a network.

Getting ready

For this recipe, we need to import the NetworkX package under the name `nx` and the Matplotlib `pyplot` module as `plt`.

How to do it...

Follow these steps to find a minimum spanning tree and dominating set for a network:

1. First, we will create a sample network to analyze:

```
G = nx.gnm_random_graph(15, 22, seed=12345)
```

2. Next, as usual, we will draw the network before doing any analysis:

```
fig, ax = plt.subplots()
pos = nx.circular_layout(G)
nx.draw(G, pos=pos, ax=ax, with_labels=True)
ax.set_title("Network with minimum spanning tree overlaid")
```

3. The minimum spanning tree can be computed using the `nx.minimum_spanning_tree` routine:

```
min_span_tree = nx.minimum_spanning_tree(G)
print(list(min_span_tree.edges))
# [(0, 13), (0, 7), (0, 5), (1, 13), (1, 11),
#   (2, 5), (2, 9), (2, 8), (2, 3), (2, 12),
#   (3, 4), (4, 6), (5, 14), (8, 10)]
```

4. Next, we will overlay the edges of the minimum spanning tree onto the plot:

```
nx.draw_networkx_edges(min_span_tree, pos=pos, ax=ax, width=1.5,
    edge_color="r")
```

5. Finally, we will find a dominating set – a set where every node in the network is adjacent to at least one node from the set – for the network using the `nx.dominating_set` routine:

```
dominating_set = nx.dominating_set(G)
print("Dominating set", dominating_set)
# Dominating set {0, 1, 2, 4, 10, 14}
```

A plot of the network with the minimum spanning tree overlaid can be seen in the following figure:

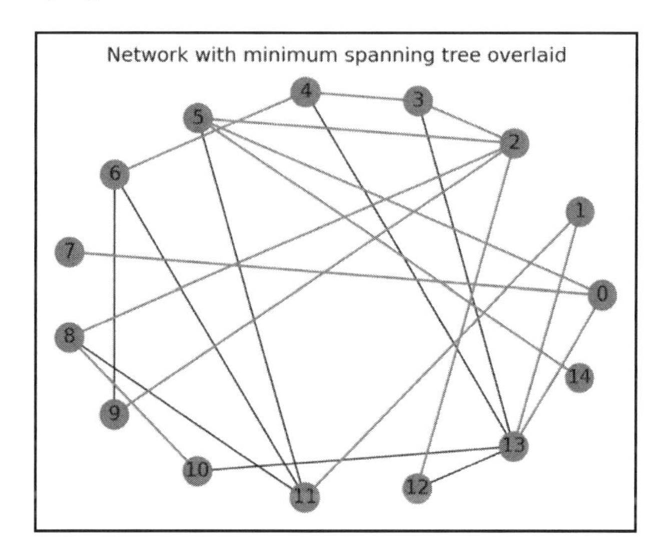

Figure 5.8: The network drawn with the minimum spanning tree overlaid

How it works...

A *spanning tree* of a network is a tree contained in the network that contains all the nodes. A *minimum* spanning tree is a spanning tree that contains the fewest edges possible – or, alternatively, has the lowest total weight. Minimum spanning trees are useful for distribution problems over a network. A simple algorithm for finding minimum spanning trees is to simply select edges (of smallest weight first, if the network is weighted) in such a way that it does not create cycles until this is no longer possible.

A *dominating set* for a network is a set of vertices where every node in the network is adjacent to at least one node in the dominating set. Dominating sets have applications in communication networks. We are often interested in finding minimal dominating sets, but this is computationally difficult. In fact, testing whether there is a dominating set that's smaller than a given size is NP-complete. However, there are some efficient algorithms for finding the smallest dominating sets for certain classes of graphs. Informally speaking, the problem is that once you've identified a candidate for a minimum size dominating set, you have to verify that there are no dominating sets that are smaller in size. This is obviously very difficult if you do not know all the possible dominating sets in advance.

Further reading

There are several classical texts on graph theory, including books by Bollobás and Diestel:

- *Diestel, R., 2010. Graph Theory. 3rd ed. Berlin: Springer.*
- *Bollobás, B., 2010. Modern Graph Theory. New York, NY: Springer.*

6
Working with Data and Statistics

One of the most attractive features of Python for people who need to analyze data is the huge ecosystem of data manipulation and analysis packages, as well as the active community of data scientists working with Python. Python is easy to use, while also offering very powerful, fast libraries, which enables even relatively novice programmers to quickly and easily process vast sets of data. At the heart of many data science packages and tools is the pandas library. Pandas provides two data container types that build on top of NumPy arrays and have good support for labels (other than simple integers). They also make working with large sets of data extremely easy.

Statistics is the systematic study of data using mathematical—specifically, probability—theory. There are two aspects to statistics. The first is to find numerical values that describe a set of data, including characteristics such as the center (mean or median) and spread (standard deviation or variance) of the data. The second aspect of statistics is inference, describing a much larger set of data (a population) using a relatively small sample dataset.

In this chapter, we will see how to leverage Python and pandas to work with large sets of data and perform statistical tests.

This chapter contains the following recipes:

- Creating Series and DataFrame objects
- Loading and storing data from a DataFrame
- Manipulating data in DataFrames
- Plotting data from a DataFrame
- Getting descriptive statistics from a DataFrame
- Understanding a population using sampling
- Testing hypotheses using t-tests

- Testing hypotheses using ANOVA
- Testing hypotheses for non-parametric data
- Creating interactive plots with Bokeh

Technical requirements

For this chapter, we will mostly make use of the pandas library for data manipulation, which provides R like data structures, such as `Series` and `DataFrame` objects, for storing, organizing, and manipulating data. We will also use the Bokeh data visualization library in the final recipe of this chapter. These libraries can be installed using your favorite package manager, such as pip:

```
python3.8 -m pip install pandas bokeh
```

We will also make use of the NumPy and SciPy packages.

The code for this chapter can be found in the `Chapter 06` folder of the GitHub repository at `https://github.com/PacktPublishing/Applying-Math-with-Python/tree/master/Chapter%2006`.

Check out the following video to see the Code in Action: `https://bit.ly/2OQs6NX`.

Creating Series and DataFrame objects

Most data handling in Python is done using the pandas library, which builds on NumPy to provide R-like structures for holding data. These structures allow the easy indexing of rows and columns, using strings or other Python objects besides just integers. Once data is loaded into a pandas `DataFrame` or `Series`, it can be easily manipulated, just as if it were in a spreadsheet. This makes Python when combined with pandas a powerful tool for processing and analyzing data.

In this recipe, we will see how to create new pandas `Series` and `DataFrame` objects and access items from `Series` or `DataFrame`.

Getting ready

For this recipe, we will import the pandas library as pd using the following command:

```
import pandas as pd
```

The NumPy package is `np`. We also create a (seeded) random number generator from NumPy, as follows:

```
from numpy.random import default_rng
rng = default_rng(12345)
```

How to do it...

The following steps outline how to create a `Series` and `DataFrame` object that holds data:

1. First, create the random data that we will store in the `Series` and `DataFrame` objects:

    ```
    diff_data = rng.normal(0, 1, size=100)
    cumulative = np.add.accumulate(diff_data)
    ```

2. Next, create a `Series` object that holds `diff_data`. We'll print `Series` to produce a view of the data:

    ```
    data_series = pd.Series(diff_data)
    print(data_series)
    ```

3. Now, create a `DataFrame` object with two columns:

    ```
    data_frame = pd.DataFrame({
       "diffs": data_series,
        "cumulative": cumulative
    })
    ```

4. Print the `DataFrame` object to produce a view of the data it holds:

    ```
    print(data_frame)
    ```

How it works...

The pandas package provides the `Series` and `DataFrame` classes, which mirror the function and capabilities of their R counterparts. `Series` is used to store one-dimensional data, such as time-series data, and `DataFrame` is used to store multidimensional data; you can think of a `DataFrame` object as a "spreadsheet."

What separates `Series` from a simple NumPy `ndarray` is the way that `Series` indexes its items. A NumPy array is indexed by integers, which is also the default for a `Series` object. However, `Series` can be indexed by any hashable Python object, including strings and `datetime` objects. This makes `Series` useful for storing time-series data. A `Series` can be created in a number of ways. In this recipe, we used a NumPy array, but any Python iterable, such as a list, can be used instead.

Each column in a `DataFrame` object is a series containing rows, just as in a traditional database or spreadsheet. In this recipe, the columns are given labels when the `DataFrame` object is constructed via the keys of the dictionary.

The `DataFrame` and `Series` objects create a summary of the data they contain when printed. This includes column names, the number of rows and columns, and the first and last five rows of the frame (series). This is useful for quickly obtaining an overview of the object and the spread of data it contains.

There's more...

The individual rows (records) of a `Series` object can be accessed using the usual index notation by providing the corresponding index. We can also access the rows by their numerical position using the special `iloc` property object. This allows us to access the rows by their numerical (integer) index, such as with Python lists or NumPy arrays.

The columns in a `DataFrame` object can be accessed using the usual index notation, providing the name of the column. The result of this is a `Series` object that contains the data from the selected column. DataFrames also provides two properties that can be used to access data. The `loc` attribute provides access to individual rows by their index, whatever this object may be. The `iloc` attribute provides access to the rows by numerical index, just as for the `Series` object.

You can provide selection criteria to `loc` (or just using index notation for the object) to select data. This includes a single label, a list of labels, a slice of labels, or a Boolean array (of an appropriate size). The `iloc` selection method accepts similar criteria.

There are other ways to select data from a `Series` or `DataFrame` object beyond the simple methods we describe here. For example, we can use the `at` attribute to access a single value at a specified row (and column) in the object.

See also

The pandas documentation contains a detailed description of the different ways to create and index a `DataFrame` or `Series` object, at `https://pandas.pydata.org/docs/user_guide/indexing.html`.

Loading and storing data from a DataFrame

It is fairly unusual to create a `DataFrame` object from the raw data in a Python session. In practice, the data will often come from an external source, such as an existing spreadsheet or CSV file, database, or API endpoint. For this reason, pandas provides numerous utilities for loading and storing data to file. Out of the box, pandas supports loading and storing data from CSV, Excel (`xls` or `xlsx`), JSON, SQL, Parquet, and Google BigQuery. This makes it very easy to import your data into pandas and then manipulate and analyze this data using Python.

In this recipe, we will see how to load and store data into a CSV file. The instructions will be similar for loading and storing data to other file formats.

Getting ready

For this recipe, we will need to import the pandas package under the `pd` alias and the NumPy library as `np`, and we create a default random number generator from NumPy using the following commands:

```
from numpy.random import default_rng
rng = default_rng(12345) # seed for example
```

How to do it...

Follow these steps to store data to a file and then load the data back into Python:

1. First, we'll create a sample `DataFrame` object using random data. We then print this `DataFrame` object so that we can compare it to the data that we will read later:

   ```
   diffs = rng.normal(0, 1, size=100)
   cumulative = np.add.accumulate(diffs)

   data_frame = pd.DataFrame({
   ```

```
        "diffs": diffs,
        "cumulative": cumulative
    })
    print(data_frame)
```

2. We will store the data in this `DataFrame` object into the `sample.csv` file using the `to_csv` method on the `DataFrame` object. We will use the `index=False` keyword argument so that the index is not stored in the CSV file:

```
    data_frame.to_csv("sample.csv", index=False)
```

3. Now, we can use the `read_csv` routine from pandas to read the `sample.csv` file into a new `DataFrame` object. We will print this object to show the result:

```
    df = pd.read_csv("sample.csv", index_col=False)
    print(df)
```

How it works...

The core of this recipe is the `read_csv` routine in pandas. This routine takes path- or file-like objects as an argument and reads the contents of the file as CSV data. We can customize the delimiter using the `sep` keyword argument, which is a comma (`,`) by default. There are also options to customize the column headers and customize the type of each column.

The `to_csv` method in a `DataFrame` or `Series` stores the contents into a CSV file. We used the `index` keyword argument here so that the indices are not printed into the file. This means that pandas will infer the index from the row number in the CSV file. This behavior is desirable if the data is indexed by integers, but this might not be the case if the data is indexed by times or dates, for example. We can also use this keyword argument to specify which column in the CSV file is the indexing column.

See also

See the pandas documentation for a list of supported file formats at `https://pandas.pydata.org/docs/reference/io.html`.

Manipulating data in DataFrames

Once we have data in a `DataFrame`, we often need to apply some simple transformations or filters to the data before we can perform any analysis. This could include, for example, filtering the rows that are missing data or applying a function to individual columns.

In this recipe, we will see how to perform some basic manipulation of `DataFrame` objects to prepare the data for analysis.

Getting ready

For this recipe, we will need the `pandas` package imported under the `pd` alias, the NumPy package imported under the `np` alias, and a default random number generator object from NumPy created using the following commands:

```
from numpy.random import default_rng
rng = default_rng(12345)
```

How to do it...

The following steps illustrate how to perform some basic filtering and manipulations on a pandas `DataFrame`:

1. We will first create a sample `DataFrame` using random data:

```
three = rng.uniform(-0.2, 1.0, size=100)
three[three < 0] = np.nan

data_frame = pd.DataFrame({
    "one": rng.random(size=100),
    "two": np.add.accumulate(rng.normal(0, 1, size=100)),
    "three": three
})
```

2. Next, we have to generate a new column from an existing column. This new column will hold `True` if the corresponding entry of column `"one"` is greater than `0.5`, and `False` otherwise:

```
data_frame["four"] = data_frame["one"] > 0.5
```

3. We now have to create a new function that we will apply to our `DataFrame`. This function multiplies the row `"two"` value by the maximum of row `"one"` and `0.5` (there are more concise ways to write this function):

    ```
    def transform_function(row):
        if row["four"]:
            return 0.5*row["two"]
        return row["one"]*row["two"]
    ```

4. We will now apply the previously defined function to each row in the DataFrame to generate a new column. We will also print the updated DataFrame for comparison later:

    ```
    data_frame["five"] = data_frame.apply(transform_function, axis=1)
    print(data_frame)
    ```

5. Finally, we have to filter out the rows in the DataFrame that contain a **Not a Number** (**NaN**) value. We will print the resulting DataFrame:

    ```
    df = data_frame.dropna()
    print(df)
    ```

How it works...

New columns can be added to an existing `DataFrame` by simply assigning them to the new column index. However, some care needs to be taken here. In some situations, pandas will create a "view" to a `DataFrame` object rather than copying, and in this case, assigning to a new column might not have the desired effect. This is discussed in the pandas documentation (`https://pandas.pydata.org/pandas-docs/stable/user_guide/indexing.html#returning-a-view-versus-a-copy`).

Pandas `Series` objects (columns in a `DataFrame`) support the rich comparison operators, such as equality and less than or greater than (in this recipe, we used the greater than operator). These comparison operators return a `Series` containing Boolean values corresponding to the positions at which the comparison was true and false. This can, in turn, be used to index the original Series and get just the rows where the comparison was true. In this recipe, we have simply added this Series of Boolean values to the original `DataFrame`.

The `apply` method takes a function (or other callable function) and applies it to each column in the DataFrame. In this recipe, we instead wanted to apply the function to each row, so we used the `axis=1` keyword argument to apply the function to each row in the DataFrame. In either case, the function is provided with a `Series` object indexed by the rows (columns). We have also applied a function to each row, which returned a value computed using the data from each row. In practice, this application would be quite slow if the DataFrame contains a large number of rows. If possible, you should operate on the columns as a whole, using functions designed to operate on NumPy arrays, for better efficiency. This is especially true for performing simple arithmetic on values in columns of a DataFrame. Just like NumPy arrays, `Series` objects implement standard arithmetic operations, which can greatly improve the operation time for large DataFrames.

In the final step of this recipe, we used the `dropna` method to quickly select only the rows from the DataFrames that do not contain a NaN value. Pandas uses NaN to represent missing data in a DataFrame, so this method selects the rows that don't contain a missing value. This method returns a view to the original `DataFrame` object, but it can also modify the original DataFrame by passing the `inplace=True` keyword argument. As used in this recipe, this is roughly equivalent to using the indexing notation to select rows using an indexing array containing Boolean values.

You should always be cautious when modifying original data directly since it might not be possible to return to this data to repeat your analysis later. If you do need to modify the data directly, you should make sure that it is either backed up or that the modifications do not remove data that you might later need.

There's more...

Most pandas routines deal with missing data (NaN) in a sensible way. However, if you do need to remove or replace missing data in a DataFrame, then there are several ways to do this. In this recipe, we have used the `dropna` method to simply drop the rows from the DataFrames that are missing data. We could instead fill all the missing values with a specific value using the `fillna` method, or interpolate missing values using the surrounding values using the `interpolate` method.

More generally, we can use the `replace` method to replace specific (non-NaN) values with other values. This method can work with both numeric values or string values, including pattern-matching with regex.

The `DataFrame` class has many useful methods. We've only covered the very basic methods here, but there are two other methods that we should also mention. These are the `agg` method and the `merge` method.

The `agg` method aggregates the results of one or more operations over a given axis of the DataFrame. This allows us to quickly produce summary information for each column (or row) by applying an aggregating function. The output is a DataFrame that has the names of the functions applied as the rows, and the labels for the chosen axis (column labels, for instance) for the columns.

The `merge` method performs a SQL-like join over two DataFrames. This will produce a new DataFrame that contains the result of the join. There are various parameters that can be passed to the `how` keyword argument to specify the type of merge to be performed, with the default being `inner`. The name of the column or index over which to perform the join should be passed to either the `on` keyword argument—if both `DataFrame` objects contain the same key—or to `left_on` and `right_on`.

Plotting data from a DataFrame

As with many mathematical problems, one of the first steps to find some way to visualize the problem and all the information is to formulate a strategy. For data-based problems, this usually means producing a plot of the data and visually inspecting it for trends, patterns, and the underlying structure. Since this is such a common operation, pandas provides a quick and simple interface for plotting data in various forms, using Matplotlib under the hood by default, directly from a `Series` or `DataFrame`.

In this recipe, we will see how to plot data directly from a `DataFrame` or `Series` to understand the underlying trends and structure.

Getting ready

For this recipe, we will need the pandas library import as `pd`, the NumPy library import as `np`, the matplotlib `pyplot` module imported as `plt`, and a default random number generator instance created using the following commands:

```
from numpy.random import default_rng
rng = default_rng(12345)
```

How to do it...

Follow these steps to create a simple DataFrame using random data and produce plots of the data it contains:

1. Create a sample DataFrame using random data:

    ```
    diffs = rng.standard_normal(size=100)
    walk = np.add.accumulate(diffs)
    df = pd.DataFrame({
        "diffs": diffs,
        "walk": walk
    })
    ```

2. Next, we have to create a blank figure with two subplots ready for plotting:

    ```
    fig, (ax1, ax2) = plt.subplots(1, 2, tight_layout=True)
    ```

3. We have to plot the `walk` column as a standard line graph. This is done by using the `plot` method on the `Series` (column) object without additional arguments. We will force the plotting on `ax1` by passing the `ax=ax1` keyword argument:

    ```
    df["walk"].plot(ax=ax1, title="Random walk")
    ax1.set_xlabel("Index")
    ax1.set_ylabel("Value")
    ```

4. Now, we have to plot a histogram of the `diffs` column by passing the `kind="hist"` keyword argument to the `plot` method:

    ```
    df["diffs"].plot(kind="hist", ax=ax2, title="Histogram of diffs")
    ax2.set_xlabel("Difference")
    ```

The resulting plots are shown here:

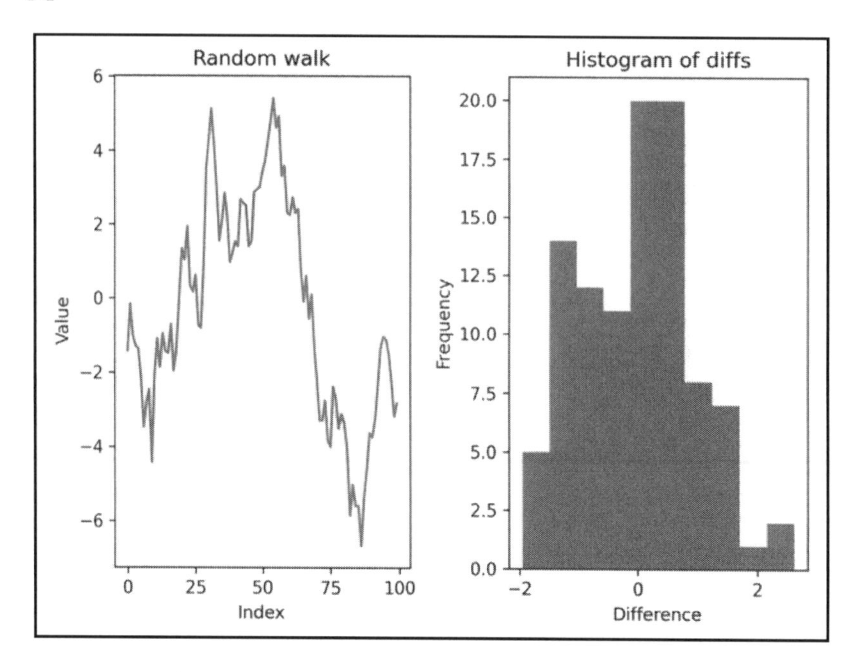

Figure 6.1 – Plot of the walk value and a histogram of differences from a DataFrame

How it works...

The `plot` method on a `Series` (or a `DataFrame`) is a quick way to plot the data it contains against the row index. The `kind` keyword argument is used to control the type of plot that is produced, with a line plot being the default. There are lots of options for the plotting type, including `bar` for a vertical bar chart, `barh` for a horizontal bar chart, `hist` for a histogram (also seen in this recipe), `box` for a box plot, and `scatter` for a scatter plot. There are several other keyword arguments to customize the plot that it produces. In this recipe, we also provided the `title` keyword argument to add a title to each subplot.

Since we wanted to put both plots on the same figure side by side using subplots that we had already created, we used the `ax` keyword argument to pass in the respective axes handles to the plotting routine. Even if you let the `plot` method construct its own figure, you may still need to use the `plt.show` routine in order to display the figure with certain settings.

There's more...

We can produce several common types of plots using the pandas interface. This includes, in addition to those mentioned in this recipe, scatter plots, bar plots (horizontal bars and vertical bars), area plots, pie charts, and box plots. The `plot` method also accepts various keyword arguments to customize the appearance of the plot.

Getting descriptive statistics from a DataFrame

Descriptive statistics, or summary statistics, are simple values associated with a set of data, such as the mean, median, standard deviation, minimum, maximum, and quartile values. These values describe the location and spread of a dataset in various ways. The mean and median are measures of the center (location) of the data, and the other values measure the spread of the data from the mean and median. These statistics are vital in understanding a dataset and form the basis for many techniques for analysis.

In this recipe, we will see how to generate descriptive statistics for each column in a DataFrame.

Getting ready

For this recipe, we need the pandas package imported as `pd`, the NumPy package imported as `np`, the matplotlib `pyplot` module imported as `plt`, and a default random number generator created using the following commands:

```
from numpy.random import default_rng
rng = default_rng(12345)
```

How to do it...

The following steps show how to generate descriptive statistics for each column in a DataFrame:

1. We will first create some sample data that we can analyze:

```
uniform = rng.uniform(1, 5, size=100)
normal = rng.normal(1, 2.5, size=100)
bimodal = np.concatenate([rng.normal(0, 1, size=50),
    rng.normal(6, 1, size=50)])
df = pd.DataFrame({
    "uniform": uniform,
    "normal": normal,
    "bimodal": bimodal
})
```

2. Next, we plot histograms of the data so that we can understand the distribution of the data in the DataFrame:

```
fig, (ax1, ax2, ax3) = plt.subplots(1, 3, tight_layout=True)

df["uniform"].plot(kind="hist", title="Uniform", ax=ax1)
df["normal"].plot(kind="hist", title="Normal", ax=ax2)
df["bimodal"].plot(kind="hist", title="Bimodal", ax=ax3, bins=20)
```

3. Pandas `DataFrame` objects have a method for getting several common descriptive statistics for each column. The `describe` method creates a new DataFrame, where the column headers are the same as from the original object and each row contains a different descriptive statistic:

```
descriptive = df.describe()
```

4. We also compute the *kurtosis* and add this to the new DataFrame we just obtained. We also print the descriptive statistics to the console to see what the values are:

```
descriptive.loc["kurtosis"] = df.kurtosis()
print(descriptive)
#              uniform      normal    bimodal
# count    100.000000 100.000000 100.000000
# mean       2.813878   1.087146   2.977682
# std        1.093795   2.435806   3.102760
# min        1.020089  -5.806040  -2.298388
# 25%        1.966120  -0.498995   0.069838
# 50%        2.599687   1.162897   3.100215
# 75%        3.674468   2.904759   5.877905
```

```
# max          4.891319   6.375775   8.471313
# kurtosis    -1.055983   0.061679  -1.604305
```

5. Finally, we add vertical lines to the histograms to illustrate the value of the mean in each case:

```
uniform_mean = descriptive.loc["mean", "uniform"]
normal_mean = descriptive.loc["mean", "normal"]
bimodal_mean = descriptive.loc["mean", "bimodal"]
ax1.vlines(uniform_mean, 0, 20)
ax2.vlines(uniform_mean, 0, 25)
ax3.vlines(uniform_mean, 0, 20)
```

The resulting histograms are shown here:

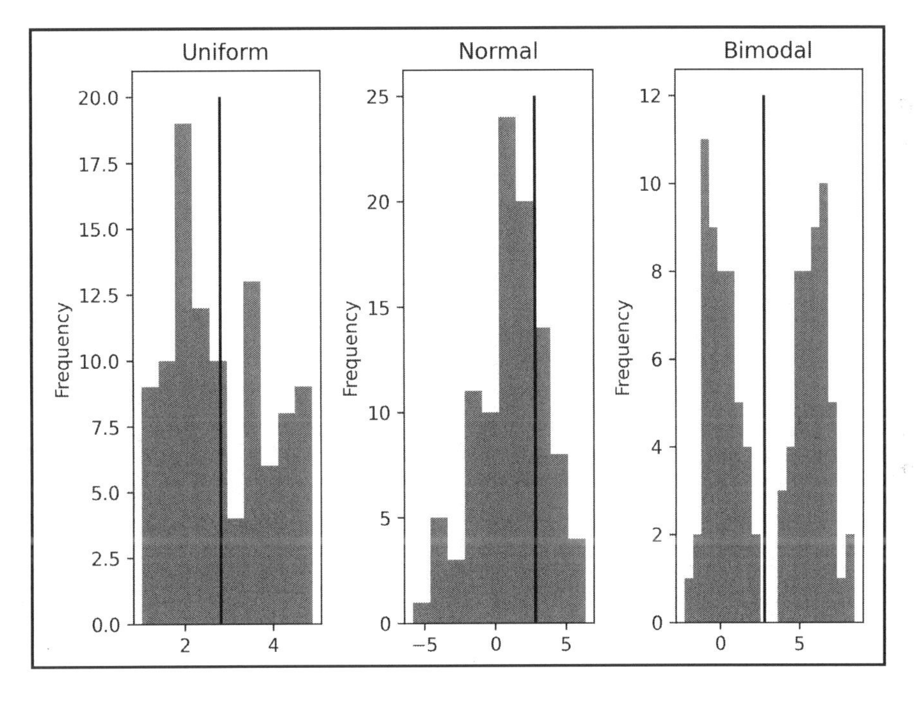

Figure 6.2 – Histograms of three sets of data with their mean values indicated

How it works...

The `describe` method returns a DataFrame with rows for the following descriptive statistics of the data: the count, mean, standard deviation, minimum value, 25% quartile, median (50% quartile), 75% quartile, and maximum value. The count is fairly self-explanatory, as are the minimum and maximum values. The mean and the median are two different *averages* of the data, which roughly represent the central value of the data. The mean is defined in a familiar way as the sum of all values divided by the number of values. We can express this quantity using the following formula:

$$\bar{x} = \frac{1}{N}\sum_{i=1}^{N} x_i$$

Here, the x_i values represent the data values and N is the number (count) of values. Here, we also adopt the common notation of the bar to represent the mean value. The median is the "middle value" when all the data is sorted (taking an average of the two middle values if there are an odd number of values). The quartile values at 25% and 75% are similarly defined, but taking the value at 25% or 75% of the way through the ordered values. You might also think of the minimum as the 0% quartile and the maximum as the 100% quartile.

Standard deviation is a measure of the spread of the data from the mean and is related to another quantity that is frequently mentioned in statistics, the **variance**. The variance is the square of the standard deviation and is defined as follows:

$$s^2 = \frac{1}{N}\sum_{i=1}^{N} (x_i - \bar{x})^2$$

You might also see $N - 1$ appear in the fraction here, which is a correction for **bias** when estimating population parameters from a sample. We will discuss population parameters and their estimation in the next recipe. Standard deviation, variance, the quartiles, and the maximum and minimum values describe the spread of the data. For example, if the maximum value is 5, the minimum value is 0, the 25% quartile is 2, and the 75% quartile is 4, then this indicates that most (at least 50% of the values, in fact) of the data is concentrated between 2 and 4.

The *kurtosis* is a measure of how much the data is concentrated in the "tails" of the distribution (far from the mean). This is not as common as the other quantities we have discussed in this recipe, but it does appear in some analysis. We have included it here mostly as a demonstration of how to compute summary statistic values that do not appear in the DataFrame returned from the `describe` method using the appropriately named method—here, `kurtosis`. There are, of course, separate methods for computing the mean (`mean`), standard deviation (`std`), and the other quantities from the `describe` method.

When pandas computes the quantities described in this recipe, it will automatically ignore any "missing values" represented by NaN. This will also be reflected in the count reported in the descriptive statistics.

There's more...

The third dataset that we included in our statistics illustrates the importance of looking at the data to make sure the values we have calculated make sense. Indeed, we compute the mean as approximately `2.9`, but looking at the histogram, it is clear that most of the data is relatively far from this value. We should always check whether the summary statistics that we calculate give an accurate summary of the data in our sample. Simply quoting the mean might give an inaccurate representation of the sample.

Understanding a population using sampling

One of the central problems in statistics is to make estimations—and quantify how good these estimations are—of the distribution of an entire population given only a small (random) sample. A classic example is to estimate the average height of all the people in a country when measuring the height of a randomly selected sample of people. These kinds of problems are particularly interesting when the true population distribution, by which we usually mean the mean of the whole population, cannot feasibly be measured. In this case, we must rely on our knowledge of statistics and a (usually much smaller) randomly selected sample to estimate the true population mean and standard deviation, and also quantify how good our estimations are. It is the latter that is the source of confusion, misunderstanding, and misrepresentation of statistics in the wider world.

In this recipe, we will see how to estimate the population mean and give a **confidence interval** for these estimates.

Getting ready

For this recipe, we need the pandas package import as `pd`, the `math` module from the Python standard library, and the SciPy `stats` module, imported using the following command:

```
from scipy import stats
```

How to do it...

In the following steps, we will give an estimation of the mean height of males in the United Kingdom, based on a randomly selected sample of 20 people:

1. We have to load our sample data into a pandas `Series`:

```
sample_data = pd.Series(
    [172.3, 171.3, 164.7, 162.9, 172.5, 176.3, 174.8, 171.9,
     176.8, 167.8, 164.5, 179.7, 157.8, 170.6, 189.9, 185. ,
     172.7, 165.5, 174.5, 171.5]
)
```

2. Next, we will compute the sample mean and standard deviation:

```
sample_mean = sample_data.mean()
sample_std = sample_data.std()
print(f"Mean {sample_mean}, st. dev {sample_std}")
# Mean 172.15, st. dev 7.473778724383846
```

3. Then, we will compute the **standard error**, as follows:

```
N = sample_data.count()
std_err = sample_std/math.sqrt(N)
```

4. We will compute the **critical values** for the confidence values we desire from the student *t* distribution:

```
cv_95, cv_99 = stats.t.ppf([0.975, 0.995], df=N-1)
```

5. Now, we can compute the 95% and 99% confidence intervals for the true population mean using the following code:

```
pm_95 = cv_95*std_err
conf_interval_95 = [sample_mean - pm_95, sample_mean + pm_95]
pm_99 = cv_99*std_err
conf_interval_99 = [sample_mean - pm_99, sample_mean + pm_99]
```

```
print("95% confidence", conf_interval_95)
# 95% confidence [168.65216388659374, 175.64783611340627]
print("99% confidence", conf_interval_99)
# 99% confidence [167.36884119608774, 176.93115880391227]
```

How it works...

The key to parameter estimation is normal distribution, which we discussed in `Chapter 4`, *Working with Randomness and Probability*. If we find the critical value of z for which the probability that a standard, normally distributed random number lies below this value z is 97.5%, then the probability that such a number lies between the values of $-z$ and z is 95% (2.5% in each tail). This critical value of z turns out to be 1.96, rounded to 2 decimal places. That is, we can be 95% sure that the value of a standard normally distributed random number lies between $-z$ and z. Similarly, the critical value of 99% confidence is 2.58 (rounded to 2 decimal places).

If our sample is "large," we could invoke the **central limit theorem**, which tells us that even if the population is not normally distributed itself, the means of random samples drawn from this population will be normally distributed with the same mean as the whole population. However, this is only valid assuming our samples are large. In this recipe, the sample is not large—it only has 20 values, which is certainly not large compared to the male population of the UK. This means that, rather than the normal distribution, we have to use a student t distribution with N-1 degrees of freedom to find our critical values, where N is the size of our sample. For this, we use the `stats.t.ppf` routine from the SciPy `stats` module.

The student t distribution is related to the normal distribution but has a parameter—the degree of freedom—that changes the shape of the distribution. As the number of degrees of freedom increases, the student t distribution will look more and more like a normal distribution. The point at which you consider the distributions to be sufficiently similar depends on your application and your data. A general rule of thumb says that a sample size of 30 is sufficient to invoke the central limit theorem and simply use the normal distribution, but it is by no means a good rule. You should be very careful when making deductions based on a sample, especially if the sample is very small compared to the total population. (Clearly, using a sample size of 20 would be pretty descriptive if the total population consists of 30 people, but not if the total population consists of 30 million people.)

Once we have the critical values, the confidence interval for the true population mean can be computed by multiplying the critical value by the standard error of the sample and adding and subtracting this from the sample mean. The standard error is an approximation of the spread of the distribution of sample means of a given sample size from the true population mean. This is why we use the standard error to give the confidence interval for our estimation of the population mean. When we multiply the standard error by the critical value taken from the student t distribution (in this case), we obtain an estimate of the maximum difference between the observed sample mean and the true population mean at the given confidence level.

In this recipe, that means that we are 95% certain that the mean height of UK males lies between 168.7 cm and 175.6 cm, and we are 99% certain that the mean height of UK males lies between 167.4 cm and 176.9 cm. In fact, our sample was drawn from a population with a mean of 175.3 cm and a standard deviation of 7.2 cm. This true mean (175.3 cm) does indeed lie within both of our confidence intervals, but only just.

See also

There is a useful package called `uncertainties` for doing computations involving values with some uncertainty attached. See the *Accounting for uncertainty in calculations* recipe in `Chapter 10`, *Miscellaneous Topics*.

Testing hypotheses using t-tests

One of the most common tasks in statistics is to test the validity of a hypothesis about the mean of a normally distributed population given that you have collected sample data from that population. For example, in quality control, we might wish to test that the thickness of a sheet produced at a mill is 2 mm. To test this, we would randomly select sample sheets and measure the thickness to obtain our sample data. Then, we can use a **t-test** to test our null hypothesis, H_0, that the mean paper thickness is 2 mm, against the alternative hypothesis, H_1, that the mean paper thickness is not 2 mm. We use the SciPy `stats` module to compute a t statistic and a p value. If the p value is below 0.05, then we accept the null hypothesis with 5% significance (95% confidence). If the p value is larger than 0.05, then we must reject the null hypothesis in favor of our alternative hypothesis.

In this recipe, we will see how to use a t-test to test whether the assumed population mean is valid given a sample.

Getting ready

For this recipe we will need the pandas package imported as `pd` and the SciPy `stats` module imported using the following command:

```
from scipy import stats
```

How to do it...

Follow these steps to use a t-test to test the validity of a proposed population mean given some sample data:

1. We will first load the data into a pandas `Series`:

```
sample = pd.Series([
    2.4, 2.4, 2.9, 2.6, 1.8, 2.7, 2.6, 2.4, 2.8, 2.4, 2.4,
    2.4, 2.7, 2.7, 2.3, 2.4, 2.4, 3.2, 2.2, 2.5, 2.1, 1.8,
    2.9, 2.5, 2.5, 3.2, 2. , 2.3, 3. , 1.5, 3.1, 2.5, 3.1,
    2.4, 3. , 2.5, 2.7, 2.1, 2.3, 2.2, 2.5, 2.6, 2.5, 2.8,
    2.5, 2.9, 2.1, 2.8, 2.1, 2.3
])
```

2. Now, set the hypothesized population mean and the significance level that we will be testing at:

```
mu0 = 2.0
significance = 0.05
```

3. Next, use the `ttest_1samp` routine from the SciPy `stats` module to generate the t statistic and the p value:

```
t_statistic, p_value = stats.ttest_1samp(sample, mu0)
print(f"t stat: {t_statistic}, p value: {p_value}")
# t stat: 9.752368720068665, p value: 4.596949515944238e-13
```

4. Finally, test whether the p value is smaller than the significance level we chose:

```
if p_value <= significance:
    print("Reject H0 in favour of H1: mu != 2.0")
else:
    print("Accept H0: mu = 2.0")
# Reject H0 in favour of H1: mu != 2.0
```

How it works...

The t statistic is computed using the following formula:

$$t = \frac{\bar{x} - \mu_0}{s/\sqrt{N}}$$

Here, μ_0 is the hypothesized mean (from the null hypothesis), x bar is the sample mean, s is the sample standard deviation, and N is the size of the sample. The t statistic is an estimation of the difference between the observed sample mean and the hypothesized population mean, μ_0, normalized by the standard error. Assuming the population is normally distributed, the t statistic will follow a t distribution with N-1 degrees of freedom. Looking at where the t statistic lies within in the corresponding student t distribution gives us an idea of how likely it is that the sample mean we observed came from the population with the hypothesized mean. This is given in the form of a p value.

The p value is the probability of observing a more extreme value than the sample mean we have observed, given the assumption that the population mean is equal to μ_0. If the p value is smaller than the significance value we have chosen, then we cannot expect the true population mean to be the value, μ_0, that we assumed. In this case, we have to accept the alternative hypothesis that the true population norm is not equal to μ_0.

There's more...

The test that we demonstrated in this recipe is the most basic use of a t-test. Here, we compared the sample mean to a hypothesized population mean to decide whether it was reasonable that the mean of the whole population is this hypothesized value. More generally, we can use t-tests to compare two independent populations given samples taken from each using a **2-sample t-test**, or compare the populations where data is paired (in some way) using a **paired t-test**. This makes the t-test an important tool for a statistician.

Significance and confidence are two concepts that occur frequently in statistics. A statistically significant result is one that has a high probability of being correct. In many contexts, we consider any result that has a probability of being wrong below a certain threshold (usually either 5% or 1%) to be statistically significant. Confidence is a quantification of how certain we are about a result. The confidence of a result is 1 minus the significance.

Unfortunately, the significance of a result is something that is often misused or misunderstood. To say that a result is statistically significant at 5% is to say that there is a 5% chance that we have wrongly accepted the null hypothesis. That is, if we repeated the same test on 20 other samples from the population, we would expect at least one of them to give the opposite result. That, however, is not to say that one of them is guaranteed to do so.

High significance indicates that we are more sure that the conclusion we have reached is correct, but it is certainly not a guarantee that this is indeed the case. In fact, the results found in this recipe are evidence for this; the sample that we used was in fact drawn from a population with a mean of `2.5` and a standard deviation of `0.35`. (Some rounding was applied to the sample after creating, which will have altered the distribution slightly.) This is not to say that our analysis is wrong, or that the conclusion we reached from our sample is not the right one.

It is important to remember that t-tests are only valid when the underlying populations follow a normal distribution, or at least approximately do so. If this is not the case, then you might need to use a non-parametric test instead. We will discuss this in the *Testing hypotheses for non-parametric data* recipe.

Testing hypotheses using ANOVA

Suppose we have designed an experiment that tests two new processes against the current process and we want to test whether the results of these new processes are different from the current process. In this case, we can use **Analysis of Variance** (**ANOVA**) to help us determine whether there are any differences between the mean values of the three sets of results (for this, we need to assume that each sample is drawn from a normal distribution with a common variance).

In this recipe, we will see how to use ANOVA to compare multiple samples with one another.

Getting ready

For this recipe, we need the SciPy `stats` module. We will also need a default random number generator instance created using the following commands:

```
from numpy.random import default_rng
rng = default_rng(12345)
```

How to do it...

Follow these steps to perform a (oneway) ANOVA test to test for differences between three different processes:

1. First, we will create some sample data, which we will analyze:

```
current = rng.normal(4.0, 2.0, size=40)
process_a = rng.normal(6.2, 2.0, size=25)
process_b = rng.normal(4.5, 2.0, size=64)
```

2. Next, we will set the significance level for our test:

```
significance = 0.05
```

3. Then, we will use the `f_oneway` routine from the SciPy `stats` module to generate the F-statistic and the *p* value:

```
F_stat, p_value = stats.f_oneway(current, process_a, process_b)
print(f"F stat: {F_stat}, p value: {p_value}")
# F stat: 9.949052026027028, p value: 9.732322721019206e-05
```

4. Now, we must test whether the *p* value is sufficiently small to see whether we should accept or reject our null hypothesis that all mean values are equal:

```
if p_value <= significance:
    print("Reject H0: there is a difference between means")
else:
    print("Accept H0: all means equal")
# Reject H0: there is a difference between means
```

How it works...

ANOVA is a powerful technique for comparing multiple samples against one another simultaneously. It works by comparing the variation in the samples relative to the overall variation. ANOVA is especially powerful when comparing three or more samples since no cumulative error is incurred from running multiple tests. Unfortunately, if ANOVA detects that not all the mean values are equal, then there is no way from the test information to determine which sample(s) are significantly different from the others. For this, you would need to use an extra test to find the differences.

The `f_oneway` SciPy `stats` package routine performs a one-way ANOVA test—the test statistic generated in ANOVA follows an F-distribution. Again, the *p* value is the crucial piece of information coming from the test. We accept the null hypothesis if the *p* value is less than our predefined significance level (in this recipe, 5%) and reject the null hypothesis otherwise.

There's more...

The ANOVA method is very flexible. The one-way ANOVA test that we presented here is the most simple case as there is only a single factor to test. A two-way ANOVA test can be used to test for differences over two different factors. This is useful in clinical trials of medicines, for example, where we test against a control but also measure the effects of gender (for instance) on the outcomes. Unfortunately, SciPy does not have a routine for performing two-way ANOVA in the `stats` module. You will need to use an alternative package, such as the `statsmodels` package. We will use this package in `Chapter 7`, *Regression and Forecasting*.

As mentioned, ANOVA can only detect whether there are differences. It cannot detect where these differences occur if there are significant differences. For example, we can use Durnett's test to test whether the other sample mean values differ from a control sample, or Tukey's range test to test each group mean against every other group mean.

Testing hypotheses for non-parametric data

Both t-tests and ANOVA have a major drawback: the population that is being sampled must follow a normal distribution. In many applications, this is not too restrictive because many real-world population values follow a normal distribution, or some rules, such as the central limit theorem, allow us to analyze some related data. However, it is simply not true that all possible population values follow a normal distribution in any reasonable way. For these (thankfully, rare) cases, we need some alternative test statistics to use as replacements for t-tests and ANOVA.

In this recipe, we will use a Wilcoxon rank-sum test and the Kruskal-Wallis test to test for differences between two (or more, in the latter case) populations.

Getting ready

For this recipe, we will need the pandas package imported as `pd`, the SciPy `stats` module, and a default random number generator instance created using the following commands:

```
from numpy.random import default_rng
rng = default_rng(12345)
```

How to do it...

Follow these steps to compare the populations of two or more populations that are not normally distributed:

1. First, we will generate some sample data to use in our analysis:

```
sample_A = rng.uniform(2.5, 4.5, size=22)
sample_B = rng.uniform(3.0, 4.4, size=25)
sample_C = rng.uniform(3.0, 4.4, size=30)
```

2. Next, we set the significance level that we will use in this analysis:

```
significance = 0.05
```

3. Now, we use the `stats.kruskal` routine to generate the test statistic and the *p* value for the null hypothesis that the populations have the same median value:

```
statistic, p_value = stats.kruskal(sample_A, sample_B, sample_C)
print(f"Statistic: {statistic}, p value: {p_value}")
# Statistic: 5.09365664638392, p value: 0.07832970895845669
```

4. We will use a conditional statement to print a statement about the outcome of the test:

```
if p_value <= significance:
    print("Accept H0: all medians equal")
else:
    print("There are differences between population medians")
# There are differences between population medians
```

5. Now, we use Wilcoxon rank-sum tests to obtain the p values for the comparisons between each pair of samples:

```
_, p_A_B = stats.ranksums(sample_A, sample_B)
_, p_A_C = stats.ranksums(sample_A, sample_C)
_, p_B_C = stats.ranksums(sample_B, sample_C)
```

6. Next, we use conditional statements to print out messages for those comparisons that indicate a significant difference:

```
if p_A_B > significance:
    print("Significant differences between A and B, p value",
        p_A_B)
# Significant differences between A and B, p value
     0.08808151166219029

if p_A_C > significance:
    print("Significant differences between A and C, p value",
        p_A_C)
# Significant differences between A and C, p value
     0.4257804790323789

if p_B_C > significance:
    print("Significant differences between B and C, p value",
        p_B_C)
else:
    print("No significant differences between B and C, p value",
        p_B_C)
# No significant differences between B and C, p value
     0.037610047044153536
```

How it works...

We say that data is non-parametric if the population from which the data was sampled does not follow a distribution that can be described by a small number of parameters. This usually means that the population is not normally distributed but is broader than this. In this recipe, we sampled from uniform distributions, but this is still a more structured example than we would generally have when non-parametric tests are necessary. Non-parametric tests can and should be used in any situation where we are not sure about the underlying distribution. The cost of doing this is that the tests are slightly less powerful.

The first step of any (real) analysis should be to plot a histogram of the data and inspect the distribution visually. If you draw a random sample from a normally distributed population, you might also expect the sample to be normally distributed (we have seen this several times in this book). If your sample shows the characteristic bell curve of a normal distribution, then it is fairly likely that the population is itself normally distributed. You might also use a **kernel density estimation** plot to help determine the distribution. This is available on the pandas plotting interface as `kind="kde"`. If you still aren't sure whether the population is normal, you can apply a statistical test, such as D'Agostino's K-squared test or Pearson's Chi-squared test for normality. These two tests are combined into a single routine to test for normality called `normaltest` in the SciPy `stats` module, along with several other tests for normality.

The Wilcoxon rank-sum test—also called the Mann-Whitney U test—is a non-parametric replacement for a two-sample t-test. Unlike the t-test, the rank-sum test does not compare the sample mean values to quantify whether the populations have different distributions. Instead, it combines the data of the samples and ranks them in order of size. The test statistic is generated from the sum of the ranks from the sample with the fewest elements. From here, as usual, we generate a p value for the null hypothesis that the two populations have the same distribution.

The Kruskal-Wallis test is a non-parametric replacement for a one-way ANOVA test. Like the rank-sum test, it uses the ranking of the sample data to generate a test statistic and p values for the null hypothesis that all the populations have the same median value. As with one-way ANOVA, we can only detect whether all of the populations have the same median, and not where the differences lie. For this, we would have to use additional tests.

In this recipe, we used the Kruskal-Wallis test to determine whether there were any significant differences between the populations corresponding to our three samples. A difference was detected with a p value of `0.07`, which is not far from being significant at 5%. We then used rank-sum tests to determine where significant differences occur between the populations. Here, we found that sample A is significantly different from samples B and C, and samples B and C are not significantly different. This is hardly surprising given the way that these samples were generated.

Unfortunately, since we have used multiple tests in this recipe, our overall confidence in our conclusions is not as high as we might expect it to be. We performed four tests with 95% confidence, which means our overall confidence in our conclusion is only approximately 81%. This is because errors aggregate over multiple tests, reducing the overall confidence. To correct for this, we would have to adjust our significance threshold for each test, using the Bonferroni correction (or similar).

Creating interactive plots with Bokeh

Test statistics and numerical reasoning are good for systematically analyzing sets of data. However, they don't really give us a good picture of the whole set of data like a plot would. Numerical values are definitive but can be difficult to understand, especially in statistics, whereas a plot instantly illustrates differences between sets of data and trends. For this reason, there is a large number of libraries for plotting data in ever more creative ways. One particularly interesting package for producing plots of data is Bokeh, which allows us to create interactive plots in the browser by leveraging JavaScript libraries.

In this recipe, we will see how to use Bokeh to create an interactive plot that can be displayed in the browser.

Getting ready

For this recipe, we will need the pandas package imported as `pd`, the NumPy package imported as `np`, an instance of the default random number generator constructed with the following code, and the `plotting` module from Bokeh, which we have imported under the `bk` alias:

```
from bokeh import plotting as bk
from numpy.random import default_rng
rng = default_rng(12345)
```

How to do it...

These steps show how to create an interactive plot in the browser using Bokeh:

1. We first need to create some sample data to plot:

    ```
    date_range = pd.date_range("2020-01-01", periods=50)
    data = np.add.accumulate(rng.normal(0, 3, size=50))
    series = pd.Series(data, index=date_range)
    ```

2. Next, we specify the output file where the HTML code for the plot will be stored by using the `output_file` routine:

    ```
    bk.output_file("sample.html")
    ```

3. Now, we create a new figure and set the title and axes labels, and set the *x*-axis type to `datetime` so that our date index will be correctly displayed:

```
fig = bk.figure(title="Time series data",
                x_axis_label="date",
                x_axis_type="datetime",
                y_axis_label="value")
```

4. We add the data to the figure as a line:

```
fig.line(date_range, series)
```

5. Finally, we use either the `show` routine or the `save` routine to save or update the HTML in the specified output file. We use `show` here to cause the plot to open in the browser:

```
bk.show(fig)
```

Bokeh plots are not static objects and are supposed to be interactive via the browser. The data as it will appear in the Bokeh plot has been recreated here, using `matplotlib` for comparison:

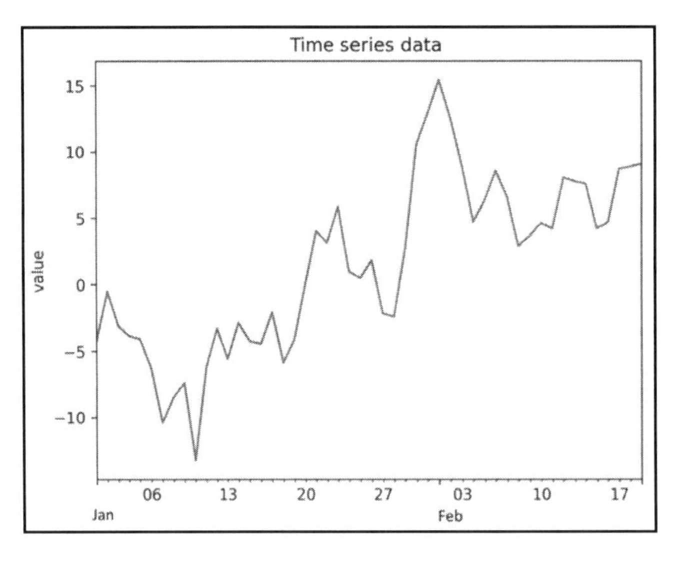

Figure 6.3 – Plot of Time series data created using Matplotlib

How it works...

Bokeh uses a JavaScript library to render a plot in a browser, using data provided by the Python backend. The advantage of this is that it can generate plots that a user can inspect for themselves. For instance, we can zoom in to see detail in the plot that might otherwise be hidden, or pan through the data in a natural way. The example given in this recipe is just a taster of what is possible using Bokeh.

The `figure` routine creates an object representing the plot, which we add elements to—such as a line through the data points—in the same way that we would add plots to a matplotlib `Axes` object. In this recipe, we created a simple HTML file that contains JavaScript code to render the data. This HTML code is dumped to the specified file whenever we save or, as is in the recipe, call the `show` routine. In practice, the smaller the p value, the more confident we can be that the hypothesized population mean is correct.

There's more...

The capabilities of Bokeh go far beyond what is described here. Bokeh plots can be embedded in files such as Jupyter notebooks, which are also rendered in the browser, or into existing websites. If you are using a Jupyter notebook, you should use the `output_notebook` routine instead of the `output_file` routine to print the plot directly into the notebook. It has a wide array of different plotting styles, supports the sharing of data between plots (data can be selected in one plot and highlighted in the other(s), for example), and supports streaming data.

Further reading

There are a large number of textbooks on statistics and statistical theory. The following book was used as reference for this chapter:

- *Mendenhall, W., Beaver, R., and Beaver, B., (2006), Introduction To Probability And Statistics, 12th ed., (Belmont, Calif.: Thomson Brooks/Cole)*

The pandas documentation (`https://pandas.pydata.org/docs/index.html`) and the following pandas book serve as good references for working with pandas:

- *McKinney, W., (2017), Python for Data Analysis, 2nd ed., (Sebastopol: O'Reilly Media, Inc, US)*

The SciPy documentation (`https://docs.scipy.org/doc/scipy/reference/tutorial/stats.html`) also contains detailed information about the statistics module that was used several times in this chapter.

7 Regression and Forecasting

One of the most important tasks that a statistician or data scientist has is to generate a systematic understanding of the relationship between two sets of data. This can mean a "continuous" relationship between two sets of data, where one value depends directly on the value of another variable. Alternatively, it can mean a categorical relationship, where one value is categorized according to another. The tool for working with these kinds of problems is *regression*. In its most basic form, regression involves fitting a straight line through a scatter plot of the two sets of data and performing some analysis to see how well this line "fits" the data. Of course, we often need something more sophisticated to model more complex relationships that exist in the real world.

Time series represent a specialized class of these regression type problems, where we have a value that is evolving over a period of time. Unlike more simple problems, time series data usually has complex dependencies between consecutive values; for instance, a value may depend on both of the previous values, and perhaps even on the previous "noise". Time series modeling is important across science and economics, and there are a variety of tools for modeling time series data. The basic technique for working with time series data is called **ARIMA**, which stands for **autoregressive integrated moving average**. This model incorporates two underlying components, an **autoregressive** (**AR**) component and a **moving average** (**MA**) component, to construct a model for the observed data.

In this chapter, we will learn how to model the relationship between two sets of data, quantify how strong this relationship is, and generate forecasts about other values (the future). Then, we will learn how to use logistic regression, which is a variation of a simple linear model, in classification problems. Finally, we will build models for time series data using ARIMA and build on these models for different kinds of data. We will finish this chapter by using a library called Prophet to automatically generate a model for time series data.

In this chapter, we will cover the following recipes:

- Using basic linear regression
- Using multilinear regression
- Classifying using logarithmic regression
- Modeling time series data with ARMA
- Forecasting from time series data using ARIMA
- Forecasting seasonal data using ARIMA
- Using Prophet to model time series

Let's get started!

Technical requirements

In this chapter, as usual, we will need the NumPy package imported under the alias `np`, the Matplotlib `pyplot` module imported as `plt`, and the Pandas package imported as `pd`. We can do this using the following commands:

```
import numpy as np
import matplotlib.pyplot as plt
import pandas as pd
```

We will also need some new packages in this chapter. The statsmodels package is used for regression and time series analysis, the `scikit-learn` package (`sklearn`) provides general data science and machine learning tools, and the Prophet package (`fbprophet`) is used for automatically modeling time series data. These packages can be installed using your favorite package manager, such as `pip`:

```
python3.8 -m pip install statsmodels sklearn fbprophet
```

The Prophet package can prove difficult to install on some operating systems because of its dependencies. If installing `fbprophet` causes a problem, you might want to try using the Anaconda distribution of Python and its package manager, `conda`, which handles the dependencies more rigorously:

```
conda install fbprophet
```

Finally, we also need a small module called `tsdata` that is contained in the repository for this chapter. This module contains a series of utilities for producing sample time series data.

The code for this chapter can be found in the `Chapter 07` folder of the GitHub repository at `https://github.com/PacktPublishing/Applying-Math-with-Python/tree/master/Chapter%2007`.

Check out the following video to see the Code in Action: `https://bit.ly/2Ct8m0B`.

Using basic linear regression

Linear regression is a tool for modeling the dependence between two sets of data so that we can eventually use this model to make predictions. The name comes from the fact that we form a linear model (straight line) of one set of data based on a second. In the literature, the variable that we wish to model is frequently called the *response* variable, and the variable that we are using in this model is the *predictor* variable.

In this recipe, we'll learn how to use the statsmodels package to perform simple linear regression to model the relationship between two sets of data.

Getting ready

For this recipe, we will need the statsmodels `api` module imported under the alias `sm`, the NumPy package imported as `np`, the Matplotlib `pyplot` module imported as `plt`, and an instance of a NumPy default random number generator. All this can be achieved with the following commands:

```
import statsmodels.api as sm
import numpy as np
import matplotlib.pyplot as plt
from numpy.random import default_rng
rng = default_rng(12345)
```

How to do it...

The following steps outline how to use the statsmodels package to perform a simple linear regression on two sets of data:

1. First, we generate some example data that we can analyze. We'll generate two sets of data that will illustrate a good fit and a less good fit:

```
x = np.linspace(0, 5, 25)
rng.shuffle(x)
```

```
trend = 2.0
shift = 5.0
y1 = trend*x + shift + rng.normal(0, 0.5, size=25)
y2 = trend*x + shift + rng.normal(0, 5, size=25)
```

2. A good first step in performing regression analysis is to create a scatter plot of the datasets. We'll do this on the same set of axes:

```
fig, ax = plt.subplots()
ax.scatter(x, y1, c="b", label="Good correlation")
ax.scatter(x, y2, c="r", label="Bad correlation")
ax.legend()
ax.set_xlabel("X"),
ax.set_ylabel("Y")
ax.set_title("Scatter plot of data with best fit lines")
```

3. We need to use the `sm.add_constant` utility routine so that the modeling step will include a constant value:

```
pred_x = sm.add_constant(x)
```

4. Now, we can create an `OLS` model for our first set of data and use the `fit` method to fit the model. We then print a summary of the data using the `summary` method:

```
model1 = sm.OLS(y1, pred_x).fit()
print(model1.summary())
```

5. We repeat the model fitting for the second set of data and print the summary:

```
model2 = sm.OLS(y2, pred_x).fit()
print(model2.summary())
```

6. Now, we create a new range of x values using `linspace` that we can use to plot the trend lines on our scatter plot. We need to add the `constant` column to interact with the models that we have created:

```
model_x = sm.add_constant(np.linspace(0, 5))
```

7. Next, we use the `predict` method on the model objects so that we can use the model to predict the response value at each of the x values we generated in the previous step:

```
model_y1 = model1.predict(model_x)
model_y2 = model2.predict(model_x)
```

8. Finally, we plot the model data computed in the previous two steps on top of the scatter plot:

```
ax.plot(model_x[:, 1], model_y1, 'b')
ax.plot(model_x[:, 1], model_y2, 'r')
```

The scatter plot, along with the best fit lines (the models) we added, can be seen in the following figure:

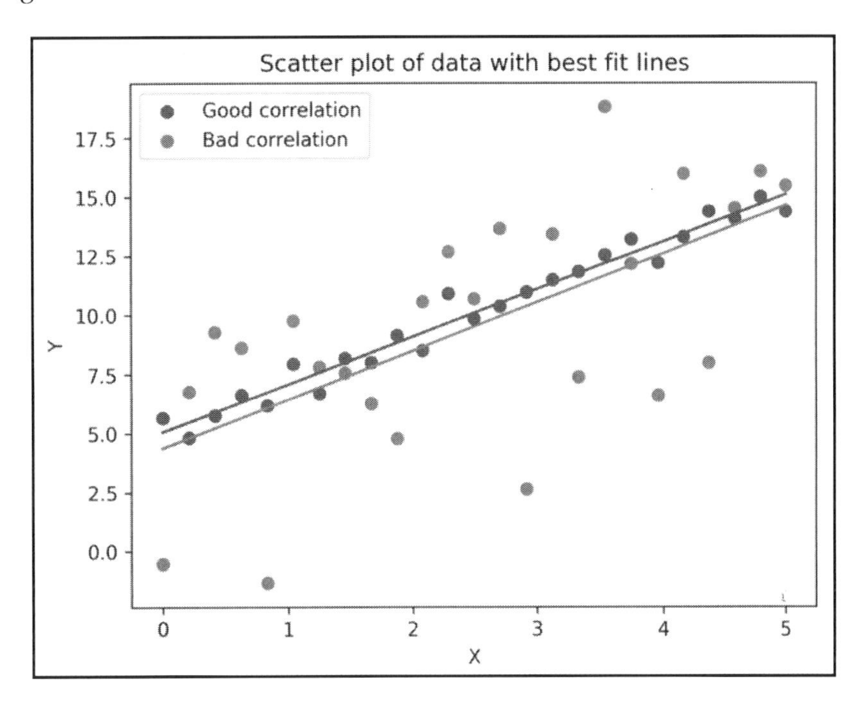

Figure 7.1: Scatter plot of data with lines of best fit computed using least squares regression

How it works...

Elementary mathematics tells us that the equation of a straight line is given by the following:

$$y = c + mx$$

Here, c is the value at which the line meets the y axis, usually called the *y intercept*, and m is the *gradient* of the line. In the linear regression context, we are trying to find a relationship between the response variable, Y, and the predictor variable, X, that has the form of a straight line so that the following occurs:

$$Y \approx c + mX$$

Here, c and m are now parameters that are to be found. We can write this in a different way, as follows:

$$Y = c + mX + E$$

Here, E is an error term, which, in general, depends on X. To find the "best" model, we need to find values for the c and m parameters, for which the error term, E, is minimized (in an appropriate sense). The basic method for finding the values of the parameters such that this error is minimized is the method of least squares, which gives its name to the type of regression used here: *ordinary least squares*. Once we have used this method to establish some relationship between a response variable and a predictor variable, our next task is to assess how well this model actually represents this relationship. For this, we form the *residuals* given by the following equation:

$$E_i = Y_i - (c + mX_i)$$

We do this for each of the data points, X_i and Y_i. In order to provide a rigorous statistical analysis of how well we have modeled the relationship between the data, we need the residuals to satisfy certain assumptions. First, we need them to be independent in the sense of probability. Second, we need them to be normally distributed about 0 with a common variance. (In practice, we can relax these slightly and still make reasonable comments about the accuracy of the model.)

In this recipe, we generated response data from the predictor data using a linear relationship. The difference between the two response datasets we created is the "size" of the error at each value. For the first dataset, `y1`, the residuals were normally distributed with a standard deviation of 0.5, whereas for the second dataset, `y2`, the residuals have a standard deviation of 5.0. We can see this variability in the scatter plot shown in the *Figure 7.1*, where the data for `y1` is generally very close to the best fit line – which closely matches the actual relationship that was used to generate the data – whereas the `y2` data is much further from the best fit line.

The `OLS` object from the statsmodels package is the main interface for ordinary least squares regression. We provide the response data and the predictor data as arrays. In order to have a constant term in the model, we need to add a column of ones in the predictor data. The `sm.add_constant` routine is a simple utility for adding this constant column. The `fit` method of the `OLS` class computes the parameters for the model and returns a results object (`model1` and `model2`) that contains the parameters for the best fit model. The `summary` method creates a string containing information about the model and various statistics about the goodness of fit. The `predict` method applies the model to new data. As the name suggests, it can be be used to make predictions using the model.

There are two statistics reported in the summary besides the parameter values themselves. The first is the R^2 value, or the adjusted version, which measures the variability explained by the model against the total variability. This value will be between 0 and 1. A higher value indicates a better fit. The second is the F statistic p value, which indicates the overall significance of the model. As with ANOVA testing, a small F statistic indicates that the model is significant, meaning that the model is more likely to accurately model the data.

In this recipe, the first model, `model1`, has an adjusted R^2 value of 0.986, indicating that the model very closely fits the data, and a p value of 6.43e-19, indicating high significance. The second model has an adjusted R^2 value of 0.361, which indicates that the model less closely fits the data, and a p value of 0.000893, which also indicates high significance. Even though the second model less closely fits the data, in terms of statistics, that is not to say that it is not useful. The model is still significant, though less so than the first model, but it doesn't account for all of the variability (or at least a significant portion of it) in the data. This could be indicative of additional (non-linear) structures in the data, or that the data is less correlated, which means there is a weaker relationship between the response and predictor data (due to the way we constructed the data, we know that the latter is true).

There's more...

Simple linear regression is a good general-purpose tool in a statistician's toolkit. It is excellent for finding the nature of the relationship between two sets of data that are known (or suspected) to be connected in some way. The statistical measurement of how much one set of data depends on another is called *correlation*. We can measure correlation using a correlation coefficient, such as *Spearman's rank correlation coefficient*. A high positive correlation coefficient indicates a strong positive relationship between the data, such as that seen in this recipe, while a high negative correlation coefficient indicates a strong negative relationship, where the slope of the best fit line through the data is negative. A correlation coefficient of 0 means that the data is not correlated: there is no relationship between the data.

If the sets of data are clearly related but not in a linear (straight line) relationship, then it might follow a polynomial relationship where, for example, one value is related to the other squared. Sometimes, you can apply a transformation, such as a logarithm, to one set of data and then use linear regression to fit the transformed data. Logarithms are especially useful when there is a power-law relationship between the two sets of data.

Using multilinear regression

Simple linear regression, as seen in the previous recipe, is excellent for producing simple models of a relationship between one response variable and one predictor variable. Unfortunately, it is far more common to have a single response variable that depends on many predictor variables. Moreover, we might not know which variables from a collection make good predictor variables. For this task, we need multilinear regression.

In this recipe, we will learn how to use multilinear regression to explore the relationship between a response variable and several predictor variables.

Getting ready

For this recipe, we will need the NumPy package imported as `np`, the Matplotlib `pyplot` module imported as `plt`, the Pandas package imported as `pd`, and an instance of the NumPy default random number generator created using the following commands:

```
from numpy.random import default_rng
rng = default_rng(12345)
```

We will also need the statsmodels `api` module imported as `sm`, which can be imported using the following command:

```
import statsmodels.api as sm
```

How to do it...

The following steps show you how to use multilinear regression to explore the relationship between several predictors and a response variable:

1. First, we need to create the predictor data to analyze. This will take the form of a Pandas `DataFrame` with four terms. We will add the constant term at this stage by adding a column of ones:

```
p_vars = pd.DataFrame({
 "const": np.ones((100,)),
 "X1": rng.uniform(0, 15, size=100),
 "X2": rng.uniform(0, 25, size=100),
 "X3": rng.uniform(5, 25, size=100)
})
```

2. Next, we will generate the response data using only the first two variables:

```
residuals = rng.normal(0.0, 12.0, size=100)
Y = -10.0 + 5.0*p_vars["X1"] - 2.0*p_vars["X2"] + residuals
```

3. Now, we'll produce scatter plots of the response data against each of the predictor variables:

```
fig, (ax1, ax2, ax3) = plt.subplots(1, 3, sharey=True,
   tight_layout=True)
ax1.scatter(p_vars["X1"], Y)
ax2.scatter(p_vars["X2"], Y)
ax3.scatter(p_vars["X3"], Y)
```

4. Then, we'll add axis labels and titles to each scatter plot since this is good practice:

```
ax1.set_title("Y against X1")
ax1.set_xlabel("X1")
ax1.set_ylabel("Y")
ax2.set_title("Y against X2")
ax2.set_xlabel("X2")
ax3.set_title("Y against X3")
ax3.set_xlabel("X3")
```

The resulting plots can be seen in the following figure:

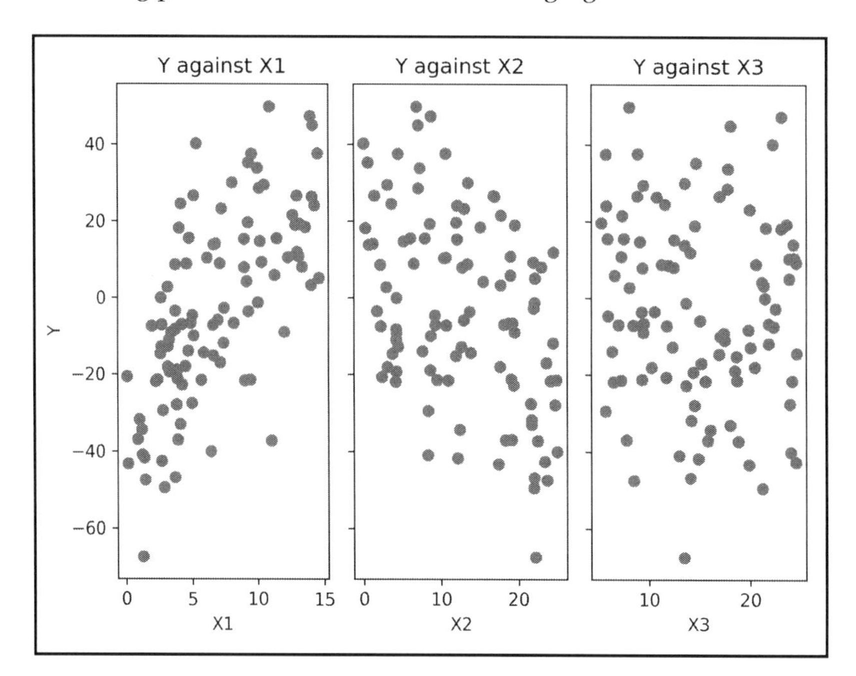

Figure 7.2: Scatter plots of the response data against each of the predictor variables

As we can see, there appears to be some correlation between the response data and the first two predictor columns, `X1` and `X2`. This is what we expect, given how we generated the data.

5. We use the same `OLS` class to perform multilinear regression; that is, providing the response array and the predictor `DataFrame`:

```
model = sm.OLS(Y, p_vars).fit()
print(model.summary())
```

The output of the `print` statement is as follows:

```
                        OLS Regression Results
===================================================================
Dep. Variable: y                    R-squared: 0.770
Model: OLS Adj.                     R-squared: 0.762
Method: Least Squares               F-statistic: 106.8
Date: Thu, 23 Apr 2020              Prob (F-statistic): 1.77e-30
Time: 12:47:30                      Log-Likelihood: -389.38
No. Observations: 100               AIC: 786.8
```

```
Df Residuals: 96                    BIC: 797.2
Df Model: 3
Covariance Type: nonrobust
==============================================================================
             coef    std err          t      P>|t|      [0.025      0.975]
------------------------------------------------------------------------------
const     -9.8676      4.028     -2.450      0.016     -17.863      -1.872
X1         4.7234      0.303     15.602      0.000       4.122       5.324
X2        -1.8945      0.166    -11.413      0.000      -2.224      -1.565
X3        -0.0910      0.206     -0.441      0.660      -0.500       0.318
==============================================================================
Omnibus: 0.296                    Durbin-Watson: 1.881
Prob(Omnibus): 0.862              Jarque-Bera (JB): 0.292
Skew: 0.123                       Prob(JB): 0.864
Kurtosis: 2.904                   Cond. No. 72.9
==============================================================================
```

In the summary data, we can see that the `X3` variable is not significant since it has a p value of 0.66.

6. Since the third predictor variable is not significant, we eliminate this column and perform the regression again:

```
second_model = sm.OLS(Y, p_vars.loc[:, "const":"X2"]).fit()
print(second_model.summary())
```

This results in a small increase in the goodness of fit statistics.

How it works...

Multilinear regression works in much the same way as simple linear regression. We follow the same procedure here as in the previous recipe, where we use the statsmodels package to fit a multilinear model to our data. Of course, there are some differences behind the scenes. The model we produce using multilinear regression is very similar in form to the simple linear model from the previous recipe. It has the following form:

$$Y = \beta_0 + \beta_1 X_1 + \cdots + \beta_n X_n + E$$

Here, Y is the response variable, X_i represents the predictor variables, E is the error term, and β_i is the parameters to be computed. The same requirements are also necessary for this context: residuals must be independent and normally distributed with a mean of 0 and a common standard deviation.

In this recipe, we provided our predictor data as a Pandas `DataFrame` rather than a plain NumPy array. Notice that the names of the columns have been adopted in the summary data that we printed. Unlike the first recipe, *Using basic linear regression*, we included the constant column in this `DataFrame`, rather than using the `add_constant` utility from statsmodels.

In the output of the first regression, we can see that the model is a reasonably good fit with an adjusted R^2 value of 0.762, and is highly significant (we can see this by looking at the regression F statistic p value). However, looking closer at the individual parameters, we can see that both of the first two predictor values are significant, but the constant and the third predictor are less so. In particular, the third predictor parameter, `X3`, is not significantly different from 0 and has a p value of 0.66. Given that our response data was constructed without using this variable, this shouldn't come as a surprise. In the final step of the analysis, we repeat the regression without the predictor variable, `X3`, which is a mild improvement to the fit.

Classifying using logarithmic regression

Logarithmic regression solves a different problem to ordinary linear regression. It is commonly used for classification problems where, typically, we wish to classify data into two distinct groups, according to a number of predictor variables. Underlying this technique is a transformation that's performed using logarithms. The original classification problem is transformed into a problem of constructing a model for the **log-odds**. This model can be completed with simple linear regression. We apply the inverse transformation to the linear model, which leaves us with a model of the probability that the desired outcome will occur, given the predictor data. The transform we apply here is called the **logistic function**, which gives its name to the method. The probability we obtain can then be used in the classification problem we originally aimed to solve.

In this recipe, we will learn how to perform logistic regression and use this technique in classification problems.

Getting ready

For this recipe, we will need the NumPy package imported as `np`, the Matplotlib `pyplot` module imported as `plt`, the Pandas package imported as `pd`, and an instance of the NumPy default random number generator to be created using the following commands:

```
from numpy.random import default_rng
rng = default_rng(12345)
```

We also need several components from the `scikit-learn` package to perform logistic regression. These can be imported as follows:

```
from sklearn.linear_model import LogisticRegression
from sklearn.metrics import classification_report
```

How to do it...

Follow these steps to use logistic regression to solve a simple classification problem:

1. First, we need to create some sample data that we can use to demonstrate how to use logistic regression. We start by creating the predictor variables:

```
df = pd.DataFrame({
    "var1": np.concatenate([rng.normal(3.0, 1.5, size=50),
        rng.normal(-4.0, 2.0, size=50)]),
    "var2": rng.uniform(size=100),
    "var3": np.concatenate([rng.normal(-2.0, 2.0, size=50),
        rng.normal(1.5, 0.8, size=50)])
})
```

2. Now, we use two of our three predictor variables to create our response variable as a series of Boolean values:

```
score = 4.0 + df["var1"] - df["var3"]
Y = score >= 0
```

3. Next, we scatter plot the points, styled according to the response variable, of the `var3` data against the `var1` data, which are the variables used to construct the response variable:

```
fig1, ax1 = plt.subplots()
ax1.plot(df.loc[Y, "var1"], df.loc[Y, "var3"], "bo", label="True
   data")
ax1.plot(df.loc[~Y, "var1"], df.loc[~Y, "var3"], "rx", label="False
```

```
    data")
ax1.legend()
ax1.set_xlabel("var1")
ax1.set_ylabel("var3")
ax1.set_title("Scatter plot of var3 against var1")
```

The resulting plot can be seen in the following figure:

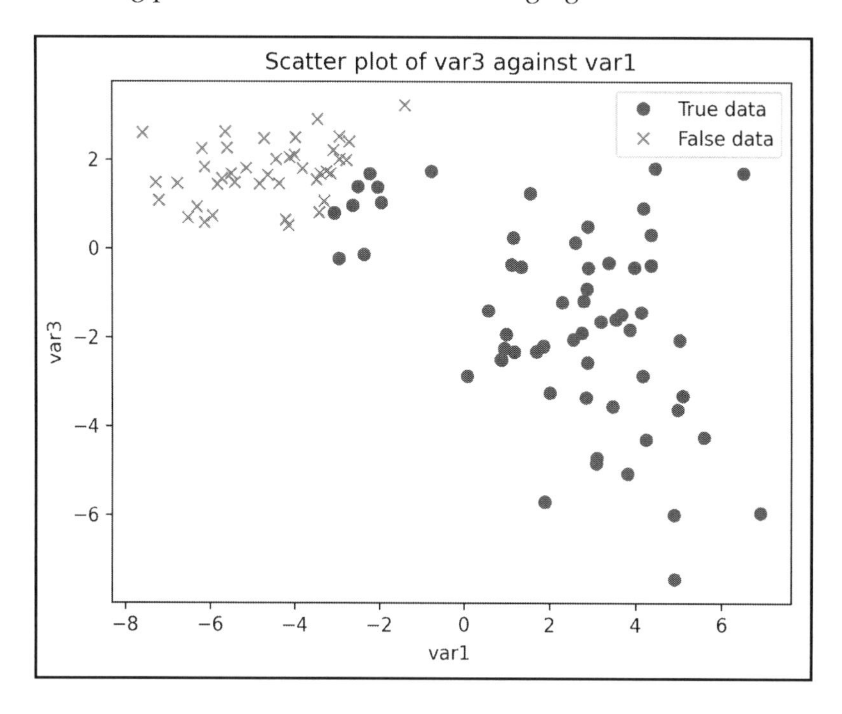

Figure 7.3: Scatter plot of the var3 data against var1, with classification marked

4. Next, we create a `LogisticRegression` object from the `scikit-learn` package and fit the model to our data:

```
model = LogisticRegression()
model.fit(df, Y)
```

5. Next, we prepare some extra data, different from what we used to fit the model, to test the accuracy of our model:

```
test_df = pd.DataFrame({
    "var1": np.concatenate([rng.normal(3.0, 1.5, size=50),
        rng.normal(-4.0, 2.0, size=50)]),
    "var2": rng.uniform(size=100),
    "var3": np.concatenate([rng.normal(-2.0, 2.0, size=50),
```

```
            rng.normal(1.5, 0.8, size=50)])
    })
    test_scores = 4.0 + test_df["var1"] - test_df["var3"]
    test_Y = test_scores >= 0
```

6. Then, we generate predicted results based on our logistic regression model:

```
test_predicts = model.predict(test_df)
```

7. Finally, we use the `classification_report` utility from `scikit-learn` to print a summary of predicted classification against known response values to test the accuracy of the model. We print this summary to the Terminal:

```
print(classification_report(test_Y, test_predicts))
```

The report that's generated by this routine looks as follows:

```
              precision    recall  f1-score   support

       False       1.00      1.00      1.00        18
        True       1.00      1.00      1.00        32

    accuracy                           1.00        50
   macro avg       1.00      1.00      1.00        50
weighted avg       1.00      1.00      1.00        50
```

How it works...

Logistic regression works by forming a linear model of the *log odds* ratio (or *logit*), which, for a single predictor variable, x, has the following form:

$$\log\left(\frac{p(x)}{1+p(x)}\right) = \beta_0 + \beta_1 x$$

Here, $p(x)$ represents the probability of a true outcome in response to the given the predictor, x. Rearranging this gives a variation of the logistic function for the probability:

$$p(x) = \frac{e^{\beta_0+\beta_1 x}}{1+e^{\beta_0+\beta_1 x}}$$

The parameters for the log odds are estimated using a maximum likelihood method.

The `LogisticRegression` class from the `linear_model` module in `scikit-learn` is an implementation of logistic regression that is very easy to use. First, we create a new model instance of this class, with any custom parameters that we need, and then use the `fit` method on this object to fit (or train) the model to the sample data. Once this fitting is done, we can access the parameters that have been estimated using the `get_params` method.

The `predict` method on the fitted model allows us to pass in new (unseen) data and make predictions about the classification of each sample. We could also get the probability estimates that are actually given by the logistic function using the `predict_proba` method.

Once we have built a model for predicting the classification of data, we need to validate the model. This means we have to test the model with some previously unseen data and check whether it correctly classifies the new data. For this, we can use `classification_report`, which takes a new set of data and the predictions generated by the model and computes the proportion of the data that was correctly predicted by the model. This is the *precision* of the model.

The classification report we generated using the `scikit-learn` utility performs a comparison between the predicted results and the known response values. This is a common method for validating a model before using it to make actual predictions. In this recipe, we saw that the reported precision for each of the categories (`True` and `False`) was 1.00, indicating that the model performed perfectly in predicting the classification with this data. In practice, it is unlikely that the precision of a model will be 100%.

There's more...

There are lots of packages that offer tools for using logistic regression for classification problems. The statsmodels package has the `Logit` class for creating logistic regression models. We used the `scikit-learn` package in this recipe, which has a similar interface. `Scikit-learn` is a general-purpose machine learning library and has a variety of other tools for classification problems.

Modeling time series data with ARMA

Time series, as the name suggests, tracks a value over a sequence of distinct time intervals. They are particularly important in the finance industry, where stock values are tracked over time and used to make predictions – known as forecasting – of the value at some future time. Good predictions coming from such data can be used to make better investments. Time series also appear in many other common situations, such as weather monitoring, medicine, and any places where data is derived from sensors over time.

Time series, unlike other types of data, do not usually have independent data points. This means that the methods that we use for modeling independent data will not be particularly effective. Thus, we need to use alternative techniques to model data with this property. There are two ways in which a value in a time series can depend on previous values. The first is where there is a direct relationship between the value and one or more previous values. This is the *autocorrelation* property and is modeled by an *autoregressive* model. The second is where the noise that's added to the value depends on one or more previous noise terms. This is modeled by a *moving average* model. The number of terms involved in either of these models is called the *order* of the model.

In this recipe, we will learn how to create a model for stationary time series data with ARMA terms.

Getting ready

For this recipe, we need the Matplotlib `pyplot` module imported as `plt` and the statsmodels package `api` module imported as `sm`. We also need to import the `generate_sample_data` routine from the `tsdata` package from this book's repository, which uses NumPy and Pandas to generate sample data for analysis:

```
from tsdata import generate_sample_data
```

How to do it...

Follow these steps to create an autoregressive moving average model for stationary time series data:

1. First, we need to generate the sample data that we will analyze:

```
sample_ts, _ = generate_sample_data()
```

2. As always, the first step in the analysis is to produce a plot of the data so that we can visually identify any structure:

```
ts_fig, ts_ax = plt.subplots()
sample_ts.plot(ax=ts_ax, label="Observed")
ts_ax.set_title("Time series data")
ts_ax.set_xlabel("Date")
ts_ax.set_ylabel("Value")
```

The resulting plot can be seen in the following figure. Here, we can see that there doesn't appear to be an underlying trend, which means that the data is likely to be stationary:

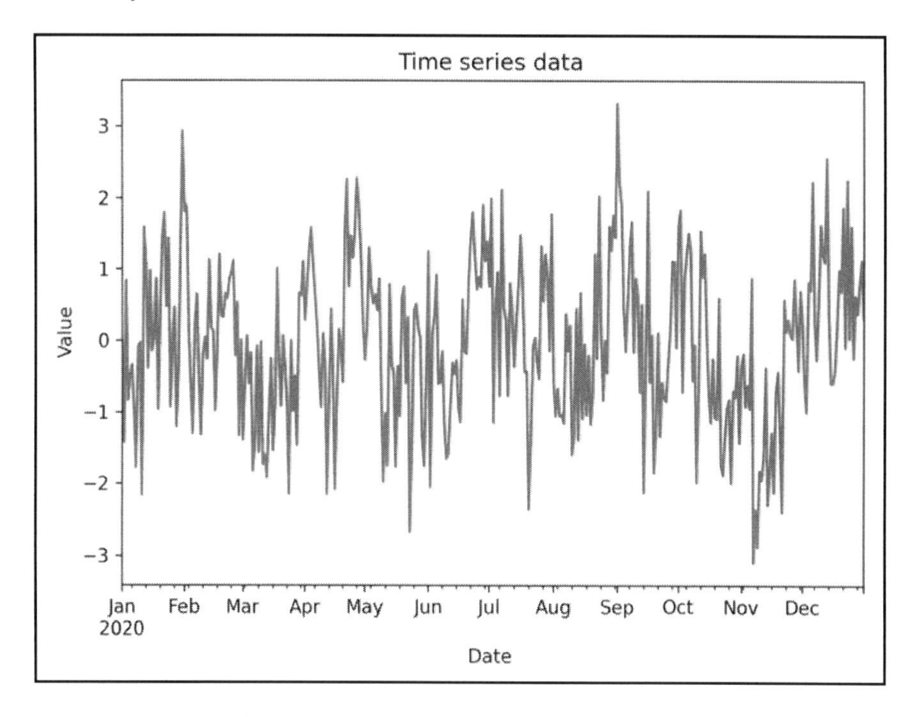

Figure 7.4: Plot of the time series data that we will analyze. There doesn't appear to be a trend in this data

3. Next, we compute the augmented Dickey-Fuller test. The null hypothesis is that the time series is not stationary:

```
adf_results = sm.tsa.adfuller(sample_ts)
adf_pvalue = adf_results[1]
print("Augmented Dickey-Fuller test:\nP-value:", adf_pvalue)
```

The reported p value is 0.000376 in this case, so we reject the null hypothesis and conclude that the series is stationary.

4. Next, we need to determine the order of the model that we should fit. For this, we'll plot the **autocorrelation function** (**ACF**) and the **partial autocorrelation function** (**PACF**) for the time series:

```
ap_fig, (acf_ax, pacf_ax) = plt.subplots(2, 1, sharex=True,
    tight_layout=True)
sm.graphics.tsa.plot_acf(sample_ts, ax=acf_ax,
    title="Observed autocorrelation")
sm.graphics.tsa.plot_pacf(sample_ts, ax=pacf_ax,
    title="Observed partial autocorrelation")
pacf_ax.set_xlabel("Lags")
pacf_ax.set_ylabel("Value")
acf_ax.set_ylabel("Value")
```

The plots of the ACF and PACF for our time series can be seen in the following figure. These plots suggest the existence of both autoregressive and moving average processes:

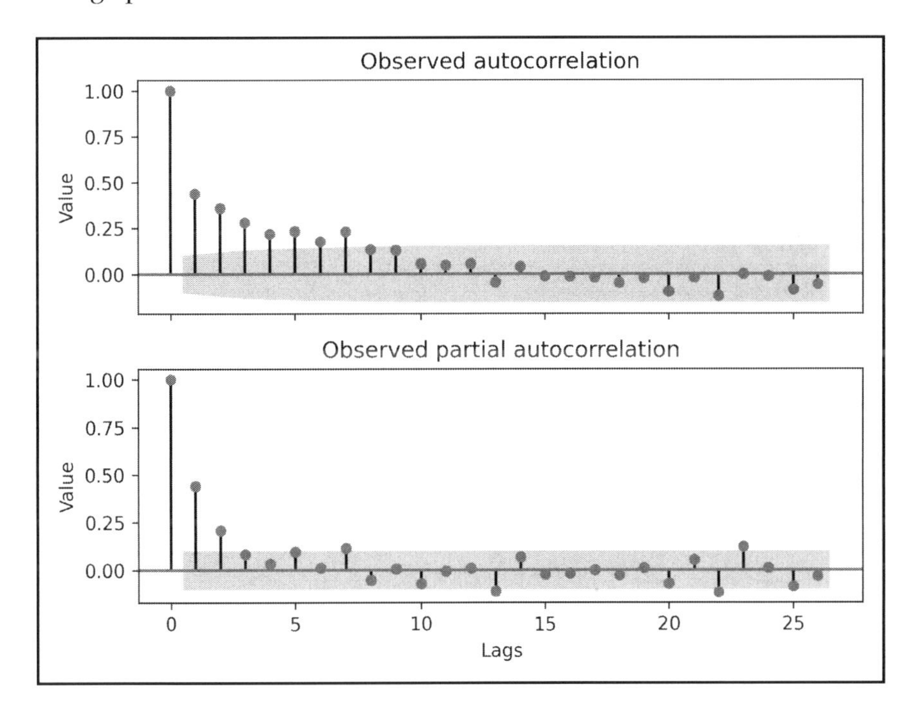

Figure 7.5: ACF and PACF for the sample time series data

5. Next, we create an ARMA model for the data, using the `ARMA` class from statsmodels, `tsa` module. This model will have an order 1 AR and an order 1 MA:

```
arma_model = sm.tsa.ARMA(sample_ts, order=(1, 1))
```

6. Now, we fit the model to the data and get the resulting model. We print a summary of these results to the Terminal:

```
arma_results = arma_model.fit()
print(arma_results.summary())
```

The summary data given for the fitted model is as follows:

```
                      ARMA Model Results
===================================================================
Dep. Variable: y             No. Observations: 366
Model: ARMA(1, 1)            Log Likelihood -513.038
Method: css-mle              S.D. of innovations 0.982
Date: Fri, 01 May 2020       AIC 1034.077
Time: 12:40:00               BIC 1049.687
Sample: 01-01-2020           HQIC 1040.280
      - 12-31-2020
===================================================================
           coef   std err      z      P>|z|    [0.025     0.975]
-------------------------------------------------------------------
const   -0.0242   0.143   -0.169   0.866   -0.305   0.256
ar.L1.y  0.8292   0.057   14.562   0.000    0.718   0.941
ma.L1.y -0.5189   0.090   -5.792   0.000   -0.695   -0.343
                             Roots
===================================================================
        Real         Imaginary          Modulus        Frequency
-------------------------------------------------------------------
AR.1    1.2059       +0.0000j           1.2059         0.0000
MA.1    1.9271       +0.0000j           1.9271         0.0000
-------------------------------------------------------------------
```

Here, we can see that both of the estimated parameters for the AR and MA components are significantly different from 0. This is because the value in the `P >|z|` column is 0 to 3 decimal places.

7. Next, we need to verify that there is no additional structure remaining in the residuals (error) of the predictions from our model. For this, we plot the ACF and PACF of the residuals:

```
residuals = arma_results.resid
rap_fig, (racf_ax, rpacf_ax) = plt.subplots(2, 1,
    sharex=True, tight_layout=True)
sm.graphics.tsa.plot_acf(residuals, ax=racf_ax,
    title="Residual autocorrelation")
sm.graphics.tsa.plot_pacf(residuals, ax=rpacf_ax,
    title="Residual partial autocorrelation")
rpacf_ax.set_xlabel("Lags")
rpacf_ax.set_ylabel("Value")
racf_ax.set_ylabel("Value")
```

The ACF and PACF of the residuals can be seen in the following figure. Here, we can see that there are no significant spikes at lags other than 0, so we conclude that there is no structure remaining in the residuals:

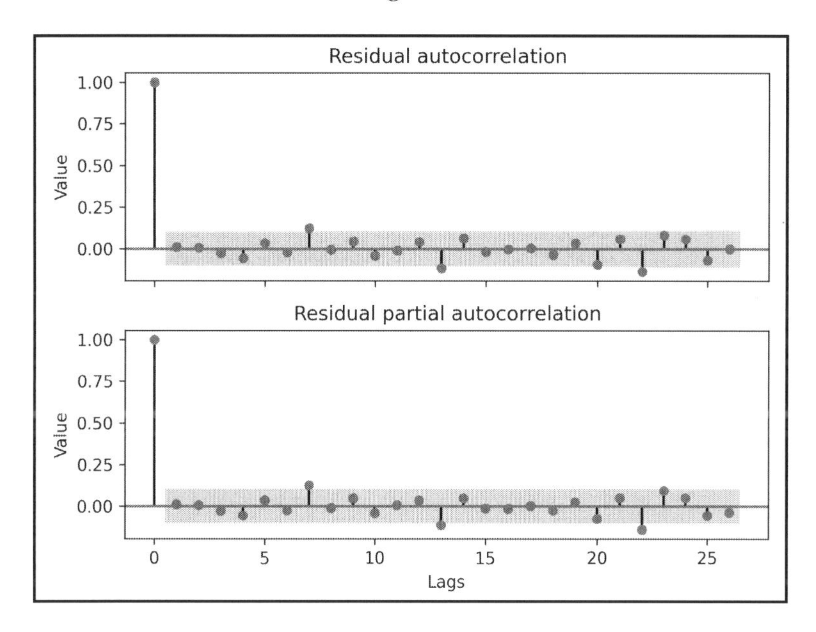

Figure 7.6: ACF and PACF for the residuals from our model

8. Now that we have verified that our model is not missing any structure, we plot the values that are fitted to each data point on top of the actual time series data to see whether the model is a good fit for the data. We plot this model in the plot we created in *step* 2:

```
fitted = arma_results.fittedvalues
fitted.plot(c="r", ax=ts_ax, label="Fitted")
ts_ax.legend()
```

The updated plot can be seen in the following figure:

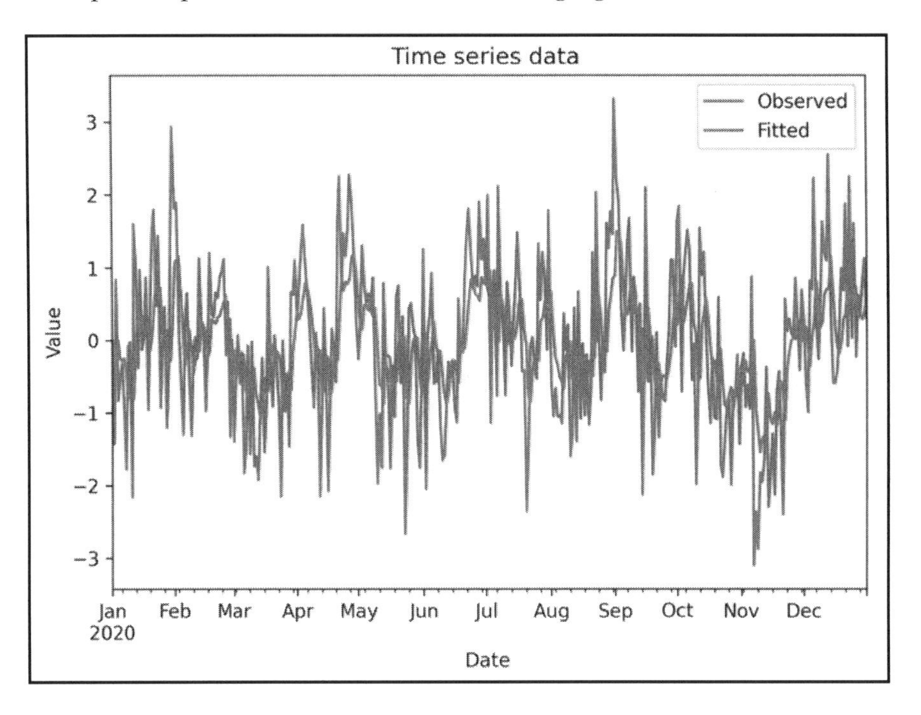

Figure 7.7: Plot of the fitted time series data over the observed time series data

The fitted values give a reasonable approximation of the behavior of the time series, but reduce the noise from the underlying structure.

How it works...

A time series is stationary if it does not have a trend. They usually have a tendency to move in one direction rather than another. Stationary processes are important because we can usually remove the trend from an arbitrary time series and model the underlying stationary series. The ARMA model that we used in this recipe is a basic means of modeling the behavior of stationary time series. The two parts of an ARMA model are the autoregressive and moving average parts, which model the dependence of the terms and noise, respectively, on previous terms and noise.

An order 1 autoregressive model has the following form:

$$Y_t = \varphi_0 + \varphi_1 Y_{t-1} + \varepsilon_t$$

Here, φ_i represents the parameters and ε_t is the noise at a given step. The noise is usually assumed to be normally distributed with a mean of 0 and a standard deviation that is constant across all the time steps. The Y_t value represents the value of the time series at the time step, t. In this model, each value depends on the previous value, though it can also depend on some constants and some noise. The model will give rise to a stationary time series precisely when the φ_1 parameter lies strictly between -1 and 1.

An order 1 moving average model is very similar to an autoregressive model and is given by the following equation:

$$Y_t = \theta_0 + \varepsilon_t + \theta_1 \varepsilon_{t-1}$$

Here, the variants of θ_i are parameters. Putting these two models together gives us an ARMA(1, 1) model, which has the following form:

$$Y_t = \varphi_0 + \varphi_1 Y_{t-1} + \varepsilon_t + \theta_1 \varepsilon_{t-1}$$

In general, we can have an ARMA(p, q) model that has an order p AR component and an order q MA component. We usually refer to the quantities, p and q, as the orders of the model.

Determining the orders of the AR and MA components is the most tricky aspect of constructing an ARMA model. The ACF and PACF give some information toward this, but even then, it can be quite difficult. For example, an autoregressive process will show some kind of decay or oscillating pattern on the ACF as lag increases, and a small number of peaks on the PACF and values that are not significantly different from 0 beyond that. The number of peaks that appear on the PAF plot can be taken as the order of the process. For a moving average process, the reverse is true. There are usually a small number of significant peaks on the ACF plot, and a decay or oscillating pattern on the PACF plot. Of course, sometimes, this isn't obvious.

In this recipe, we plotted the ACF and PACF for our sample time series data. In the autocorrelation plot in *Figure 7.5* (top), we can see that the peaks decay rapidly until they lie within the confidence interval of zero (meaning they are not significant). This suggests the presence of an autoregressive component. On the partial autocorrelation plot in *Figure 7.5* (bottom), we can see that there are only two peaks that can be considered not zero, which suggests an autoregressive process of order 1 or 2. You should try to keep the order of the model as small as possible. Due to this, we chose an order 1 autoregressive component. With this assumption, the second peak on the partial autocorrelation plot is indicative of decay (rather than an isolated peak), which suggests the presence of a moving average process. To keep the model simple, we try an order 1 moving average process. This is how the model that we used in this recipe was decided on. Notice that this is not an exact process, and you might have decided differently.

We use the augmented Dickey-Fuller test to test the likelihood that the time series that we have observed is stationary. This is a statistical test, such as those seen in `Chapter 6`, *Working with Data and Statistics*, that generates a test statistic from the data. This test statistic, in turn, determines a p-value that is used to determine whether to accept or reject the null hypothesis. For this test, the null hypothesis is that a unit root is present in the time series that's been sampled. The alternative hypothesis – the one we are really interested in – is that the observed time series is (trend) stationary. If the p-value is sufficiently small, then we can conclude with the specified confidence that the observed time series is stationary. In this recipe, the p-value was 0.000 to 3 decimal places, which indicates a strong likelihood that the series is stationary. Stationarity is an essential assumption for using the ARMA model for the data.

Once we have determined that the series is stationary, and also decided on the orders of the model, we have to fit the model to the sample data that we have. The parameters of the model are estimated using a maximum likelihood estimator. In this recipe, the learning of the parameters is done using the `fit` method, in *step 6*.

The statsmodels package provides various tools for working with time series, including utilities for calculating – and plotting – ACF and PACF of time series data, various test statistics, and creating ARMA models for time series. There are also some tools for automatically estimating the order of the model.

We can use the **Akaike information criterion** (**AIC**), **Bayesian information criterion** (**BIC**), and **Hannan-Quinn Information Criterion** (**HQIC**) quantities to compare this model to other models to see which model best describes the data. A smaller value is better in each case.

When using ARMA to model time series data, as in all kinds of mathematical modeling tasks, it is best to pick the simplest model that describes the data to the extent that is needed. For ARMA models, this usually means picking the smallest order model that describes the structure of the observed data.

There's more...

Finding the best combination of orders for an ARMA model can be quite difficult. Often, the best way to fit a model is to test multiple different configurations and pick the order that produces the best fit. For example, we could have tried ARMA(0, 1) or ARMA(1, 0) in this recipe, and compared it to the ARMA(1, 1) model we used to see which produced the best fit by considering the **Akaike Information Criteria** (**AIC**) statistic reported in the summary. In fact, if we build these models, we will see that the AIC value for ARMA(1, 1) – the model we used in this recipe – is the "best" of these three models.

Forecasting from time series data using ARIMA

In the previous recipe, we generated a model for a stationary time series using an ARMA model, which consists of an **autoregressive** (**AR**) component and an **moving average** (**MA**) component. Unfortunately, this model cannot accommodate time series that have some underlying trend; that is, they are not stationary time series. We can often get around this by *differencing* the observed time series one or more times until we obtain a stationary time series that can be modeled using ARMA. The incorporation of differencing into an ARMA model is called an ARIMA model, which stands for **Autoregressive** (**AR**) **Integrated** (**I**) **Moving Average** (**MA**).

Differencing is the process of computing the difference of consecutive terms in a sequence of data. So, applying first-order differencing amounts to subtracting the value at the current step from the value at the next step (t_{i+1} - t_i). This has the effect of removing the underlying upward or downward linear trend from the data. This helps to reduce an arbitrary time series to a stationary time series that can be modeled using ARMA. Higher-order differencing can remove higher-order trends to achieve similar effects.

An ARIMA model has three parameters, usually labeled *p*, *d*, and *q*. The *p* and *q* order parameters are the order of the autoregressive component and the moving average component, respectively, just as they are for the ARMA model. The third order parameter, *d*, is the order of differencing to be applied. An ARIMA model with these orders is usually written as ARIMA (*p*, *d*, *q*). Of course, we will need to determine what order differencing should be included before we start fitting the model.

In this recipe, we will learn how to fit an ARIMA model to a non-stationary time series and use this model to make forecasts about future values.

Getting ready

For this recipe, we will need the NumPy package imported as `np`, the Pandas package imported as `pd`, the Matplotlib `pyplot` module as `plt`, and the statsmodels `api` module imported as `sm`. We will also need the utility for creating sample time series data from the `tsdata` module, which is included in this book's repository:

```
from tsdata import generate_sample_data
```

How to do it...

The following steps show you how to construct an ARIMA model for time series data and use this model to make forecasts:

1. First, we load the sample data using the `generate_sample_data` routine:

```
sample_ts, test_ts = generate_sample_data(trend=0.2, undiff=True)
```

2. As usual, the next step is to plot the time series so that we can visually identify the trend of the data:

```
ts_fig, ts_ax = plt.subplots(tight_layout=True)
sample_ts.plot(ax=ts_ax, c="b", label="Observed")
ts_ax.set_title("Training time series data")
ts_ax.set_xlabel("Date")
ts_ax.set_ylabel("Value")
```

The resulting plot can be seen in the following figure. As we can see, there is a clear upward trend in the data, so the time series is certainly not stationary:

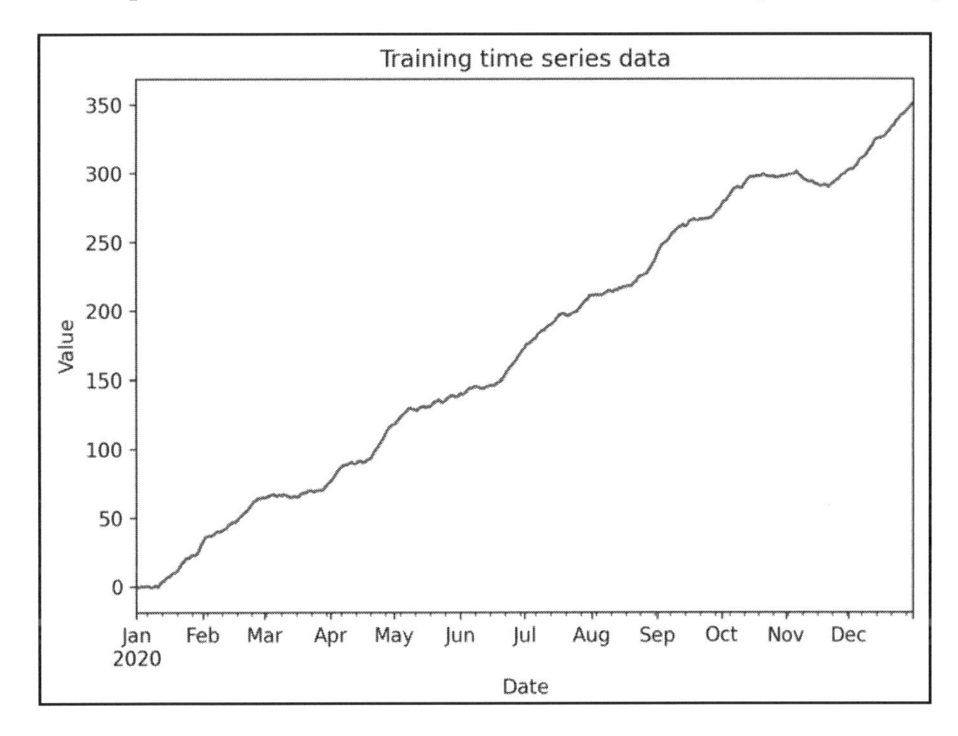

Figure 7.8: Plot of the sample time series. There is an obvious positive trend in the data.

3. Next, we difference the series to see if one level of differencing is sufficient to remove the trend:

```
diffs = sample_ts.diff().dropna()
```

4. Now, we plot the ACF and PACF for the differenced time series:

```
ap_fig, (acf_ax, pacf_ax) = plt.subplots(1, 2,
   tight_layout=True, sharex=True)
sm.graphics.tsa.plot_acf(diffs, ax=acf_ax)
sm.graphics.tsa.plot_pacf(diffs, ax=pacf_ax)
acf_ax.set_ylabel("Value")
pacf_ax.set_xlabel("Lag")
pacf_ax.set_ylabel("Value")
```

The ACF and PACF can be seen in the following figure. We can see that there does not appear to be any trends left in the data and that there appears to be both an autoregressive component and a moving average component:

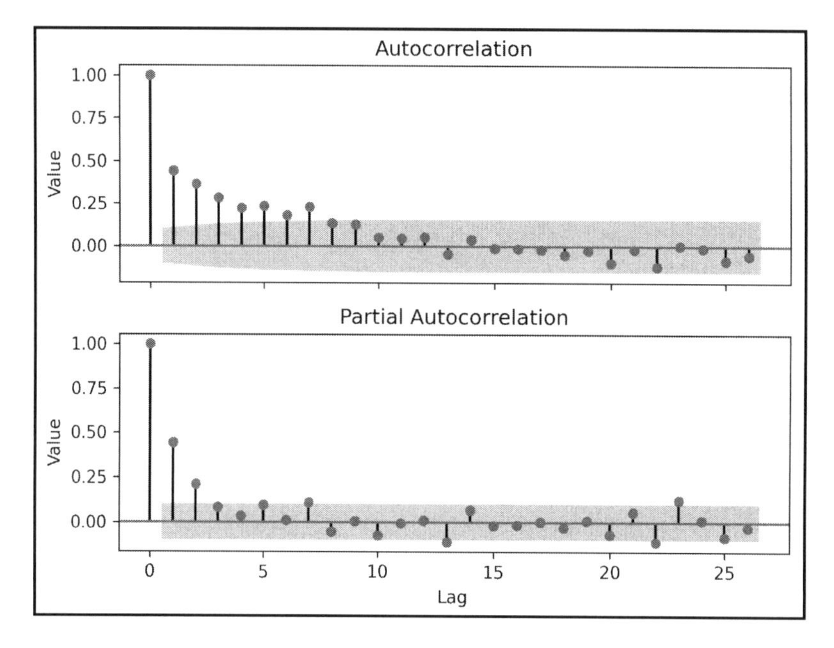

Figure 7.9: ACF and PACF for the differenced time series

5. Now, we construct the ARIMA model with order 1 differencing, an autoregressive component, and a moving average component. We fit this to the observed time series and print a summary of the model:

```
model = sm.tsa.ARIMA(sample_ts, order=(1,1,1))
fitted = model.fit(trend="c")
print(fitted.summary())
```

The summary information that's printed looks as follows:

```
                          ARIMA Model Results
==============================================================================
Dep. Variable: D.y                  No. Observations: 365
Model: ARIMA(1, 1, 1)               Log Likelihood -512.905
Method: css-mle                     S.D. of innovations 0.986
Date: Sat, 02 May 2020              AIC 1033.810
Time: 14:47:25                      BIC 1049.409
Sample: 01-02-2020                  HQIC 1040.009
      - 12-31-2020
==============================================================================
              coef     std err      z        P>|z|      [0.025      0.975]
------------------------------------------------------------------------------
const        0.9548    0.148       6.464     0.000       0.665      1.244
ar.L1.D.y 0.8342       0.056      14.992     0.000       0.725      0.943
ma.L1.D.y -0.5204      0.088      -5.903     0.000      -0.693     -0.348
                                 Roots
==============================================================================
               Real        Imaginary          Modulus         Frequency
------------------------------------------------------------------------------
AR.1         1.1987         +0.0000j           1.1987            0.0000
MA.1         1.9216         +0.0000j           1.9216            0.0000
------------------------------------------------------------------------------
```

Here, we can see that all three of our estimated coefficients are significantly different from 0 due to the fact that all three have 0 to 3 decimal places in the `P>|z|` column.

6. Now, we can use the `forecast` method to generate predictions of future values. This also returns the standard error and confidence intervals for predictions:

```
forecast, std_err, fc_ci = fitted.forecast(steps=50)
forecast_dates = pd.date_range("2021-01-01", periods=50)
forecast = pd.Series(forecast, index=forecast_dates)
```

7. Next, we plot the forecast values and their confidence intervals on the figure containing the time series data:

```
forecast.plot(ax=ts_ax, c="g", label="Forecast")
ts_ax.fill_between(forecast_dates, fc_ci[:, 0], fc_ci[:, 1],
                   color="r", alpha=0.4)
```

8. Finally, we add the actual future values to generate, along with the sample in *step 1*, to the plot (it might be easier if you repeat the plot commands from *step 1* to regenerate the whole plot here):

```
test_ts.plot(ax=ts_ax, c="k", label="Actual")
ts_ax.legend()
```

The final plot containing the time series with the forecast and the actual future values can be seen in the following figure:

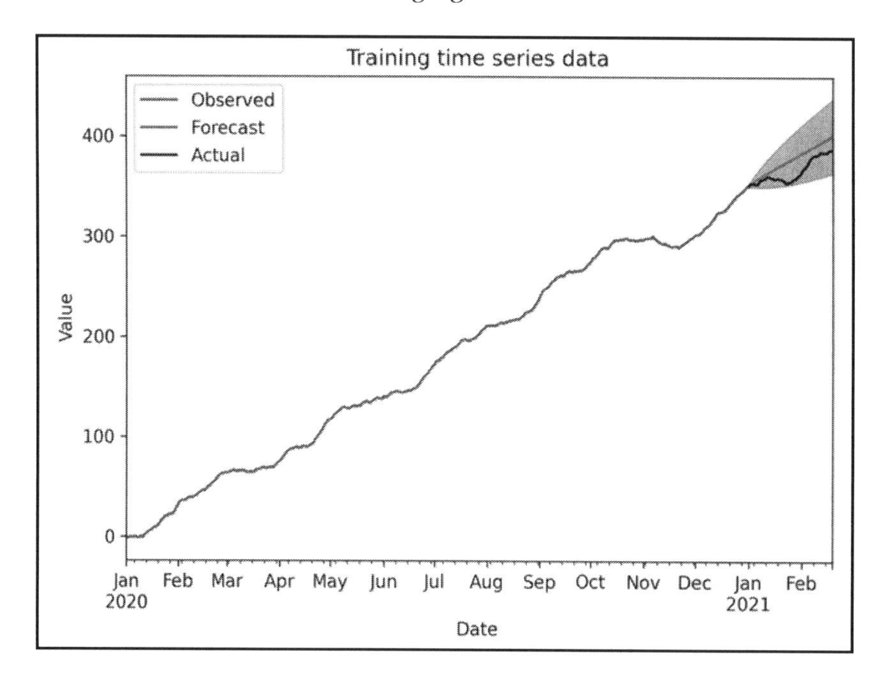

Figure 7.10: Plot of the sample time series with forecast values and actual future values for comparison

Here, we can see that the actual future values are within the confidence interval for the forecast values.

How it works...

The ARIMA model – with orders *p*, *d*, and *q* – is simply an ARMA (*p*, *q*) model that's applied to a time series. This is obtained by applying differencing of order *d* to the original time series data. It is a fairly simple way to generate a model for time series data. The statsmodels `ARIMA` class handles the creation of a model, while the `fit` method fits this model to the data. We passed the `trend="c"` keyword argument because we know, from *Figure 7.9*, that the time series has a constant trend.

The model is fit to the data using a maximum likelihood method and the final estimates for the parameters – in this case, one parameter for the autoregressive component, one for the moving average component, the constant trend parameter, and the variance of the noise. These parameters are reported in the summary. From this output, we can see that the estimates for the AR coefficient (0.8342) and the MA constant (-0.5204) are very good approximations of the true estimates that were used to generate the data, which were 0.8 for the AR coefficient and -0.5 for the MA coefficient. These parameters are set in the `generate_sample_data` routine from the `tsdata.py` file in the code repository for this chapter. This generates the sample data in *step 1*. You might have noticed that the constant parameter (0.9548) is not 0.2, as specified in the `generate_sample_data` call in *step 1*. In fact, it is not so far from the actual drift of the time series.

The `forecast` method on the fitted model (the output of the `fit` method) uses the model to make predictions about the value after a given number of steps. In this recipe, we forecast for up to 50 time steps beyond the range of the sample time series. The output of the `forecast` method is a tuple containing the forecast values, the standard error for the forecasts, and the confidence interval (by default, 95% confidence) for the forecasts. Since we provided the time series as a Pandas series, these are returned as `Series` objects (the confidence interval is a `DataFrame`).

When you construct an ARIMA model for time series data, you need to make sure you use the smallest order differencing that removes the underlying trend. Applying more differencing than is necessary is called *overdifferencing* and can lead to problems with the model.

Forecasting seasonal data using ARIMA

Time series often display periodic behavior so that peaks or dips in the value appear at regular intervals. This behavior is called *seasonality* in the analysis of time series. The methods we have used to far in this chapter to model time series data obviously do not account for seasonality. Fortunately, it is relatively easy to adapt the standard ARIMA model to incorporate seasonality, resulting in what is sometimes called a SARIMA model.

In this recipe, we will learn how to model time series data that includes seasonal behavior and use this model to produce forecasts.

Getting ready

For this recipe, we will need the NumPy package imported as `np`, the Pandas package imported as `pd`, the Matplotlib `pyplot` module as `plt`, and the statsmodels `api` module imported as `sm`. We will also need the utility for creating sample time series data from the `tsdata` module, which is included in this book's repository:

```
from tsdata import generate_sample_data
```

How to do it...

Follow these steps to produce a seasonal ARIMA model for sample time series data and use this model to produce forecasts:

1. First, we use the `generate_sample_data` routine to generate a sample time series to analyze:

```
sample_ts, test_ts = generate_sample_data(undiff=True,
    seasonal=True)
```

2. As usual, our first step is to visually inspect the data by producing a plot of the sample time series:

```
ts_fig, ts_ax = plt.subplots(tight_layout=True)
sample_ts.plot(ax=ts_ax, title="Time series", label="Observed")
ts_ax.set_xlabel("Date")
ts_ax.set_ylabel("Value")
```

The plot of the sample time series data can be seen in the following figure. Here, we can see that there seem to be periodic peaks in the data:

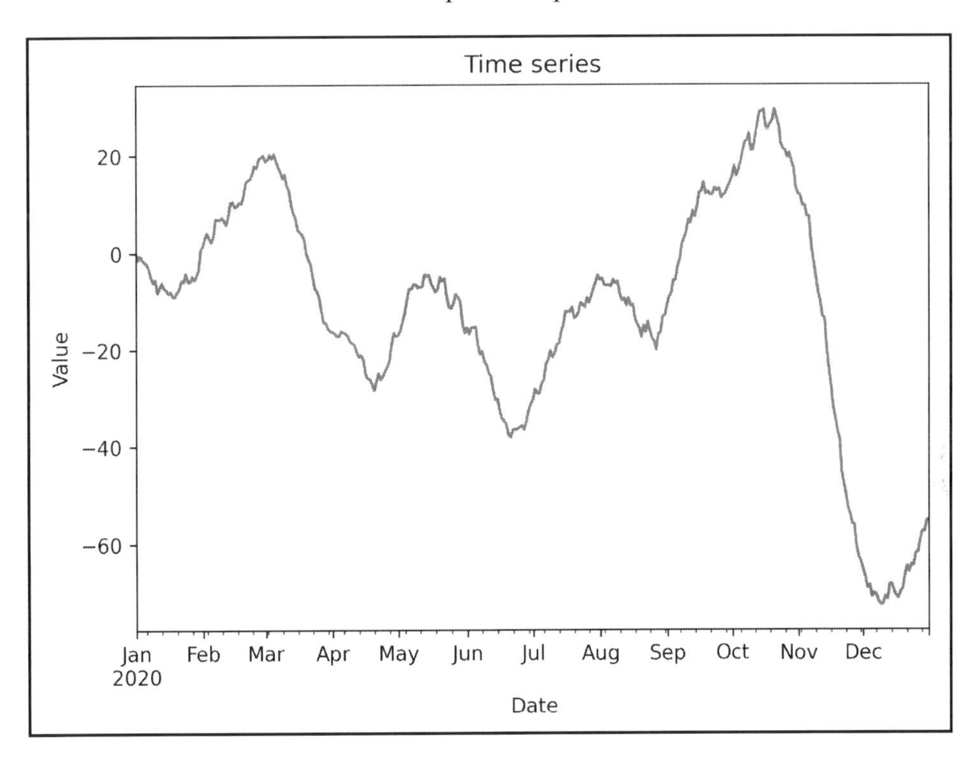

Figure 7.11: Plot of the sample time series data

3. Next, we plot the ACF and PACF for the sample time series:

```
ap_fig, (acf_ax, pacf_ax) = plt.subplots(2, 1,
   sharex=True, tight_layout=True)
sm.graphics.tsa.plot_acf(sample_ts, ax=acf_ax)
sm.graphics.tsa.plot_pacf(sample_ts, ax=pacf_ax)
pacf_ax.set_xlabel("Lag")
acf_ax.set_ylabel("Value")
pacf_ax.set_ylabel("Value")
```

The ACF and PACF for the sample time series can be seen in the following figure:

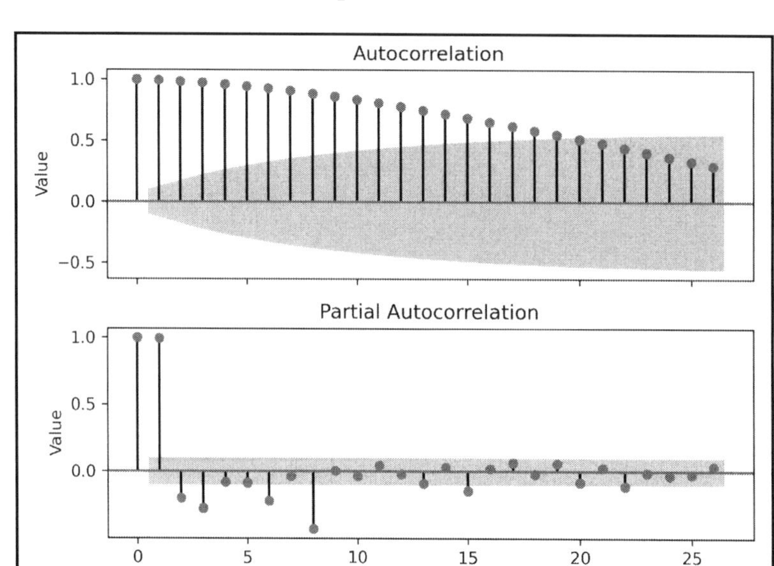

Figure 7.12: ACF and PACF for the sample time series

These plots possibly indicate the existence of autoregressive components, but also a significant spike on the PACF with lag 7.

4. Next, we difference the time series and produce plots of the ACF and PACF for the differenced series. This should make the order of the model clearer:

```
diffs = sample_ts.diff().dropna()
dap_fig, (dacf_ax, dpacf_ax) = plt.subplots(2, 1, sharex=True,
   tight_layout=True)
sm.graphics.tsa.plot_acf(diffs, ax=dacf_ax,
   title="Differenced ACF")
sm.graphics.tsa.plot_pacf(diffs, ax=dpacf_ax,
   title="Differenced PACF")
dpacf_ax.set_xlabel("Lag")
dacf_ax.set_ylabel("Value")
dpacf_ax.set_ylabel("Value")
```

The ACF and PACF for the differenced time series can be seen in the following figure. We can see that there is definitely a seasonal component with lag 7:

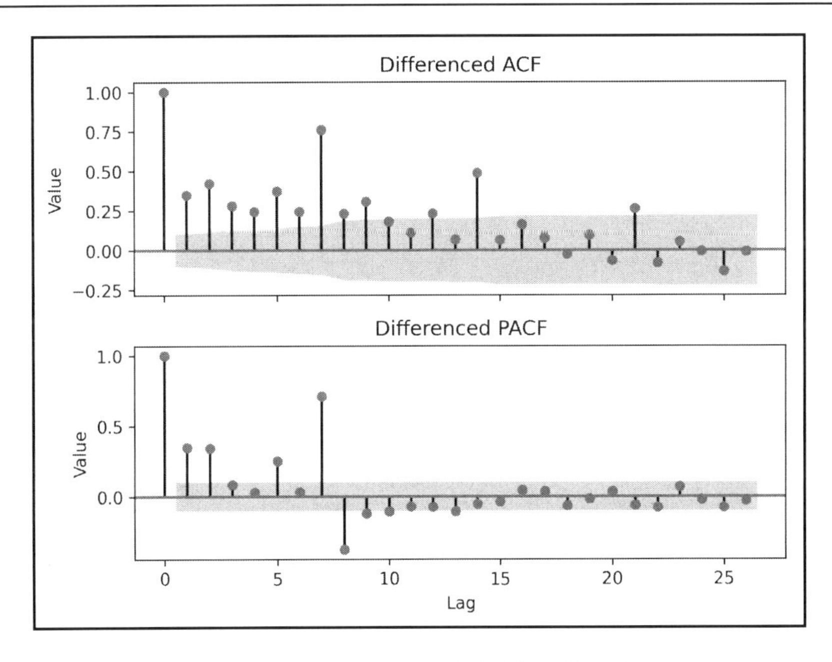

Figure 7.13: Plot of the ACF and PACF for the differenced time series

5. Now, we need to create a `SARIMAX` object that holds the model, with ARIMA order `(1, 1, 1)` and seasonal ARIMA order `(1, 0, 0, 7)`. We fit this model to the sample time series and print summary statistics. We plot the predicted values on top of the time series data:

```
model = sm.tsa.SARIMAX(sample_ts, order=(1, 1, 1),
    seasonal_order=(1, 0, 0, 7))
fitted_seasonal = model.fit()
print(fitted_seasonal.summary())
fitted_seasonal.fittedvalues.plot(ax=ts_ax, c="r",
    label="Predicted")
```

The summary statistics that are printed to the Terminal look as follows:

```
                     SARIMAX Results
=====================================================================
Dep. Variable: y                      No. Observations: 366
Model: SARIMAX(1, 1, 1)x(1, 0, [], 7) Log Likelihood -509.941
Date: Mon, 04 May 2020                AIC 1027.881
Time: 18:03:27                        BIC 1043.481
Sample: 01-01-2020                    HQIC 1034.081
      - 12-31-2020
Covariance Type:                      opg
=====================================================================
```

```
            coef     std err         z        P>|z|      [0.025      0.975]
-----------------------------------------------------------------------------
ar.L1     0.7939       0.065    12.136       0.000       0.666       0.922
ma.L1    -0.4544       0.095    -4.793       0.000      -0.640      -0.269
ar.S.L7   0.7764       0.034    22.951       0.000       0.710       0.843
sigma2    0.9388       0.073    12.783       0.000       0.795       1.083
=============================================================================
Ljung-Box (Q): 31.89                    Jarque-Bera (JB): 0.47
Prob(Q): 0.82                           Prob(JB): 0.79
Heteroskedasticity (H): 1.15            Skew: -0.03
Prob(H) (two-sided): 0.43               Kurtosis: 2.84
=============================================================================

Warnings:
[1] Covariance matrix calculated using the outer product
    of gradients (complex-step).
```

6. This model appears to be a reasonable fit, so we move ahead and forecast `50` time steps into the future:

```
forecast_result = fitted_seasonal.get_forecast(steps=50)
forecast_index = pd.date_range("2021-01-01", periods=50)
forecast = forecast_result.predicted_mean
```

7. Finally, we add the forecast values to the plot of the sample time series, along with the confidence interval for these forecasts:

```
forecast.plot(ax=ts_ax, c="g", label="Forecasts")
conf = forecast_result.conf_int()
ts_ax.fill_between(forecast_index, conf["lower y"],
   conf["upper y"], color="r", alpha=0.4)
test_ts.plot(ax=ts_ax, color="k", label="Actual future")
ts_ax.legend()
```

The final plot of the time series, along with the predictions and the confidence interval for the forecasts, can be seen in the following figure:

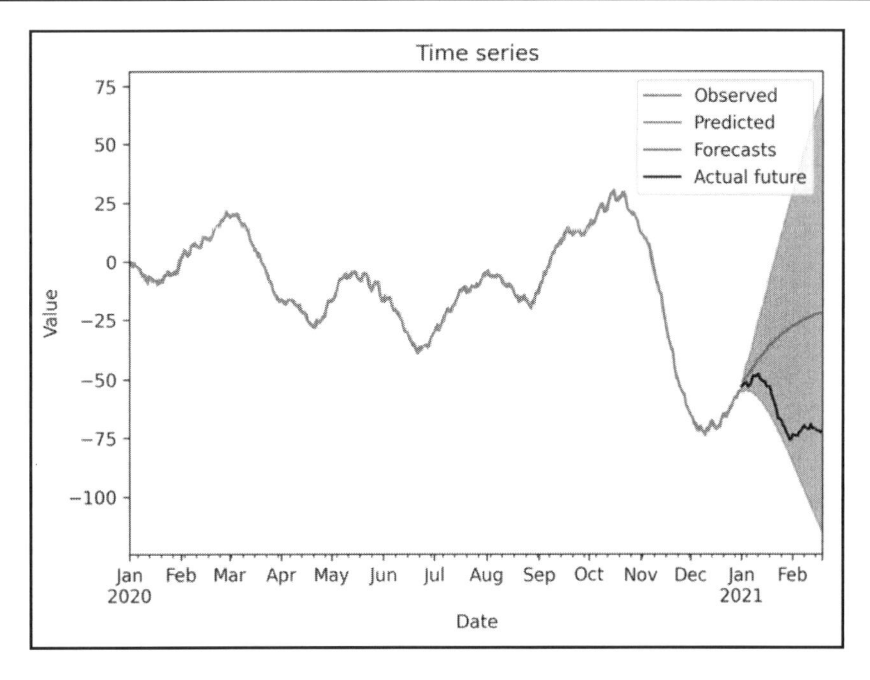

Figure 7.14: Plot of the sample time series, along with the forecasts and confidence interval

How it works...

Adjusting an ARIMA model to incorporate seasonality is a relatively simple task. A seasonal component is similar to an autoregressive component, where the lag starts at some number larger than 1. In this recipe, the time series exhibits seasonality with period 7 (weekly), which means that the model is approximately given by the following equation:

$$Y_t = \varphi_1 Y_{t-1} + \varepsilon_t + \Phi_1 Y_{t-7}$$

Here φ_1 and Φ_1 are the parameters and ε_t is the noise at time step t. The standard ARIMA model is easily adapted to include this additional lag term.

The SARIMA model incorporates this additional seasonality into the ARIMA model. It has four additional order terms on top of the three for the underlying ARIMA model. These four additional parameters are the seasonal AR, differencing, and MA components, along with the period of the seasonality. In this recipe, we took the seasonal AR to be order 1, with no seasonal differencing or MA components (order 0), and a seasonal period of 7. This gives us the additional parameters (1, 0, 0, 7) that we used in *step 5* of this recipe.

Seasonality is clearly important in modeling time series data that is measured over a period of time covering days, months, or years. It usually incorporates some kind of seasonal component based on the time frame that they occupy. For example, a time series of national power consumption measured hourly over several days would probably have a 24-hour seasonal component since power consumption will likely fall during the night hours.

Long-term seasonal patterns might be hidden if the time series data that you are analyzing does not cover a sufficiently large time period for the pattern to emerge. The same is true for trends in the data. This can lead to some interesting problems when trying to produce long-term forecasts from a relatively short period represented by observed data.

The `SARIMAX` class from the statsmodels package provides the means of modeling time series data using a seasonal ARIMA model. In fact, it can also model external factors that have an additional effect on the model, sometimes called *exogenous regressors*. (We will not cover these here.) This class works much like the `ARMA` and `ARIMA` classes that we used in the previous recipes. First, we create the model object by providing the data and orders for both the ARIMA process and the seasonal process, and then use the `fit` method on this object to create a fitted model object. We use the `get_forecasts` method to generate an object holding the forecasts and confidence interval data that we can then plot, thus producing the *Figure 7.14*.

There's more...

There is a small difference in the interface between the `SARIMAX` class used in this recipe and the `ARIMA` class used in the previous recipe. At the time of writing, the statsmodels package (v0.11) includes a second `ARIMA` class that builds on top of the `SARIMAX` class, thus providing the same interface. However, at the time of writing, this new `ARIMA` class does not offer the same functionality as that used in this recipe.

Using Prophet to model time series data

The tools we have seen so far for modeling time series data are very general and flexible methods, but they require some knowledge of time series analysis in order to be set up. The analysis needed to construct a good model that can be used to make reasonable predictions into the future can be intensive and time-consuming, and may not be viable for your application. The Prophet library is designed to automatically model time series data quickly, without the need for input from the user, and make predictions into the future.

In this recipe, we will learn how to use Prophet to produce forecasts from a sample time series.

Getting ready

For this recipe, we will need the Pandas package imported as `pd`, the Matplotlib `pyplot` package imported as `plt`, and the `Prophet` object from the Prophet library, which can be imported using the following command:

```
from fbprophet import Prophet
```

We also need to import the `generate_sample_data` routine from the `tsdata` module, which is included in the code repository for this book:

```
from tsdata import generate_sample_data
```

How to do it...

The following steps show you how to use the Prophet package to generate forecasts for a sample time series:

1. First, we use `generate_sample_data` to generate the sample time series data:

```
sample_ts, test_ts = generate_sample_data(undiff=True, trend=0.2)
```

2. We need to convert the sample data into a `DataFrame` that Prophet expects:

```
df_for_prophet = pd.DataFrame({
    "ds": sample_ts.index,   # dates
    "y": sample_ts.values    # values
})
```

3. Next, we make a model using the `Prophet` class and fit it to the sample time series:

```
model = Prophet()
model.fit(df_for_prophet)
```

4. Now, we create a new `DataFrame` that contains the time intervals for the original time series, plus the additional periods for the forecasts:

```
forecast_df = model.make_future_dataframe(periods=50)
```

5. Then, we use the `predict` method to produce the forecasts along the time periods we just created:

```
forecast = model.predict(forecast_df)
```

6. Finally, we plot the predictions on top of the sample time series data, along with the confidence interval and the true future values:

```
fig, ax = plt.subplots(tight_layout=True)
sample_ts.plot(ax=ax, label="Observed", title="Forecasts")
forecast.plot(x="ds", y="yhat", ax=ax, c="r",
    label="Predicted")
ax.fill_between(forecast["ds"].values,
forecast["yhat_lower"].values,
    forecast["yhat_upper"].values, color="r", alpha=0.4)
test_ts.plot(ax=ax, c="k", label="Future")
ax.legend()
ax.set_xlabel("Date")
ax.set_ylabel("Value")
```

The plot of the time series, along with forecasts, can be seen in the following figure:

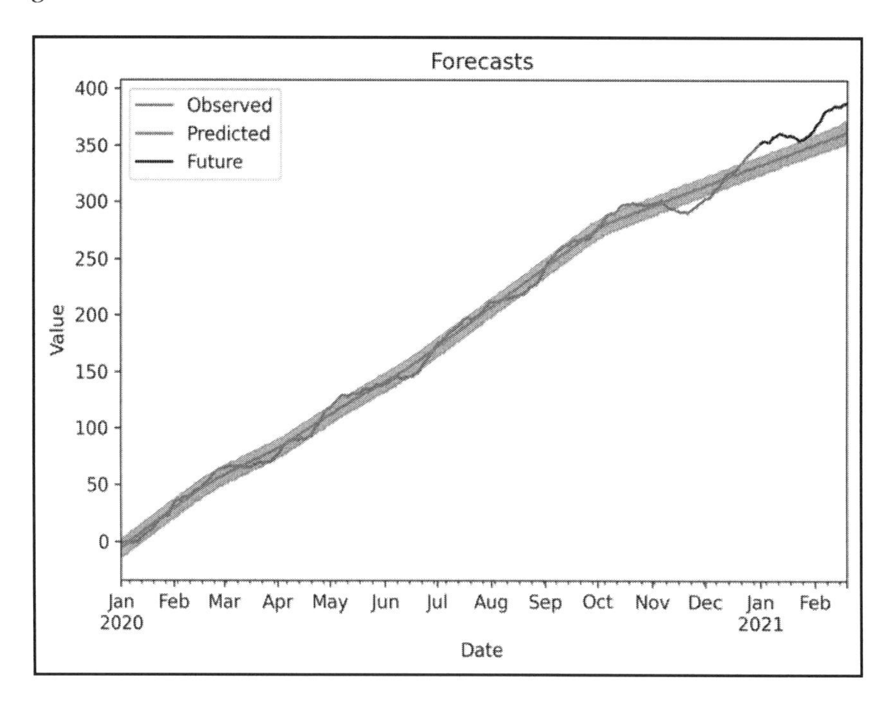

Figure 7.15: Plot of sample time series data, along with forecasts and a confidence interval

How it works...

Prophet is a package that's used to automatically produce models for time series data based on sample data, with little extra input needed from the user. In practice, it is very easy to use; we just need to create an instance of the `Prophet` class, call the `fit` method, and then we are ready to produce forecasts and understand our data using the model.

The `Prophet` class expects the data in a specific format: a `DataFrame` with columns named `ds` for the date/time index, and `y` for the response data (the time series values). This `DataFrame` should have integer indices. Once the model has been fit, we use `make_future_dataframe` to create a `DataFrame` in the correct format, with appropriate date intervals, and with additional rows for future time intervals. The `predict` method then takes this `DataFrame` and produces values using the model to populate these time intervals with predicted values. We also get other information, such as the confidence intervals, in this forecast's `DataFrame`.

There's more...

Prophet does a fairly good job of modeling time series data without any input from the user. However, the model can be customized using various methods from the `Prophet` class. For example, we could provide information about the seasonality of the data using the `add_seasonality` method of the `Prophet` class, prior to fitting the model.

There are alternative packages for automatically generating models for time series data. For example, popular machine learning libraries such as TensorFlow can be used to model time series data.

Further reading

A good textbook on regression in statistics is the book *Probability and Statistics* by Mendenhall, Beaver, and Beaver, as mentioned in `Chapter 6`, *Working with Data and Statistics*. The following books provide a good introduction to classification and regression in modern data science:

- *James, G. and Witten, D., 2013. An Introduction To Statistical Learning: With Applications In R. New York: Springer.*
- *Müller, A. and Guido, S., 2016. Introduction To Machine Learning With Python. Sebastopol: O'Reilly Media.*

A good introduction to time series analysis can be found in the following book:

- *Cryer, J. and Chan, K., 2008. Time Series Analysis. New York: Springer.*

8
Geometric Problems

This chapter describes solutions to several problems concerning two-dimensional geometry. Geometry is a branch of mathematics concerned with the characteristics of points, lines, and other figures (shapes), the interaction between such figures, and the transformation of such figures. In this chapter, we'll focus on the characteristics of two-dimensional figures and the interactions between these objects.

There are several problems we must overcome when working with geometric objects in Python. The biggest hurdle is the problem of representation. Most geometric objects occupy a region in the two-dimensional plane, and as such, it is impossible to store every point that lies within the region. Instead, we have to find a more compact way to represent the region that can be stored as a relatively small number of points. For example, we might store a selection of points along the boundary of an object that we can reconstruct the boundary and the object itself from. Moreover, we reformulate geometric problems into questions that can be answered using the representative data.

The second biggest problem is converting purely geometric questions into a form that can be understood and solved using software. This can be relatively simple – for example, finding the point at which two straight lines intersect is a matter of solving a matrix equation – or it can be extremely complex, depending on the type of question being asked. A common technique that's used to solve these problems is to represent the figure in question using more simple objects and solve the (hopefully) easier problem using each of the simple objects. This should then give us an idea of the solution to the original problem.

We will start by showing you how to visualize two-dimensional shapes, and then learn how to determine whether a point is contained within another figure. Then, we'll move on and look at edge detection, triangulation, and finding convex hulls. We'll conclude this chapter by constructing Bezier curves.

This chapter covers the following recipes:

- Visualizing two-dimensional geometric shapes
- Finding interior points
- Finding edges in an image
- Triangulating planar figures
- Computing convex hulls
- Constructing Bezier curves

Let's get started!

Technical requirements

For this chapter, we will need the `numpy` package and the `matplotlib` package, as usual. We will also need the Shapely package and the `scikit-image` package, which can be installed using your favorite package manager, such as `pip`:

```
python3.8 -m pip install numpy matplotlib shapely scikit-image
```

The code for this chapter can be found in the `Chapter 08` folder of the GitHub repository at `https://github.com/PacktPublishing/Applying-Math-with-Python/tree/master/Chapter%2008`.

Check out the following video to see the Code in Action: `https://bit.ly/3hpeKEF`.

Visualizing two-dimensional geometric shapes

The focus of this chapter is on two-dimensional geometry, so our first task is to learn how to visualize two-dimensional geometric figures. Some of the techniques and tools mentioned here might be applicable to three-dimensional geometric figures, but generally, this will require more specialized packages and tools.

A *geometric figure*, at least in the context of this book, is any point, line, curve, or closed region (including the boundary) whose boundary is a collection of lines and curves. Simple examples include points and lines (obviously), rectangles, polygons, and circles.

In this recipe, we will learn how to visualize geometric figures using Matplotlib.

Getting ready

For this recipe, we need the NumPy package imported as `np`, and the Matplotlib `pyplot` module imported as `plt`. We also need to import the `Circle` class from the Matplotlib `patches` module and the `PatchCollection` class from the Matplotlib `collections` module. This can be done with the following commands:

```
import numpy as np
import matplotlib.pyplot as plt
from matplotlib.patches import Circle
from matplotlib.collections import PatchCollection
```

We will also need the `swisscheese-grid-10411.csv` data file from the code repository for this chapter.

How to do it...

The following steps show you to visualize a two-dimensional geometric figure:

1. First, we load the data from the `swisscheese-grid-10411.csv` file from this book's code repository:

   ```
   data = np.loadtxt("swisscheese-grid-10411.csv")
   ```

2. We create a new patch object that represents a region on a plot. This is going to be a circle (disk) with the center at the origin and a radius of `1`. We create a new set of axes and add this patch to them:

   ```
   fig, ax = plt.subplots()
   outer = Circle((0.0, 0.0), 1.0, zorder=0, fc="k")
   ax.add_patch(outer)
   ```

3. Next, we create a `PatchCollection` object from the data we loaded in *step 1*, which contains centers and radii for a number of other circles. We then add this `PatchCollection` to the axes we created in *step 2*:

   ```
   col = PatchCollection(
       (Circle((x, y), r) for x, y, r in data),
       facecolor="white", zorder=1, linewidth=0.2,
       ls="-", ec="k"
   )
   ax.add_collection(col)
   ```

4. Finally, we set the x- and y-axis ranges so that the whole image is displayed and then turns the axes off:

```
ax.set_xlim((-1.1, 1.1))
ax.set_ylim((-1.1, 1.1))
ax.set_axis_off()
```

The resulting image is of a *Swiss Cheese*, as shown here:

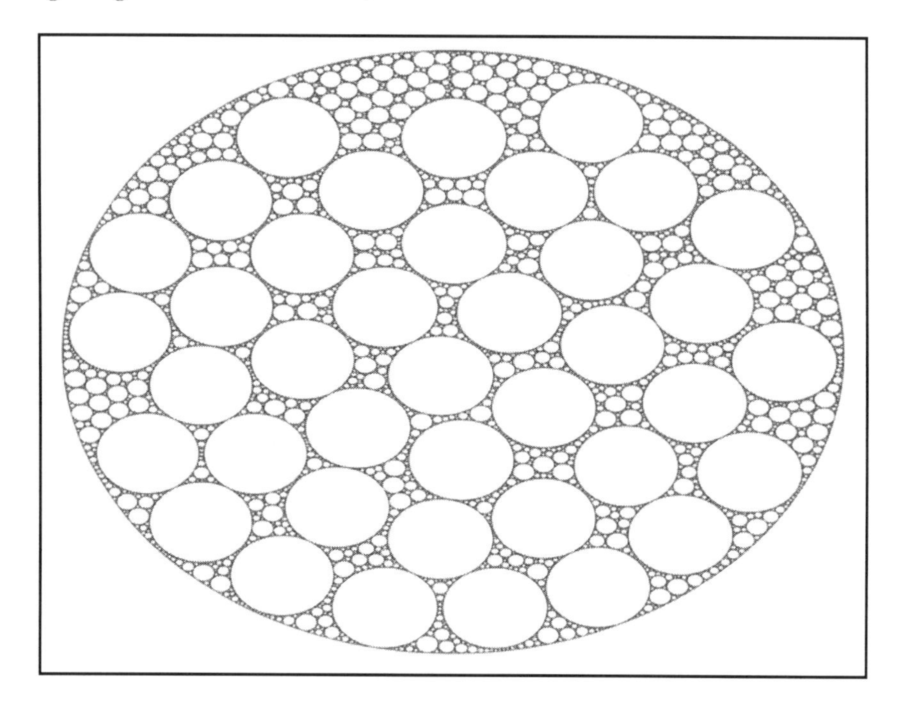

Figure 8.1: Plot of a Swiss cheese

How it works...

The keys to this recipe are the `Circle` and `PatchCollection` objects, which represent the regions of the plot area on Matplotlib `Axes`. In this case, we are creating one large circular patch, centered at the origin and with a radius of `1`, that has a black face color and uses `zorder=0` to place it behind other patches. This patch is added to the `Axes` object using the `add_patch` method.

The next step is to create an object that will render the circles represented by the data that we loaded from the CSV file in *step 1*. This data consisted of x, y, and r values for the center (x, y) and the radius, r, of the individual circles (10,411 in total). The `PatchCollection` object combines a sequence of patches into a single object that can be added to an `Axes` object. Here, we add one `Circle` for each row in our data, which is then added to the `Axes` object using the `add_collection` method. Notice that we have applied the face color to the whole collection, rather than to each individual `Circle` constituent. We set the face color to white (using the `facecolor="w"` argument), the edge color to black (using `ec="k"`), the line width (of the edge lines) to 0.2 (using `linewidth=0.2`), and the edge style to a continuous line. All of this, when put together, results in our image.

The image that we have created here is called a "Swiss Cheese". These were first used in rational approximation theory in 1938 by Alice Roth; they were subsequently rediscovered, and similar constructions have been used many times since. We used this example because it consists of one large individual part, plus a large collection of smaller individual parts. Roth's Swiss Cheese is an example of a set in the plane that has a positive area but no topological interior. (It is fairly amazing that such a set can even exist!) More importantly, there are continuous functions defined on this Swiss Cheese that cannot be approximated by rational functions. This property has made similar constructions useful in the theory of *uniform algebra*.

The `Circle` class is a subclass of the more general `Patch` class. There are numerous other `Patch` classes that represent different planar figures, such as `Polygon` and `PathPatch`, which represent the region bounded by a path (curve or collection of curves). These can be used to generate complex patches that can be rendered in a Matplotlib figure. Collections can be used to apply settings to a number of patch objects simultaneously, which can be especially useful if, as in this recipe, you have a large number of objects that will all be rendered in the same style.

There's more...

There are many different patch types available in Matplotlib. In this recipe, we used the `Circle` patch class, which represents a circular region on the axes. There is also the `Polygon` patch class, which represents a polygon (regular or otherwise). There are also `PatchPath` objects, which are regions that are surrounded by a curve that does not necessarily consist of straight-line segments. This is similar to the way a shaded region can be constructed in many vector graphics software packages.

In addition to the single patch types in Matplotlib, there are a number of collection types that gather a number of patches together to be used as a single object. In this recipe, we used the `PatchCollection` class to gather a large number of `Circle` patches. There are more specialized patch collections that can be used to generate these internal patches automatically, rather than us generating them ourselves.

See also

A more detailed history of Swiss Cheeses in mathematics can be found in the following biographical article: *Daepp, U., Gauthier, P., Gorkin, P. and Schmieder, G., 2005. Alice in Switzerland: The life and mathematics of Alice Roth. The Mathematical Intelligencer, 27(1), pp.41-54.*

Finding interior points

One problem with working with two-dimensional figures in a programming environment is that you can't possibly store all the points that lie within the figure. Instead, we usually store far fewer points that represent the figure in some way. In most cases, this will be a number of points (connected by lines) that describe the boundary of the figure. This is efficient in terms of memory and makes it easy to visualize them on screen using Matplotlib `Patches`, for example. However, this approach makes it more difficult to determine whether a point, or another figure, lies within a given figure. This is a crucial question in many geometric problems.

In this recipe, we will learn how to represent geometric figures and determine whether a point lies within a figure or not.

Getting ready

For this recipe, we will need to import the `matplotlib` package (as a whole) as `mpl` and the `pyplot` module as `plt`:

```
import matplotlib as mpl
import matplotlib.pyplot as plt
```

We also need to import the `Point` and `Polygon` objects from the `geometry` module of the Shapely package. The Shapely package contains many routines and objects for representing, manipulating, and analyzing two-dimensional geometric figures:

```
from shapely.geometry import Polygon, Point
```

How to do it...

The following steps show you how to create a Shapely representation of a polygon and then test whether a point lies within this polygon:

1. Create a sample polygon to test:

```
polygon = Polygon(
    [(0, 2), (-1, 1), (-0.5, -1), (0.5, -1), (1, 1)],
)
```

2. Next, we plot the polygon on a new figure. First, we need to convert the polygon into a Matplotlib `Polygon` patch that can be added to the figure:

```
fig, ax = plt.subplots()
poly_patch = mpl.patches.Polygon(polygon.exterior, ec="k",
   lw="1", alpha=0.5)
ax.add_patch(poly_patch)
ax.set(xlim=(-1.05, 1.05), ylim=(-1.05, 2.05))
ax.set_axis_off()
```

3. Now, we need to create two test points, one of which will be inside the polygon and one of which will be outside the polygon:

```
p1 = Point(0.0, 0.0)
p2 = Point(-1.0, -0.75)
```

4. We plot and annotate these two points on top of the polygon to show their positions:

```
ax.plot(0.0, 0.0, "k*")
ax.annotate("p1", (0.0, 0.0), (0.05, 0.0))
ax.plot(-0.8, -0.75, "k*")
ax.annotate("p2", (-0.8, -0.75), (-0.8 + 0.05, -0.75))
```

5. Finally, we test where each point lies within the polygon using the `contains` method, and then print the result to the Terminal:

```
print("p1 inside polygon?", polygon.contains(p1))
print("p2 inside polygon?", polygon.contains(p2))
```

The results show that the first point, `p1`, is contained in the polygon, while the second point, `p2`, is not. This can also be seen in the following figure, which clearly shows that one point is contained within the shaded polygon, while the other point is not:

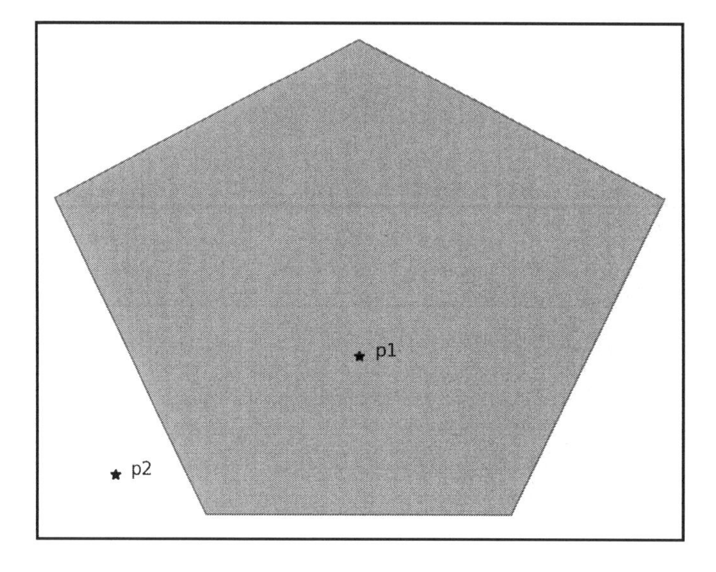

Figure 8.2: Points inside and outside a polygonal region

How it works...

The Shapely `Polygon` class is a representation of a polygon that stores its vertices as points. The region enclosed by the outer boundary – the five straight lines between the stored vertices – is obvious to us and easily identified by the eye, but the notion of being "inside" the boundary is difficult to define in a way that can be easily understood by a computer. It is not even straightforward to give a formal mathematical definition of what it means to lie "within" a given curve.

There are two main ways to determine whether a point lies within a simple closed curve – that is, a curve that starts and ends at the same place that does not contain any self-intersections. The first uses a mathematical concept called the *winding number*, which counts the number of times the curve "wraps around" a point, and the *ray crossing counting* method, where we count the number of times a ray from the point to a point at infinity crosses the curve. Fortunately, we don't need to compute these numbers ourselves since we can use the tools from the Shapely package to do this computation for us. This is what the `contains` method of a polygon does. (Under the hood, Shapely uses the GEOS library to perform this calculation.)

The Shapely `Polygon` class can be used to compute many quantities associated with these planar figures, including perimeter length and area. The `contains` method is used to determine whether a point, or a collection of points, lies within the polygon represented by the object. (There are some limitations regarding the kinds of polygons that can be represented by this class.) In fact, you can use the same method to determine whether one polygon is contained within another since, as we have seen in this recipe, a polygon is represented by a simple collection of points.

Finding edges in an image

Finding edges in images is a good way of reducing a complex image that contains a lot of noise and distractions to a very simple image containing the most prominent outlines. This can be useful as our first step of the analysis process, such as in image classification, or as the process of importing line outlines into computer graphics software packages.

In this recipe, we will learn how to use the `scikit-image` package and the Canny algorithm to find the edges in a complex image.

Getting ready

For this recipe, we will need to import the Matplotlib `pyplot` module as `plt`, the `imread` routine from the `skimage.io` module, and the `canny` routine from the `skimage.feature` module:

```
import matplotlib.pyplot as plt
from skimage.io import imread
from skimage.feature import canny
```

How to do it...

Follow these steps to learn how to use the `scikit-image` package to find edges in an image:

1. Load the image data from the source file. This can be found in the GitHub repository for this chapter. Crucially, we pass in `as_gray=True` to load the image in grayscale:

```
image = imread("mandelbrot.png", as_gray=True)
```

The following is the original image, for reference. The set itself is shown by the white region and, as you can see, the boundary, indicated by the darker shades, is very complex:

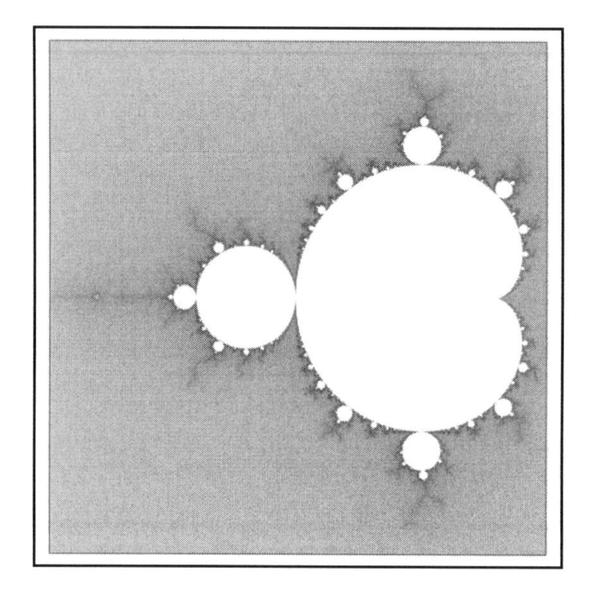

Figure 8.3: Plot of the Mandelbrot set generated using Python

2. Next, we use the `canny` routine, which needs to be imported from the `features` module of the `scikit-image` package. The `sigma` value is set to 0.5 for this image:

```
edges = canny(image, sigma=0.5)
```

3. Finally, we add the edges image to a new figure with a grayscale (reversed) colormap:

```
fig, ax = plt.subplots()
ax.imshow(edges, cmap="gray_r")
ax.set_axis_off()
```

The edges that have been detected can be seen in the following image. The edge-finding algorithm has identified most of the visible details of the boundary of the Mandelbrot set, although it is not perfect (this is an estimate, after all):

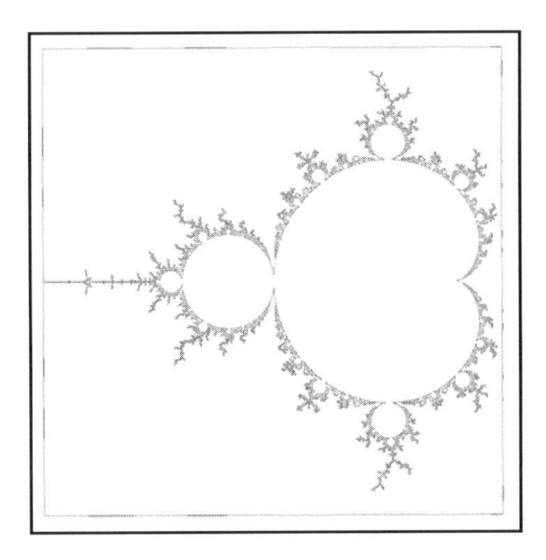

Figure 8.4: The edges of the Mandelbrot set found using the scikit-image package's Canny edge detection algorithm

How it works...

The scikit-image package provides various utilities and types for manipulating and analyzing data derived from images. As the name suggests, the canny routine uses the Canny edge detection algorithm to find edges in an image. This algorithm uses the intensity gradients in the image to detect edges, where the gradient is larger. It also performs some filtering to reduce the noise in the edges it finds.

The sigma keyword value we provided is the standard deviation of the Gaussian smoothing that's applied to the image prior to calculating the gradients for edge detection. This helps us remove some of the noise from the image. The value we set (0.5) is smaller than the default (1), but it does give us better resolution in this case. A large value would obscure some of the finer details in the boundary of the Mandelbrot set.

Triangulating planar figures

As we saw in `Chapter 3`, *Calculus and Differential Equations*, we often need to break down a continuous region into smaller, simpler regions. In earlier recipes, we reduced an interval of real numbers into a collection of smaller intervals, each with a small length. This process is usually called **discretization**. In this chapter, we are working with two-dimensional figures, so we need a two-dimensional version of this process. For this, we'll break a two-dimensional figure (in this recipe, a polygon) into a collection of smaller and simpler polygons. The simplest of all polygons are triangles, so this is a good place to start for two-dimensional discretization. The process of finding a collection of triangles that "tiles" a geometric figure is called *triangulation*.

In this recipe, we will learn how to triangulate a polygon (with a hole) using the Shapely package.

Getting ready

For this recipe, we will need the NumPy package imported as `np`, the Matplotlib package imported as `mpl`, and the `pyplot` module imported as `plt`:

```
import matplotlib as mpl
import matplotlib.pyplot as plt
import numpy as np
```

We also need the following items from the Shapely package:

```
from shapely.geometry import Polygon
from shapely.ops import triangulate
```

How to do it...

The following steps show you how to triangulate a polygon with a hole using the Shapely package:

1. First, we need to create a `Polygon` object that represents the figure that we wish to triangulate:

```
polygon = Polygon(
    [(2.0, 1.0), (2.0, 1.5), (-4.0, 1.5), (-4.0, 0.5),
        (-3.0, -1.5), (0.0, -1.5), (1.0, -2.0), (1.0, -0.5),
          (0.0, -1.0), (-0.5, -1.0), (-0.5, 1.0)],
    holes=[np.array([[-1.5, -0.5], [-1.5, 0.5], [-2.5, 0.5],
```

```
            [-2.5, -0.5]]))]
    )
```

2. Now, we should plot the figure so that we can understand the region that we will be working within:

```
fig, ax = plt.subplots()
plt_poly = mpl.patches.Polygon(polygon.exterior,
    ec="k", lw="1", alpha=0.5, zorder=0)
ax.add_patch(plt_poly)
plt_hole = mpl.patches.Polygon(polygon.interiors[0],
    ec="k", fc="w")
ax.add_patch(plt_hole)
ax.set(xlim=(-4.05, 2.05), ylim=(-2.05, 1.55))
ax.set_axis_off()
```

This polygon can be seen in the following image. As we can see, the figure has a "hole" in it that must be carefully considered:

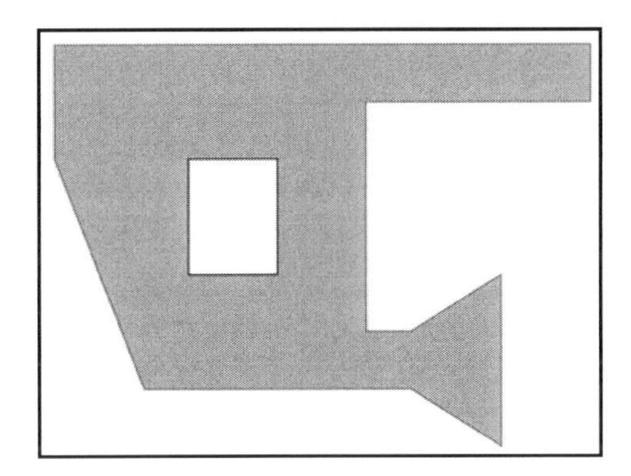

Figure 8.5: Sample polygon but with a hole

3. We use the `triangulate` routine to generate a triangulation of the polygon. This triangulation includes external edges, which is something we don't want in this recipe:

```
triangles = triangulate(polygon)
```

4. To remove the triangles that lie outside the original polygon, we need to use the built-in `filter` routine, along with the `contains` method (seen earlier in this chapter):

```
filtered = filter(lambda p: polygon.contains(p), triangles)
```

5. To plot the triangles on top of the original polygon, we need to convert the Shapely triangles into Matplotlib `Patch` objects, which we store in a `PatchCollection`:

```
patches = map(lambda p: mpl.patches.Polygon(p.exterior), filtered)
col = mpl.collections.PatchCollection(patches, fc="none", ec="k")
```

6. Finally, we add the collection of triangular patches to the figure we created earlier:

```
ax.add_collection(col)
```

The triangulation that's been plotted on top of the original polygon can be seen in the following figure. Here, we can see that every vertex has been connected to two others to form a system of triangles that cover the entire original polygon:

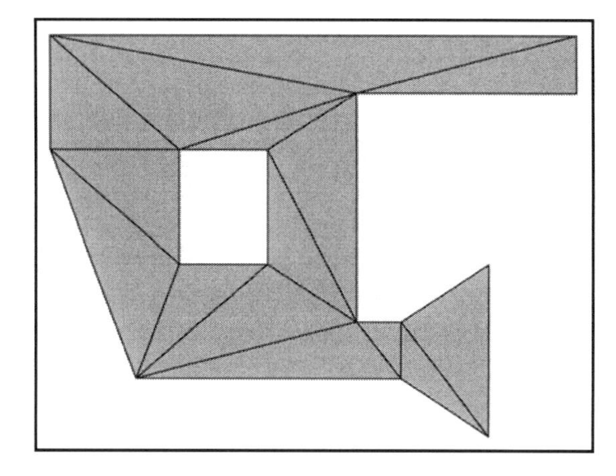

Figure 8.6: Triangulation of a sample polygon with a hole

How it works...

The `triangulate` routine uses a technique called *Delaunay triangulation* to connect a collection of points to a system of triangles. In this case, the collection of points are the vertices of the polygon. The Delaunay method finds these triangles in such a way that none of the points are contained within the circumcircle of any of the triangles. This is a technical condition of the method, but it means that the triangles are chosen efficiently, in the sense that it avoids very long, thin triangles. The resulting triangulation makes use of the edges that are present in the original polygon and also connects some of the external edges.

In order to remove the triangles that lie outside of the original polygon, we use the built-in `filter` routine, which creates a new iterable by removing the items that the criterion function fails under. This is used in conjunction with the `contains` method on Shapely `Polygon` objects to determine whether each triangle lies within the original figure. As we mentioned previously, we need to convert these Shapely items into Matplotlib patches before they can be added to the plot.

There's more...

Triangulations are usually used to reduce a complex geometric figure into a collection of triangles, which are much simpler, for some kind of computational task. However, they do have other uses. One particularly interesting application of triangulations is to solve the "art gallery problem". This problem concerns finding the maximum number of guards that are necessary to "guard" an art gallery of a particular shape. Triangulations are an essential part of Fisk's simple proof of the art gallery theorem, which was originally proved by Chvátal.

Suppose that the polygon from this recipe is the floor plan for an art gallery and that some guards need to be placed on the vertices. A small amount of work will show that you'll need three guards to be placed at the polygon's vertices for the whole museum to be covered. In the following image, we have plotted one possible arrangement:

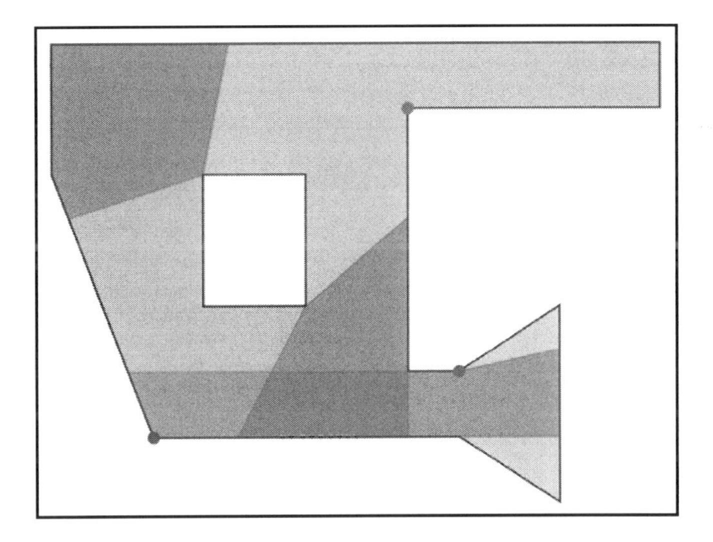

Figure 8.7: One possible solution to the art gallery problem where guards are placed on vertices. The guards are indicated by the dots, and their corresponding field of vision is shaded.

One guard is placed at each of the vertices with a circle, and their field is vision is denoted by the corresponding shaded area. Here, you can see that the whole polygon is covered by at least one color. The solution to the art gallery problem – which is actually a variation of the original problem – tells us that we need, at most, four guards.

See also

More information about the art gallery problem can be found in the classic book by O'Rourke: *ORourke, J. (1987). Art gallery theorems and algorithms. New York: Oxford University Press.*

Computing convex hulls

A geometric figure is said to be *convex* if every pair of points within the figure can be joined using a straight line that is also contained within the figure. Simple examples of convex bodies include points, straight lines, squares, circles (disks), regular polygons, and so on. The geometric figure shown in *Figure 8.5* is not convex since the points on the opposite sides of the hole cannot be connected by a straight line that remains inside the figure.

Convex figures are simple from a certain perspective, which means they are useful in a variety of applications. One particular problem involves finding the smallest convex set that contains a collection of points. This smallest convex set is called the *convex hull* of the set of points.

In this recipe, we'll learn how to find the convex hull of a set of points using the Shapely package.

Getting ready

For this recipe, we will need the NumPy package imported as `np`, the Matplotlib package imported as `mpl`, and the `pyplot` module imported as `plt`:

```
import numpy as np
import matplotlib as mpl
import matplotlib.pyplot as plt
```

We will also need a default random number generator from NumPy. We can import this as follows:

```
from numpy.random import default_rng
rng = default_rng(12345)
```

Finally, we will need to import the `MultiPoint` class from Shapely:

```
from shapely.geometry import MultiPoint
```

How to do it...

Follow these steps to find the convex hull of a collection of randomly generated points:

1. First, we generate a two-dimensional array of random numbers:

```
raw_points = rng.uniform(-1.0, 1.0, size=(50, 2))
```

2. Next, we create a new figure and plot these raw sample points on this figure:

```
fig, ax = plt.subplots()
ax.plot(raw_points[:, 0], raw_points[:, 1], "k.")
ax.set_axis_off()
```

These randomly generated points can be seen in the following figure. The points are roughly spread over a square region:

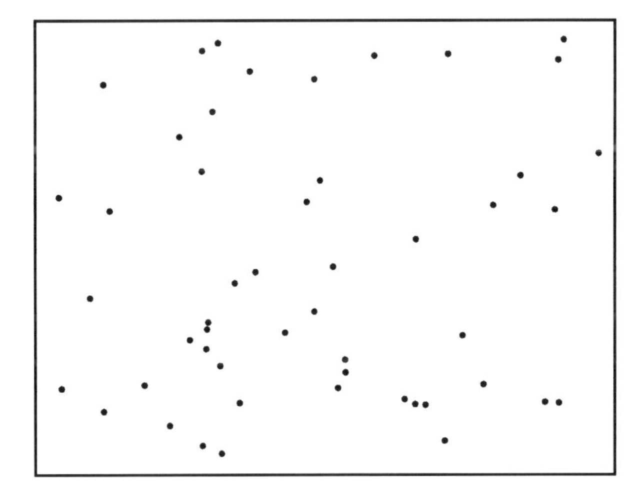

Figure 8.8: A collection of points in the plane

3. Next, we construct a `MultiPoint` object that collects all these points and put them into a single object:

```
points = MultiPoint(raw_points)
```

4. Now, we get the convex hull of this `MultiPoint` object using the `convex_hull` attribute:

```
convex_hull = points.convex_hull
```

5. Then, we create a Matplotlib `Polygon` patch that can be plotted on our figure to show the result of finding the convex hull:

```
patch = mpl.patches.Polygon(convex_hull.exterior, alpha=0.5,
    ec="k", lw=1.2)
```

6. Finally, we add the `Polygon` patch to the figure to show the convex hull:

```
ax.add_patch(patch)
```

The convex hull of the randomly generated points can be seen in the following image:

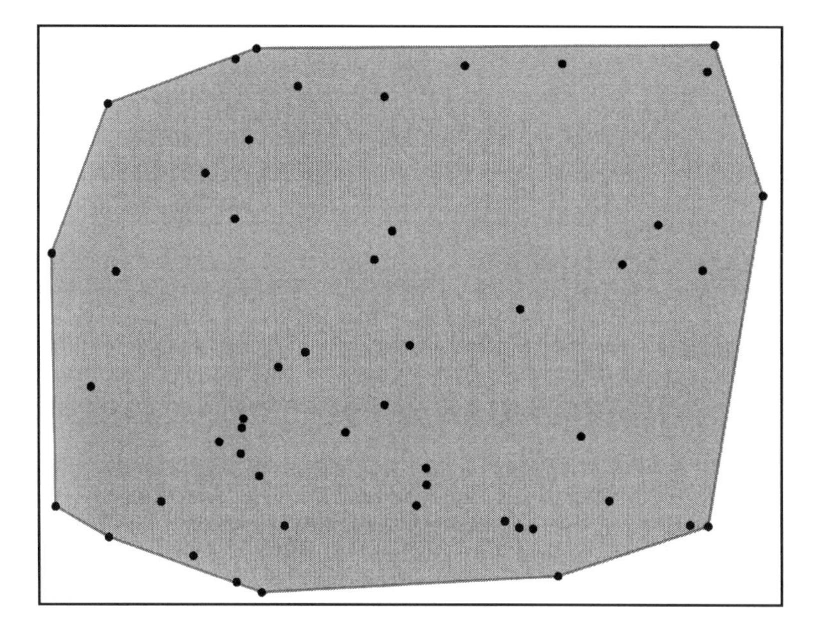

Figure 8.9: The convex hull of a collection of points in the plane

How it works...

The Shapely package is a Python wrapper around the GEOS library for geometric analysis. The `convex_hull` attribute of Shapely geometric objects calls the convex hull computation routine from the GEOS library, resulting in a new Shapely object. From this recipe, we can see that the convex hull of the collection of points is a polygon with vertices at the points that are farthest away from the "center".

Constructing Bezier curves

Bezier curves, or *B-splines*, are a family of curves that are extremely useful in vector graphics – for instance, they are commonly used in high-quality font packages. This is because they are defined by a small number of points that can then be used to inexpensively calculate a large number of points along the curve. This allows detail to be scaled according to the needs of the user.

In this recipe, we'll learn how to create a simple class representing a Bezier curve and compute a number of points along it.

Getting ready

In this recipe, we will use the NumPy package imported as `np`, the Matplotlib `pyplot` module imported as `plt`, and the `comb` routine from the Python Standard Library `math` module, imported under the alias `binom`:

```
from math import comb as binom
import matplotlib.pyplot as plt
import numpy as np
```

How to do it...

Follow these steps to define a class that represents a Bezier curve that can be used to compute points along the curve:

1. The first step is to set up the basic class. We need to provide the control points (nodes) and some associated numbers to instance attributes:

```
class Bezier:
    def __init__(self, *points):
        self.points = points
```

```
        self.nodes = n = len(points) - 1
        self.degree = l = points[0].size
```

2. Still inside the `__init__` method, we generate the coefficients for the Bezier curve and store them in a list on an instance attribute:

```
self.coeffs = [binom(n, i)*p.reshape((l, 1)) for i,
   p in enumerate(points)]
```

3. Next, we define a `__call__` method to make the class callable. We load the number of nodes from the instance into a local variable for clarity:

```
    def __call__(self, t):
        n = self.nodes
```

4. Next, we reshape the input array so that it contains a single row:

```
t = t.reshape((1, t.size))
```

5. Now, we generate a list of arrays of values using each of the coefficients in the `coeffs` attribute for the instance:

```
vals = [c @ (t**i)*(1-t)**(n-i) for i,
   c in enumerate(self.coeffs)]
```

6. Finally, we sum all the arrays that were constructed in *step 5* and return the resulting array:

```
return np.sum(vals, axis=0)
```

7. Now, we will test our class by means of an example. We'll define four control points for this example:

```
p1 = np.array([0.0, 0.0])
p2 = np.array([0.0, 1.0])
p3 = np.array([1.0, 1.0])
p4 = np.array([1.0, 3.0])
```

8. Next, we set up a new figure for plotting and plot the control points with a dashed connecting line:

```
fig, ax = plt.subplots()
ax.plot([0.0, 0.0, 1.0, 1.0], [0.0, 1.0, 1.0, 3.0], "*--k")
ax.set(xlabel="x", ylabel="y", title="Bezier curve with
    4 nodes, degree 3")
```

9. Then, we create a new instance of our `Bezier` class using the four points we defined in *step 7*:

```
b_curve = Bezier(p1, p2, p3, p4)
```

10. We can now create an array of equally spaced points between 0 and 1 using `linspace` and compute the points along the Bezier curve:

```
t = np.linspace(0, 1)
v = b_curve(t)
```

11. Finally, we plot this curve on top of the control points that we plotted earlier:

```
ax.plot(v[0,:], v[1, :])
```

The Bezier curve that we've plotted can be seen in the following diagram. As you can see, the curve starts at the first point (0, 0) and finishes at the final point (1, 3):

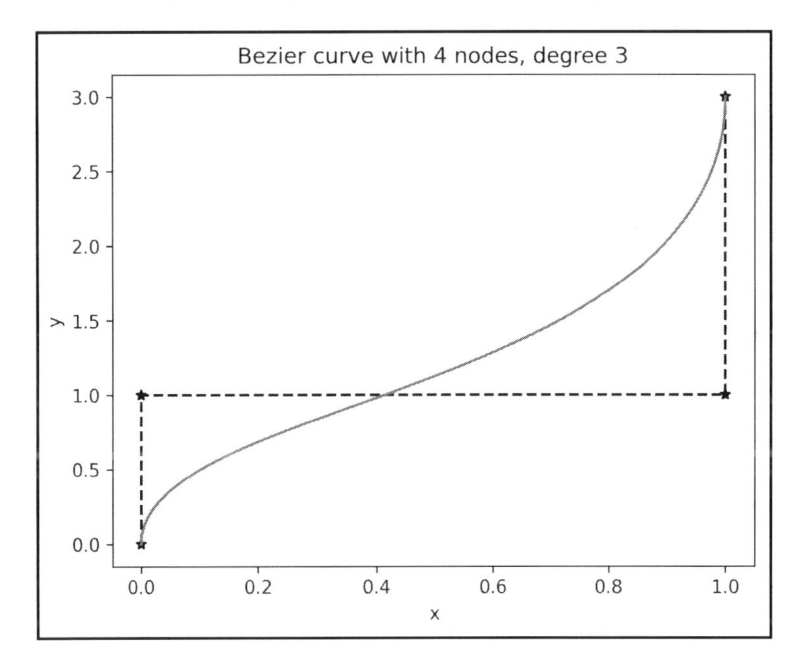

Figure 8.10: Bezier curve of degree 3 constructed using four nodes

How it works...

A Bezier curve is described by a sequence of control points, from which we construct the curve in a recursive manner. A Bezier curve with one point is a constant curve that stays at that point. A Bezier curve with two control points is a line segment between those two points:

$$B(\mathbf{p}_1, \mathbf{p}_2; t) = (1-t)\mathbf{p}_1 + t\mathbf{p}_2 \qquad (0 \le t \le 1).$$

When we add a third control point, we take the line segment between the corresponding points on the Bezier curve of curves that are constructed with one less point. This means that we construct the Bezier curve with three control points using the following formula:

$$B(\mathbf{p}_1, \mathbf{p}_2, \mathbf{p}_3; t) = (1-t)B(\mathbf{p}_1, \mathbf{p}_2; t) + tB(\mathbf{p}_2, \mathbf{p}_3; t) \qquad (0 \le t \le 1).$$

This construction can be seen in the following diagram:

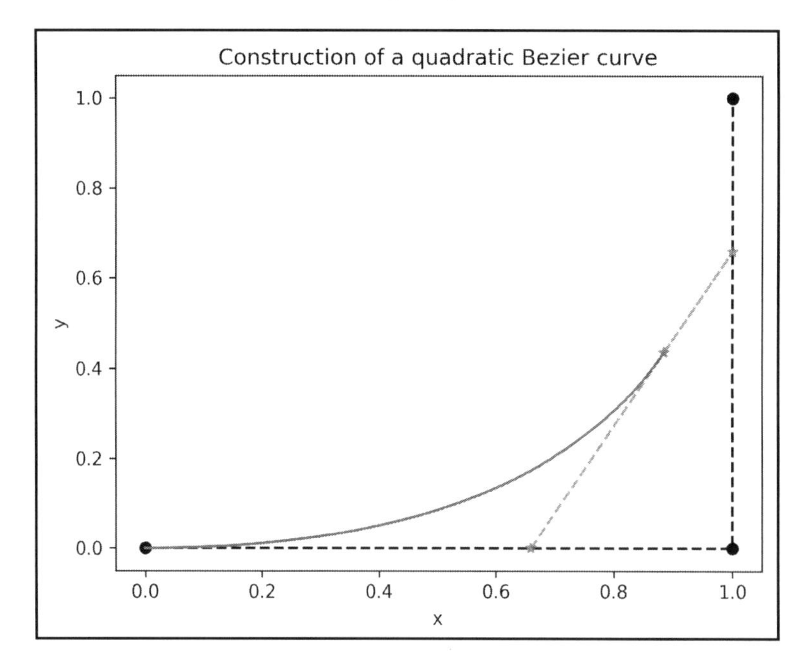

Figure 8.11: Construction of a quadratic Bezier curve using a recursive definition. The two linear Bezier curves are shown by the black dashed lines.

The construction continues in this manner to define the Bezier curve on any number of control points. Fortunately, we don't need to work with this recursive definition in practice because we can flatten the formulae into a single formula for the curve, which is given by the following formula:

$$B(\mathbf{p}_1, \mathbf{p}_2, \dots, \mathbf{p}_n; t) = \sum_{j=0}^{n} \binom{n}{j} t^j (1-t)^{n-j} \mathbf{p}_j \qquad 0 \le t \le 1.$$

Here, the $\mathbf{p}_i$ elements are the control points, t is a parameter, and

$$\binom{n}{j} = \frac{n!}{j!(n-j)!}$$

is the binomial coefficient. Remember that the t parameter is the quantity that is changing to generate the points of the curve. We can isolate the terms in the previous sum that involve t and those that do not. This defines the coefficients that we defined in *step 2*, each of which are given by the following code fragment:

```
binom(n, i)*p.reshape((l, 1))
```

We reshape each of the points, `p`, in this step to make sure it is arranged as a column vector. This means that each of the coefficients is a column vector (as a NumPy array) consisting of the control points scaled by the binomial coefficients.

Now, we need to specify how to evaluate the Bezier curve at various values of t. This is where we make use of the high-performance array operations from the NumPy package. We reshaped our control points as column vectors when forming our coefficients. In *step 4*, we reshaped the input, t, values to make a row vector. This means that we can use the matrix multiplication operator to multiply each coefficient by the corresponding (scalar) value, depending on the input, t. This is what happens in *step 5*, inside the list comprehension. In the following line, we multiply the $l \times 1$ array by the $1 \times N$ array to obtain an $l \times N$ array:

```
c @ (t**i)*(1-t)**(n-i)
```

We get one of these for each coefficient. We can then use the `np.sum` routine to sum each of these $l \times N$ arrays to get the values along the Bezier curve. In the example provided in this recipe, the top row of the output array contains the x values of the curve and the bottom row contains the y values of the curve. We have to be careful when specifying the `axis=0` keyword argument for the `sum` routine to make sure the sum takes over the list we created, and not the arrays that this list contains.

The class we defined is initialized using the control points for the Bezier curve, which are then used to generate the coefficients. The actual computation of the curve values is done using NumPy, so this implementation should have relatively good performance. Once a specific instance of this class has been created, it functions very much like a function, as you might expect. However, no type checking is done here, so we can only call this "function" with a NumPy array as an argument.

There's more...

Bezier curves are defined using an iterative construction, where the curve with n points is defined using the straight line connecting the curves defined by the first and last $n-1$ points. Keeping track of the coefficient of each of the control points using this construction will quickly lead you to the equation we used to define the preceding curve. This construction also leads to interesting – and useful – geometric properties of Bezier curves.

As we mentioned in the introduction to this recipe, Bezier curves appear in many applications that involve vector graphics, such as fonts. They also appear in many common vector graphics software packages. In these software packages, it is common to see *quadratic Bezier curves*, which are defined by a collection of three points. However, you can also define a quadratic Bezier curve by supplying the two endpoints, along with the gradient lines, at those points. This is more common in graphics software packages. The resulting Bezier curve will leave each of the endpoints along the gradient lines and connect the curve smoothly between these points.

The implementation we constructed here will have relatively good performance for small applications, but will not be sufficient for applications involving rendering curves with a large number of control points at a large number of t values. For this, it is best to use a low-level package written in a compiled language. For example, the `bezier` Python package uses a compiled Fortran backend for its computations and provides a much richer interface than the class we defined here.

Bezier curves can, of course, be extended to higher dimensions in a natural way. The result is a Bezier surface, which makes them very useful general-purpose tools for high-quality, scalable graphics.

Further reading

- A description of some common algorithms from computation geometry can be found in the following book: *Press, W.H., Teukolsky, S.A., Vetterling, W.T., and Flannery, B.P., 2007. Numerical recipes: the art of scientific computing. 3rd ed. Cambridge: Cambridge University Press.*
- For a more detailed account of some problems and techniques from computational geometry, check out the following book: *O'Rourke, J., 1994. Computational geometry in C. Cambridge: Cambridge University Press.*

9 Finding Optimal Solutions

In this chapter, we'll address various methods for finding the best outcome in a given situation. This is called *optimization* and usually involves either minimizing or maximizing an objective function. An *objective function* is a function that takes a number of parameters as arguments and returns a single scalar value that represents the cost or payoff for a given choice of parameters. The problems regarding minimizing and maximizing functions are actually equivalent to one another, so we'll only discuss minimizing object functions in this chapter. Minimizing a function, $f(x)$, is equivalent to maximizing the function $-f(x)$. More details on this will be provided when we discuss the first recipe.

The algorithms available to us for minimizing a given function depend on the nature of the function. For instance, a simple linear function containing one or more variables has different algorithms available compared to a non-linear function with many variables. The minimization of linear functions falls within the category of *linear programming*, which is a well-developed theory. For non-linear functions, we usually make use of the gradient (derivative) of a function in order to find the minimum points. We will discuss several methods for minimizing various functions of different types.

Finding the minima and maxima of the functions of a single variable is especially simple, and can be done easily if the derivatives of the function are known. If not, then the method described in the appropriate recipe will be applicable. The notes in the *Minimizing a non-linear function* recipe give some extra details about this.

We'll also provide a very short introduction to *game theory*. Broadly speaking, this is a theory surrounding decision-making and has wide-ranging implications in subjects such as economics. In particular, we'll discuss how to represent simple two-player games as objects in Python, compute payoffs associated with certain choices, and compute Nash equilibria for these games.

We will start by looking at how to minimize linear and non-linear functions containing one or more variables. Then, we'll move on and look at gradient descent methods and curve fitting using least squares. We'll conclude this chapter by analyzing two-player games and Nash equilibria.

In this chapter, we will cover the following recipes:

- Minimizing a simple linear function
- Minimizing a non-linear function
- Using gradient descent methods in optimization
- Using least squares to fit a curve to data
- Analyzing simple two-player games
- Computing Nash equilibria

Let's get started!

Technical requirements

In this chapter, we will need the NumPy package, the SciPy package, and the Matplotlib package, as usual. We will also need the Nashpy package for the final two recipes. These packages can be installed using your favorite package manager, such as `pip`:

```
python3.8 -m pip install numpy scipy matplotlib nashpy
```

The code for this chapter can be found in the `Chapter 09` folder of the GitHub repository at `https://github.com/PacktPublishing/Applying-Math-with-Python/tree/master/Chapter%2009`.

Check out the following video to see the Code in Action: `https://bit.ly/2BjzwGo`.

Minimizing a simple linear function

The most basic type of problem we face in optimization is finding the parameters where a function takes its minimum value. Usually, this problem is *constrained* by some bounds on the possible values of the parameters, which increases the complexity of the problem. Obviously, the complexity of this problem increases further if the function that we are minimizing is also complex. For this reason, we must first consider *linear functions*, which are in the following form:

$$f(\mathbf{x}) = \mathbf{c} \cdot \mathbf{x} = c_1 x_1 + c_2 x_2 + \cdots + c_n x_n$$

To solve these kinds of problems, we need to convert the constraints into a form that can be used by the computer. In this case, we usually convert them into a linear algebra problem (matrices and vectors). Once this is done, we can use the tools from the linear algebra packages in NumPy and SciPy to find the parameters we seek. Fortunately, since these kinds of problems occur quite frequently, SciPy has routines that handle this conversion and subsequent solving.

In this recipe, we'll solve the following constrained linear minimization problem using routines from the SciPy `optimize` module:

$$f(\mathbf{x}) = \mathbf{c} \cdot \mathbf{x} = x_0 + 5x_1$$

This will be subject to the following conditions:

$$\begin{aligned} 2x_0 + x_1 &\le 6 \\ x_0 + x_1 &\ge 4 \\ -3 \le x_0 &\le 14 \\ 2 \le x_1 &\le 12 \end{aligned}$$

Getting ready

For this recipe, we need to import the NumPy package under the alias `np`, the Matplotlib `pyplot` module under the name `plt`, and the SciPy `optimize` module. We also need to import the `Axes3D` class from `mpl_toolkits.mplot3d` to make 3D plotting available:

```
import numpy as np
from scipy import optimize
import matplotlib.pyplot as plt
from mpl_toolkits.mplot3d import Axes3D
```

How to do it...

Follow these steps to solve a constrained linear minimization problem using SciPy:

1. Set up the system in a form that SciPy can recognize:

```
A = np.array([
    [2, 1],    # 2*x0 + x1 <= 6
    [-1, -1]  # -x0 - x1 <= -4
])
b = np.array([6, -4])
x0_bounds = (-3, 14) # -3 <= x0 <= 14
x1_bounds = (2, 12)  # 2 <= x1 <= 12
c = np.array([1, 5])
```

2. Next, we need to define a routine that evaluates the linear function at a value of *x*, which is a vector (a NumPy array):

```
def func(x):
    return np.tensordot(c, x, axes=1)
```

3. Then, we create a new figure and add a set of `3d` axes that we can plot the function on:

```
fig = plt.figure()
ax = fig.add_subplot(projection="3d")
ax.set(xlabel="x0", ylabel="x1", zlabel="func")
ax.set_title("Values in Feasible region")
```

4. Next, we create a grid of values covering the region from the problem and plot the value of the function over this region:

```
X0 = np.linspace(*x0_bounds)
X1 = np.linspace(*x1_bounds)
x0, x1 = np.meshgrid(X0, X1)
z = func([x0, x1])
ax.plot_surface(x0, x1, z, alpha=0.3)
```

5. Now, we plot the line in the plane of function values that corresponds to the critical line, `2*x0 + x1 == 6`, and plot the values that fall within the range on top of our plot:

```
Y = (b[0] - A[0, 0]*X0) / A[0, 1]
I = np.logical_and(Y >= x1_bounds[0], Y <= x1_bounds[1])
ax.plot(X0[I], Y[I], func([X0[I], Y[I]]), "r", lw=1.5)
```

6. We repeat this plotting step for the second critical line, `x0 + x1 == -4`:

```
Y = (b[1] - A[1, 0]*X0) / A[1, 1]
I = np.logical_and(Y >= x1_bounds[0], Y <= x1_bounds[1])
ax.plot(X0[I], Y[I], func([X0[I], Y[I]]), "r", lw=1.5)
```

7. Next, we shade the region that lies within the two critical lines, which corresponds to the feasible region for the minimization problem:

```
B = np.tensordot(A, np.array([x0, x1]), axes=1)
II = np.logical_and(B[0, ...] <= b[0], B[1, ...] <= b[1])
ax.plot_trisurf(x0[II], x1[II], z[II], color="b", alpha=0.5)
```

The plot of the function values over the feasible region can be seen in the following image:

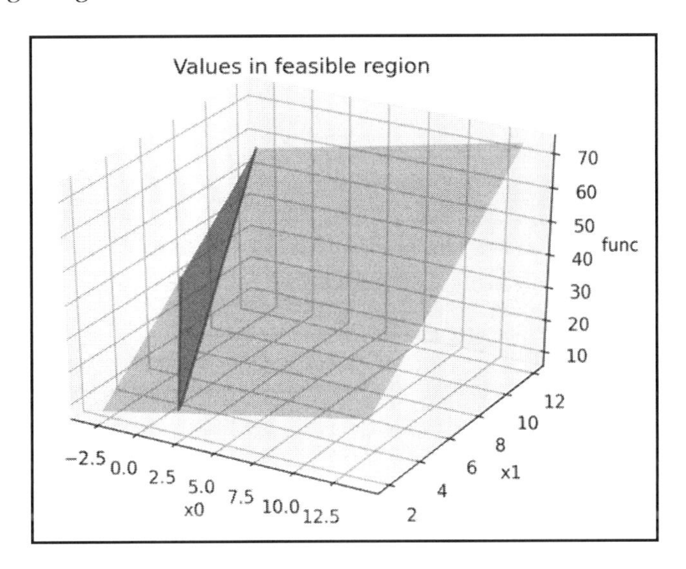

Figure 9.1: Values of the linear function with the feasible region highlighted

As we can see, the minimum value that lies within this shaded region occurs at the intersection of the two critical lines.

8. Next, we use `linprog` to solve the constrained minimization problem with the bounds we created in *Step 1*. We print the resulting object in the terminal:

```
res = optimize.linprog(c, A_ub=A, b_ub=b, bounds=
    (x0_bounds, x1_bounds))
print(res)
```

9. Finally, we plot the minimum function value on top of the feasible region:

```
ax.plot([res.x[0]], [res.x[1]], [res.fun], "k*")
```

The updated plot can be seen in the following image:

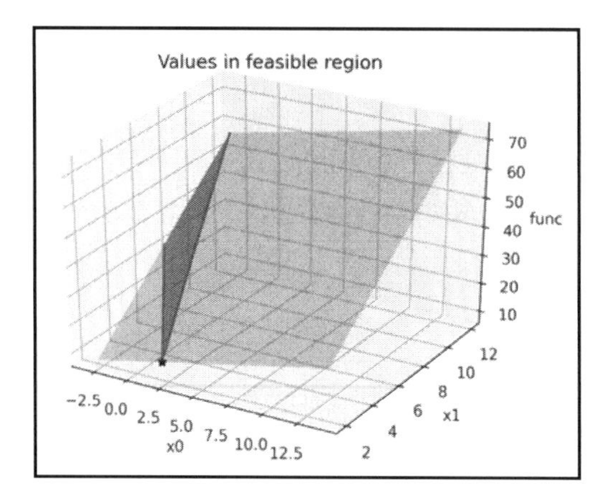

Figure 9.2: Minimum value plotted on the feasible region

Here, we can see that the `linprog` routine has indeed found that the minimum is at the intersection of the two critical lines.

How it works...

Constrained linear minimization problems are common in economic situations, where you try to minimize costs while maintaining other aspects of the parameters. In fact, a lot of the terminology from optimization theory mirrors this fact. A very simple algorithm for solving these kinds of problems is called the **simplex method**, which uses a sequence of array operations to find the minimal solution. Geometrically, these operations represent changing to different vertices of a simplex (which we won't define here), and it is this that gives the algorithm its name.

Before we continue, we'll provide a brief outline of the process used by the simplex method to solve a constrained linear optimization problem. The problem, as presented to us, is not a matrix equation problem but a matrix inequality problem. We can remedy this problem by introducing **slack variables**, which turn an inequality into an equality. For example, the first constraint inequality can be rewritten as follows by introducing the slack variable, s_1:

$$2x_0 + x_1 + s_1 = 6$$

This satisfies the desired inequality, provided that s_1 is not negative. The second constraint inequality is a greater than or equal to type inequality that we must first change so that it's of the less than or equal to type. We do this by multiplying all terms by -1. This gives us the second row of matrix `A` that we defined in the recipe. After introducing a second slack variable, s_2, we get the second equation:

$$-x_0 - x_1 + s_2 = -4$$

From this, we can construct a matrix whose columns contain the coefficients of the two parameter variables, x_1 and x_2, and the two slack variables, s_1 and s_2. The rows of this matrix represent the two bounding equations and the objective function. This system of equations can now be solved, using elementary row operations on this matrix, to obtain the values of x_1 and x_2, which minimize the objective function. Since solving matrix equations is easy and fast, this means that we can minimize linear functions quickly and efficiently.

Fortunately, we don't need to remember how to reduce our system of inequalities into a system of linear equations since routines such as `linprog` do this for us. We can simply provide the bounding inequalities as a matrix and vector pair, consisting of the coefficients of each, and a separate vector that defines the objective function. The `linprog` routine takes care of formulating and then solving the minimization problem.

In practice, the simplex method is not the algorithm used by the `linprog` routine to minimize the function. Instead, `linprog` uses an interior point algorithm, which is more efficient. (The method can actually be set to `simplex` or `revised-simplex` by providing the `method` keyword argument with the appropriate method name. In the printed resulting output, we can see that it only took five iterations to reach the solution.) The resulting object that is returned by this routine contains the parameter values at which the minimum occurs stored in the `x` attribute, the value of the function at this minimum value stored in the `fun` attribute, and various other pieces of information about the solving process. If the method had failed, then the `status` attribute would have contained a numerical code that described why the method failed.

In *step 2* of this recipe, we created a function that represents the objective function for this problem. This function takes a single array as input, which contains the parameter space values at which the function should be evaluated. Here, we used the `tensordot` routine (with `axes=1`) from NumPy to evaluate the dot product of the coefficient vector, c, with each input, x. We have to be quite careful here since the values that we pass into the function will be a $2 \times 50 \times 50$ array in a later step. The ordinary matrix multiplication (`np.dot`) would not give the 50×50 array output that we desire in this case.

In *steps 5* and *6*, we computed the points on the critical lines as those points with the following equation:

$$x_1 = (b_0 - A_{0,0}x_0)/A_{0,1} \quad \text{and} \quad x_1 = (b_1 - A_{1,0}x_0)/A_{1,1}$$

We then computed the corresponding z values so that we could plot the lines that lie on the plane defined by the objective function. We also need to "trim" the values so that we only include those that lie in the range specified in the problem.

There's more...

This recipe covered the constrained minimization problem and how to solve it using SciPy. However, the same method can be used to solve the constrained *maximization* problem. This is because maximization and minimization are *dual* to one another in the sense that maximizing a function, $f(x)$, is the same as minimizing the function $-f(x)$, and then taking the negative of this value. In fact, we used this fact in this recipe to change the second constraining inequality from ≥ to ≤.

In this recipe, we solved a problem with only two parameter variables, but the same method will work (except for the plotting steps) for a problem involving more than two such variables. We just need to add more rows and columns to each of the arrays to account for this increased number of variables – this includes the tuple of bounds supplied to the routine. The routine can also be used with sparse matrices, where appropriate, for extra efficiency when dealing with very large amounts of variables.

The `linprog` routine gets its name from *linear programming*, which is used to describe problems of this type – finding values of x that satisfy some matrix inequalities subject to other conditions. Since there is a very close connection to the theory of matrices and linear algebra, there are many very fast and efficient techniques available for linear programming problems that are not available in a non-linear context.

Minimizing a non-linear function

In the previous recipe, we saw how to minimize a very simple linear function. Unfortunately, most functions are not linear and usually don't have nice properties that we would like. For these non-linear functions, we cannot use the fast algorithms that have been developed for linear problems, so we need to devise new methods that can be used in these more general cases. The algorithm that we will use there is called the Nelder-Mead algorthim, which is a robust and general-purpose method that's used to find the minimum value of a function and does not rely on the gradient of the function.

In this recipe, we'll learn how to use the Nelder-Mead simplex method to minimize a non-linear function containing two variables.

Getting ready

In this recipe, we will use the NumPy package imported as `np`, the Matplotlib `pyplot` module imported as `plt`, the `Axes3D` class imported from `mpl_toolkits.mplot3d` to enable 3D plotting, and the SciPy `optimize` module:

```
import numpy as np
import matplotlib.pyplot as plt
from mpl_toolkits.mplot3d import Axes3D
from scipy import optimize
```

How to do it...

The following steps show you how to use the Nelder-Mead simplex method to find the minimum of a general non-linear objective function:

1. Define the objective function that we will minimize:

```
def func(x):
    return ((x[0] - 0.5)**2 + (x[1] + 0.5)**2)*
       np.cos(0.5*x[0]*x[1])
```

2. Next, create a grid of values that we can plot our objective function on:

```
x_r = np.linspace(-1, 1)
y_r = np.linspace(-2, 2)
x, y = np.meshgrid(x_r, y_r)
```

3. Now, we evaluate the function on this grid of points:

```
z = func([x, y])
```

4. Next, we create a new figure with a `3d` axes object and set the axis labels and the title:

```
fig = plt.figure(tight_layout=True)
ax = fig.add_subplot(projection="3d")
ax.tick_params(axis="both", which="major", labelsize=9)
ax.set(xlabel="x", ylabel="y", zlabel="z")
ax.set_title("Objective function")
```

5. Now, we can plot the objective function as a surface on the axes we just created:

```
ax.plot_surface(x, y, z, alpha=0.7)
```

6. We choose an initial point that our minimization routine will start its iteration at and plot this on the surface:

```
x0 = np.array([-0.5, 1.0])
ax.plot([x0[0]], [x0[1]], func(x0), "r*")
```

The plot of the objective function's surface, along with the initial point, can be seen in the following image. Here, we can see that the minimum value appears to occur at around 0.5 on the x-axis and -0.5 on the y-axis:

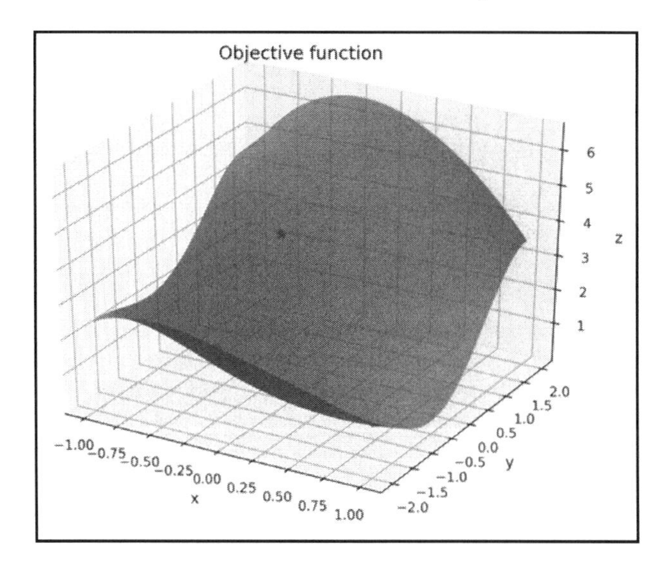

Figure 9.3: Non-linear objective function with a starting value

7. Now, we use the `minimize` routine from the `optimize` package to find the minimum value and print the `result` object that it produces:

```
result = optimize.minimize(func, x0, tol=1e-6, method=
    "Nelder-Mead")
print(result)
```

8. Finally, we plot the minimum value found by the `minimize` routine on top of the objective function surface:

```
ax.plot([result.x[0]], [result.x[1]], [result.fun], "r*")
```

The updated plot of the objective function, including the minimum point found by the `minimize` routine, can be seen in the following image:

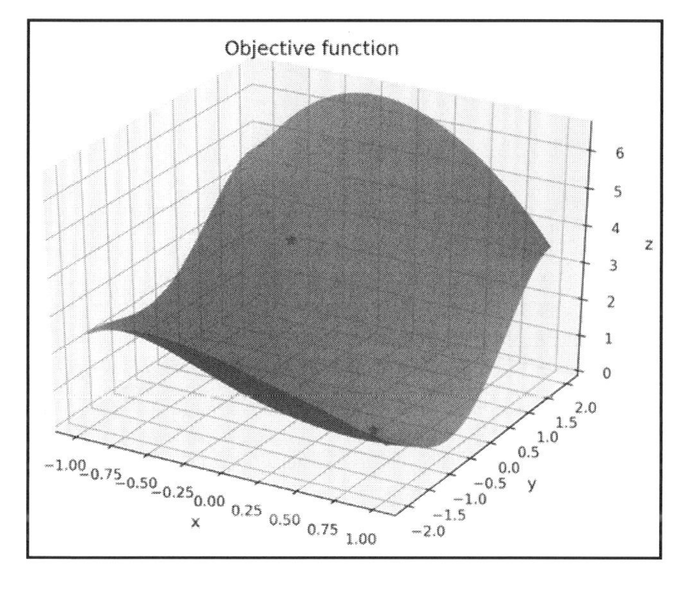

Figure 9.4: Objective function with a starting point and a minimum point

How it works...

The Nelder-Mead simplex method – not to be confused with the simplex method for linear optimization problems – is a simple algorithm for finding the minimum values of a non-linear function and works even when the objective function does not have a known derivative. (This is not the case for the function in this recipe; the only gains from using a gradient-based method is the speed of convergence.) The method works by comparing the values of the objective function at the vertices of a simplex, which is a triangle in a two-dimensional space. The vertex with the largest function value is "reflected" through the opposite edge and performs an appropriate expansion or contraction that, in effect, moves the simplex "downhill".

The `minimize` routine from the SciPy `optimize` module is an entry point for many non-linear function minimization algorithms. In this recipe, we used the Nelder-Mead simplex algorithm, but there are also a number of other algorithms available. Many of these algorithms require knowledge of the gradient of the function, which might be computed automatically by the algorithm. The algorithm can be used by providing the appropriate name to the `method` keyword argument.

The `result` object that's returned by the `minimize` routine contains lots of information about the solution that has been found – or not found, if an error occurred – by the solver. In particular, the desired parameters that the calculated minimum occurs at is stored in the `x` attribute of the result, while the value of the function is stored in the `fun` attribute.

The `minimize` routine requires the function and a starting value of `x0`. In this recipe, we also provided a tolerance value that the minimum should be computed at using the `tol` keyword argument. Changing this value will modify the accuracy that the solution is computed with.

There's more...

The Nelder-Mead algorithm is an example of a "gradient-free" minimization algorithm since it does not require any information about the gradient (derivative) of the objective function. There are several such algorithms, all of which typically involve evaluating the objective function at a number of specified points, and then using this information to move toward the minimum value. In general, gradient-free methods tend to converge more slowly than gradient descent models. However, they can be used for almost any objective function, even where it is not easy to compute the gradient either exactly or by means of approximation.

Optimizing the functions of a single variable is generally easier than the multi-dimensional case and has its own special function in the SciPy `optimize` library.
The `minimize_scalar` routine performs minimization for functions of a single variable and should be used instead of `minimize` in this case.

Using gradient descent methods in optimization

In the previous recipe, we used the Nelder-Mead simplex algorithm to minimize a non-linear function containing two variables. This is a fairly robust method that works even if very little is known about the objective function. However, in many situations, we do know more about the objective function, and this fact allows us to devise faster and more efficient algorithms for minimizing the function. We can do this by making use of properties such as the gradient of the function.

The *gradient* of a function of more than one variable describes the rate of change of the function in each of its component directions. This is a vector of the partial derivatives of the function with respect to each of the variables. From this gradient vector, we can deduce the direction in which the function is increasing most rapidly and, conversely, the direction in which the function is decreasing most rapidly from any given position. This gives us the basis for *gradient descent* methods for minimizing a function. The algorithm is very simple: given a starting position, $\mathbf{x}$, we compute the gradient at this $\mathbf{x}$ and the corresponding direction in which the gradient is most rapidly decreasing, then make a small step in that direction. After a few iterations, this will move from the starting position to the minimum of the function.

In this recipe, we will learn how to implement an algorithm based on the steepest descent algorithm to minimize an objective function within a bounded region.

Getting ready

For this recipe, we will need the NumPy package imported as `np`, the Matplotlib `pyplot` module imported as `plt`, and the `Axes3D` object imported from `mpl_toolkits.mplot3d`:

```
import numpy as np
import matplotlib.pyplot as plt
from mpl_toolkits.mplot3d import Axes3D
```

How to do it...

In the following steps, we will implement a simple gradient descent method to minimize an objective function with a known gradient function (we're actually going to use a generator function so that we can see the method as it works):

1. We will start by defining a `descend` routine, which will carry out our algorithm. The function declaration is as follows:

```
def descend(func, x0, grad, bounds, tol=1e-8, max_iter=100):
```

2. Next, we need to implement this routine. We start by defining the variables that will hold the iterate values while the method is running:

```
    xn = x0
    xnm1 = np.inf
    grad_xn = grad(x0)
```

3. We then start our loop, which will run the iterations. We immediately check whether we are making meaningful progress before continuing:

```
    for i in range(max_iter):
        if np.linalg.norm(xn - xnm1) < tol:
            break
```

4. The direction is minus the gradient vector. We compute this once and store it in the `direction` variable:

```
        direction = -grad_xn
```

5. Now, we update the previous and current values, `xnm1` and `xn`, respectively, ready for the next iteration. This concludes the code for the `descend` routine:

```
        xnm1 = xn
        xn = xn + 0.2*direction
```

6. Now, we can compute the gradient at the current value and yield all the appropriate values:

```
        grad_xn = grad(xn)
        yield i, xn, func(xn), grad_xn
```

This concludes the definition of the `descend` routine.

7. We can now define a sample objective function to minimize:

```
def func(x):
    return ((x[0] - 0.5)**2 + (x[1] +
0.5)**2)*np.cos(0.5*x[0]*x[1])
```

8. Next, we create a grid that we will evaluate and then plot the objective function on:

```
x_r = np.linspace(-1, 1)
y_r = np.linspace(-2, 2)
x, y = np.meshgrid(x_r, y_r)
```

9. Once the grid has been created, we can evaluate our function and store the result in the `z` variable:

```
z = func([x, y])
```

10. Next, we create a three-dimensional surface plot of the objective function:

```
surf_fig = plt.figure(tight_layout=True)
surf_ax = surf_fig.add_subplot(projection="3d")
surf_ax.tick_params(axis="both", which="major", labelsize=9)
surf_ax.set(xlabel="x", ylabel="y", zlabel="z")
surf_ax.set_title("Objective function")
surf_ax.plot_surface(x, y, z, alpha=0.7)
```

11. Before we can start the minimization process, we need to define an initial point, `x0`. We plot this point on the objective function plot we created in the previous step:

```
x0 = np.array([-0.8, 1.3])
surf_ax.plot([x0[0]], [x0[1]], func(x0), "r*")
```

The surface plot of the objective function, along with the initial value, can be seen in the following image:

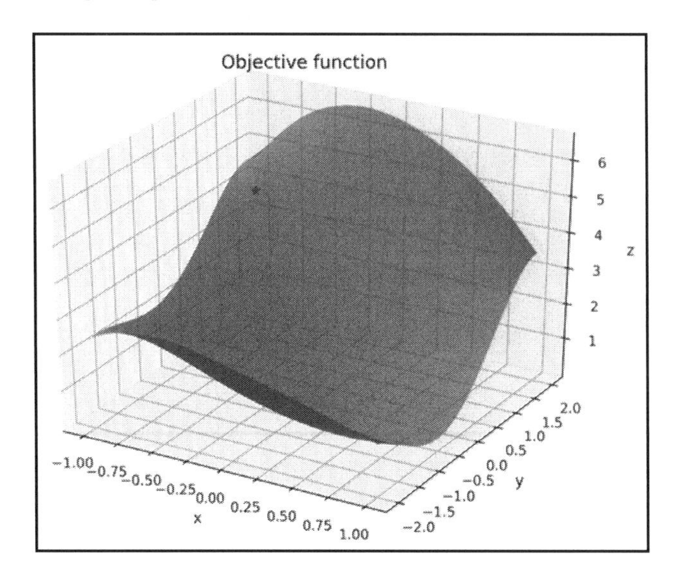

Figure 9.5: Surface of the objective function with the initial position

12. Our `descend` routine requires a function that evaluates the gradient of the objective function, so we will define one:

```
def grad(x):
    c1 = x[0]**2 - x[0] + x[1]**2 + x[1] + 0.5
    cos_t = np.cos(0.5*x[0]*x[1])
    sin_t = np.sin(0.5*x[0]*x[1])
    return np.array([
        (2*x[0]-1)*cos_t - 0.5*x[1]*c1*sin_t,
        (2*x[1]+1)*cos_t - 0.5*x[0]*c1*sin_t
    ])
```

13. We will plot the iterations on a contour plot, so we set this up as follows:

```
cont_fig, cont_ax = plt.subplots()
cont_ax.set(xlabel="x", ylabel="y")
cont_ax.set_title("Contour plot with iterates")
cont_ax.contour(x, y, z, levels=30)
```

14. Now, we create a variable that holds the bounds in the x and y directions as a tuple of tuples. These are the same bounds from the `linspace` calls in *step 10*:

```
bounds = ((-1, 1), (-2, 2))
```

15. We can now use a `for` loop to drive the `descend` generator to produce each of the iterations and add the steps to the contour plot:

```
xnm1 = x0
for i, xn, fxn, grad_xn in descend(func, x0, grad, bounds):
    cont_ax.plot([xnm1[0], xn[0]], [xnm1[1], xn[1]], "k*--")
    xnm1, grad_xnm1 = xn, grad_xn
```

16. Once the loop is complete, we print the final values to the Terminal:

```
print(f"iterations={i}")
print(f"min val at {xn}")
print(f"min func value = {fxn}")
```

The output of the preceding print statements is as follows:

```
iterations=37
min val at [ 0.49999999 -0.49999999]
min func value = 2.1287163880894953e-16
```

Here, we can see that our routine used 37 iterations to find a minimum at approximately (0.5, -0.5), which is correct.

The contour plot with its iterations plotted can be seen in the following image:

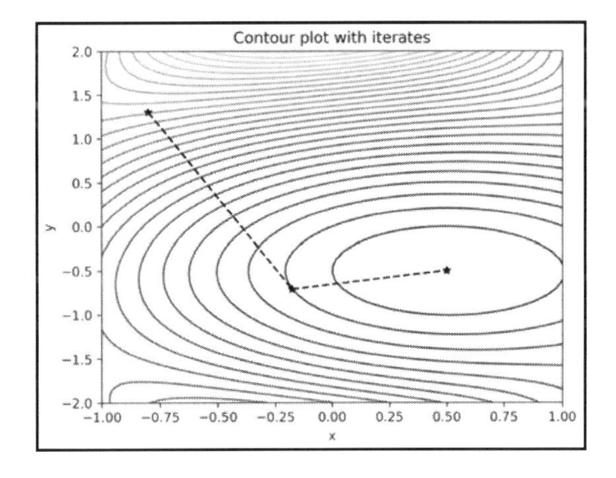

Figure 9.6: Contour plot of the objective function with gradient descent iterating to a minimum value

Here, we can see that the direction of each iteration – shown by the dashed lines – is in the direction where the objective function is decreasing most rapidly. The final iteration lies at the center of the "bowl" of the objective function, which is where the minimum occurs.

How it works...

The heart of this recipe is the `descend` routine. The process that's defined in this routine is a very simple implementation of the gradient descent method. Computing the gradient at a given point is handled by the `grad` argument, and is then used to deduce the direction of travel for the iteration by taking `direction = -grad`. We multiply this direction by a fixed scale factor (sometimes called the **learning rate**) with a value of 0.2 to obtain the scaled step, and then take this step by adding `0.2*direction` to the current position.

The solution in the recipe took 37 iterations to converge, which is a mild improvement on the Nelder-Mead simplex algorithm from the *Minimizing a non-linear function* recipe, which took 58 iterations. (This is not a perfect comparison since we changed the starting position for this recipe.) This performance is heavily dependent on the step size that we choose. In this case, we fixed the maximum step size to be 0.2 times the size of the direction vector. This keeps the algorithm simple, but it is not particularly efficient.

In this recipe, we chose to implement the algorithm as a generator function so that we could see the output of each step and plot this on our contour plot as we stepped through the iteration. In practice, we probably wouldn't want to do this and instead return the calculated minimum once the iterations have finished. To do this, we can simply remove the `yield` statement and replace it with `return xn` at the very end of the function, at the main function's indentation (that is, not inside the loop). If you want to guard against non-convergence, you can use the `else` feature of the `for` loop to catch cases where the loop finishes because it has reached the end of its iterator without hitting the `break` keyword. This `else` block could raise an exception to indicate that the algorithm has failed to stabilize to a solution. The condition we used to end the iteration in this recipe does not guarantee that the method has reached a minimum, but this will usually be the case.

There's more...

In practice, you would not usually implement the gradient descent algorithm for yourself and instead use a general-purpose routine from a library such as the SciPy `optimize` module. We can use the same `minimize` routine that we used in the previous recipe to perform minimization with a variety of different algorithms, including several gradient descent algorithms. These implementations are likely to have much higher performance and be more robust than a custom implementation such as this.

The gradient descent method we used in this recipe is a very naive implementation and can be greatly improved by allowing the routine to choose the step size at each step. (Methods that are allowed to choose their own step size are sometimes called adaptive methods.) The difficult part of this improvement is choosing the size of the step to take in this direction. For this, we need to consider the function of a single variable, which is given by the following equation:

$$g(t) = f(\mathbf{x}_n + t\mathbf{d}_n)$$

Here, $\mathbf{x}_n$ represents the current point, $\mathbf{d}_n$ represents the current direction, and t is a parameter. For simplicity, we can use a minimization routine called `minimize_scalar` for scalar-valued functions from the SciPy `optimize` module. Unfortunately, it is not quite as simple as passing in this auxiliary function and finding the minimum value. We have to bound the possible value of t so that the computed minimizing point, $\mathbf{x}_n + t\mathbf{d}_n$, lies within the region that we are interested in.

To understand how we bound the values of t, we must first look at the construction geometrically. The auxiliary function that we introduce evaluates the objective function along a single line in the given direction. We can picture this as taking a single cross-section through the surface that passes through the current $\mathbf{x}_n$ point in the $\mathbf{d}_n$ direction. The next step of the algorithm is finding the step size, t, that minimizes the values of the objective function along this line – this is a scalar function, which is much easier to minimize. The bounds should then be the range of t values during which this line lies within the rectangle defined by the x and y boundary values. We determine the four values at which this line crosses those x and y boundary lines, two of which will be negative and two of which will be positive. (This is because the current point must lie within the rectangle.) We take the minimum of the two positive values and the maximum of the two negative values and pass these bounds to the scalar minimization routine. This is achieved using the following code:

```
alphas = np.array([
        (bounds[0][0] - xn[0]) / direction[0], # x lower
        (bounds[1][0] - xn[1]) / direction[1], # y lower
        (bounds[0][1] - xn[0]) / direction[0], # x upper
```

```
        (bounds[1][1] - xn[1]) / direction[1] # y upper
])

alpha_max = alphas[alphas >= 0].min()
alpha_min = alphas[alphas < 0].max()
result = minimize_scalar(lambda t: func(xn + t*direction),
        method="bounded", bounds=(alpha_min, alpha_max))
amount = result.x
```

Once the step size has been chosen, the only remaining step is to update the current `xn` value, as follows:

```
xn = xn + amount * direction
```

Using this adaptive step size increases the complexity of the routine, but the performance is massively improved. Using this revised routine, the method converged in just three iterations, which is far fewer than the number of iterations used by the naive code in this recipe (37 iterations) or by the Nelder-Mead simplex algorithm in the previous recipe (58 iterations). This reduction in the number of iterations is exactly what we expected by providing the method with more information in the form of the gradient function.

We created a function that returned the gradient of the function at a given point. We computed this gradient by hand before we started, which will not always be easy or even possible. Instead, it is much more common to replace the "analytic" gradient used here with a numerically computed gradient that's been estimated using finite differences or a similar algorithm. This has an impact on performance and accuracy, as all approximations do, but these concerns are usually minor given the improvement in the speed of convergence offered by gradient descent methods.

Gradient descent type algorithms are particularly popular in machine learning applications. Most of the popular Python machine learning libraries – including PyTorch, TensorFlow, and Theano – offer utilities for automatically computing gradients numerically for data arrays. This allows gradient descent methods to be used in the background to improve performance.

A popular variation of the gradient descent method is **stochastic gradient descent**, where the gradient is estimated by sampling randomly rather than using the whole set of data. This can dramatically reduce the computational burden of the method – at the cost of slower convergence – especially for high-dimensional problems such as those that are common in machine learning applications. Stochastic gradient descent methods are often combined with backpropagation to form the basis for training artificial neural networks in machine learning applications.

There are several extensions of the basic stochastic gradient descent algorithm. For example, the momentum algorithm incorporates the previous increment into the calculation of the next increment. Another example is the adaptive gradient algorithm, which incorporates per-parameter learning rates to improve the rate of convergence for problems that involve a large number of sparse parameters.

Using least squares to fit a curve to data

Least squares is a powerful technique for finding a function from a relatively small family of potential functions that best describe a particular set of data. This technique is especially common in statistics. For example, least squares is used in linear regression problems – here, the family of potential functions is the collection of all linear functions. Usually, this family of functions that we try to fit has relatively few parameters that can be adjusted to solve the problem.

The idea of least squares is relatively simple. For each data point, we compute the square of the residual – the difference between the value of the point and the expected value given a function – and try to make the sum of these squared residuals as small as possible (hence least squares).

In this recipe, we'll learn how to use least squares to fit a curve to a sample set of data.

Getting ready

For this recipe, we will need the NumPy package imported, as usual, as `np`, and the Matplotlib `pyplot` module imported as `plt`:

```
import numpy as np
import matplotlib.pyplot as plt
```

We will also need an instance of the default random number generator from the NumPy `random` module imported, as follows:

```
from numy.random import default_rng
rng = default_rng(12345)
```

Finally, we need the `curve_fit` routine form the SciPy `optimize` module:

```
from scipy.optimize import curve_fit
```

How to do it...

The following steps show you how to use the `curve_fit` routine to fit a curve to a set of data:

1. The first step is to create the sample data:

```
SIZE = 100
x_data = rng.uniform(-3.0, 3.0, size=SIZE)
noise = rng.normal(0.0, 0.8, size=SIZE)
y_data = 2.0*x_data**2 - 4*x_data + noise
```

2. Next, we produce a scatter plot of the data to see if we can identify the underlying trend in the data:

```
fig, ax = plt.subplots()
ax.scatter(x_data, y_data)
ax.set(xlabel="x", ylabel="y", title="Scatter plot of sample data")
```

The scatter plot that we have produced can be seen in the following image. Here, we can see that the data certainly doesn't follow a linear trend (straight line). Since we know the trend is a polynomial, our next guess would be a quadratic trend. This is what we're using here:

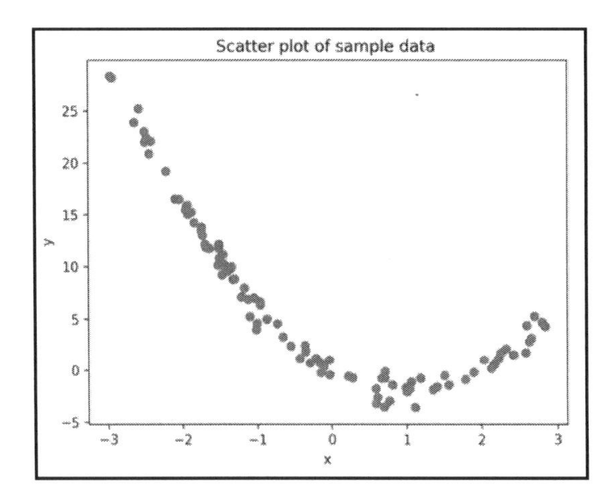

Figure 9.7: Scatter plot of the sample data. We can see that the data does not follow a linear trend

3. Next, we create a function that represents the model that we wish to fit:

```
def func(x, a, b, c):
    return a*x**2 + b*x + c
```

4. Now, we can use the `curve_fit` routine to fit the model function to the sample data:

```
coeffs, _ = curve_fit(func, x_data, y_data)
print(coeffs)
# [ 1.99611157 -3.97522213 0.04546998]
```

5. Finally, we plot the best fit curve on top of the scatter plot to evaluate how well the fitted curve describes the data:

```
x = np.linspace(-3.0, 3.0, SIZE)
y = func(x, coeffs[0], coeffs[1], coeffs[2])
ax.plot(x, y, "k--")
```

The updated scatter plot can be seen in the following image:

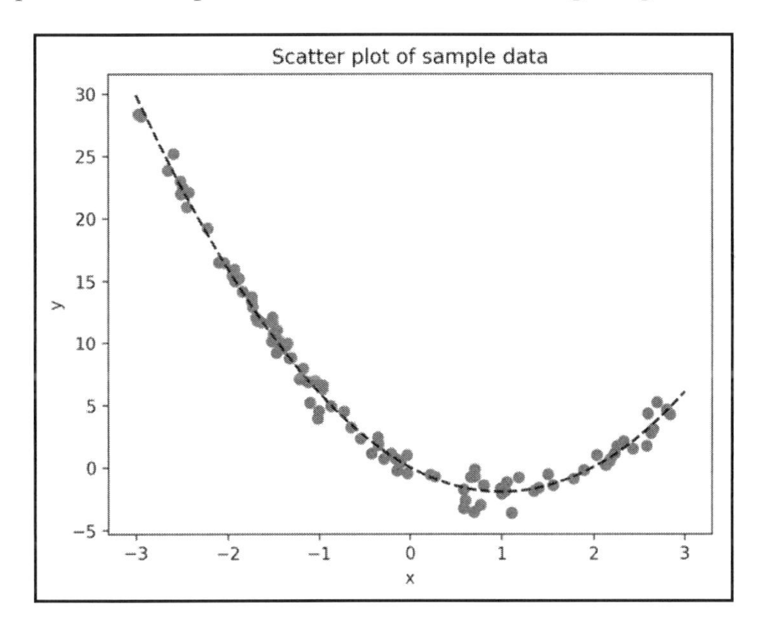

Figure 9.8: Scatter plot with the curve of best fit found using least-squares superimposed

Here, we can see that the curve we have found fits the data reasonably well.

How it works...

The `curve_fit` routine performs least-squares fitting to fit the model's curve to the sample data. In practice, this amounts to minimizing the following objective function:

$$\phi(a, b, c) = \sum_{i=0}^{99} (y_i - ax_i^2 - bx_i - c)^2$$

Here, the pairs (x_i, y_i) are the points from the sample data. In this case, we are optimizing over a three-dimensional parameter space, with one dimension for each of the parameters. The routine returns the estimated coefficients – the point in the parameter space at which the objective function is minimized – and a second variable that contains estimates for the covariance matrix for the fit. We ignored this in this recipe.

The estimated covariance matrix that's returned from the `curve_fit` routine can be used to give a confidence interval for the estimated parameters. This is done by taking the square root of the diagonal elements divided by sample size (100 in this recipe). This gives the standard error for the estimate that, when multiplied by the appropriate values corresponding to the confidence, gives us the size of the confidence interval. (We discussed confidence intervals in `Chapter 6`, *Working with Data and Statistics*.)

You might have noticed that the parameters estimated by the `curve_fit` routine are close, but not exactly equal, to the parameters that we used to define the sample data in *step 1*. The fact that these are not exactly equal is due to the normally distributed noise that we added to the data. In this recipe, we knew that the underlying structure of the data was quadratic – that is, a degree 2 polynomial – and not some other, more esoteric, function. In practice, we are unlikely to know so much about the underlying structure of the data, which is the reason we added noise to the sample.

There's more...

There is another routine in the SciPy `optimize` module for performing least-squares fitting called `least_squares`. This routine has a slightly less intuitive signature but does return a results object with more information about the optimization process. However, the way this routine is set up is perhaps more similar to the way that we constructed the underlying mathematical problem in the *How it works...* section. To use this routine, we define the objective function as follows:

```
def func(params, x, y):
    return y - (params[0]*x**2 + params[1]*x + params[2])
```

We pass this function along with a starting estimate in the parameter space, `x0`, such as `(1, 0, 0)`. The additional parameters for the objective function, `func`, can be passed using the `args` keyword argument; for example, we could use `args=(x_data, y_data)`. These arguments are passed into the `x` and `y` arguments of the objective function. To summarize, we could have estimated the parameters using the following call to `least_squares`:

```
results = least_squares(func, [1, 0, 0], args=(x_data, y_data))
```

The `results` object that's returned from the `least_squares` routine is actually the same as the one returned by the other optimization routines described in this chapter. It contains details such as the number of iterations used, whether the process was successful, detailed error messages, the parameter values, and the value of the objective function at the minimum value.

Analyzing simple two-player games

Game theory is a branch of mathematics concerned with the analysis of decision-making and strategy. It has applications in economics, biology, and behavioral science. Many seemingly complex situations can be reduced to a relatively simple mathematical game that can be analyzed in a systematic way to find "optimal" solutions.

A classic problem in game theory is the *prisoner's dilemma*, which, in its original form, is as follows: two co-conspirators are caught and must decide whether to remain quiet or to testify against the other. If both remain quiet, they both serve a 1-year sentence; if one testifies but the other does not, the testifier is released and the other serves a 3-year sentence; and if both testify against one another, they both serve a 2-year sentence. What should each conspirator do? It turns out that the best choice each conspirator can make, given any reasonable distrust of the other, is to testify. Adopting this strategy, they will either serve no sentence or a 2-year sentence maximum.

Since this book is about Python, we will use a variation of this classic problem to illustrate just how universal the idea of this problem is. Consider the following problem: you and your colleague have to write some code for a client. You think that you could write the code faster in Python, but your colleague thinks that they could write it faster in C. The question is, which language should you choose for the project?

You think that you could write the Python code 4 times faster than in C, so you write C with speed 1 and Python with speed 4. Your colleague says that they can write C slightly faster than Python, so they write C with speed 3 and Python with speed 2. If you both agree on a language, then you write the code at the speed you predicted, but if you disagree, then the productivity of the faster programmer is reduced by 1. We can summarize this as follows:

Colleague/You	**C**	**Python**
C	3 / 1	3 / 2
Python	2 / 1	2 / 4

In this recipe, we will learn how to construct an object in Python to represent this simple two-player game, and then perform some elementary analysis regarding the outcomes of this game.

Getting ready

For this recipe, we will need the NumPy package imported as `np`, and the Nashpy package imported as `nash`:

```
import numpy as np
import nashpy as nash
```

How to do it...

The following steps show you how to create and perform some simple analysis of a two-player game using Nashpy:

1. First, we need to create matrices that hold the payoff information for each player (you and your colleague, in this example):

    ```
    you = np.array([[1, 3], [1, 4]])
    colleague = np.array([[3, 2], [2, 2]])
    ```

2. Next, we create a `Game` object that holds the game represented by these payoff matrices:

    ```
    dilemma = nash.Game(you, colleague)
    ```

3. We compute the utility for the given choices using index notation:

```
print(dilemma[[1, 0], [1, 0]])  # [1 3]
print(dilemma[[1, 0], [0, 1]])  # [3 2]
print(dilemma[[0, 1], [1, 0]])  # [1 2]
print(dilemma[[0, 1], [0, 1]])  # [4 2]
```

4. We can also compute the expected utilities based on the probabilities of making a specific choice:

```
print(dilemma[[0.1, 0.9], [0.5, 0.5]]) # [2.45 2.05]
```

How it works...

In this recipe, we built a Python object that represents a very simple two-player strategic game. The idea here is that there are two "players" who have decisions to make, and each combination of both player's choices gives a specific payoff value. What we're aiming to do here is find the best choice that each player can make. The players are assumed to make a single move simultaneously, in the sense that neither is aware of the other's choice. Each player has a strategy that determines the choice they make.

In *step 1*, we create two matrices – one for each player – that are assigned to each combination of choices for the payoff value. These two matrices are wrapped by the `Game` class from Nashpy, which provides a convenient and intuitive (from a game-theoretic point of view) interface for working with games. We can quickly calculate the utility of a given combination of choices by passing in the choices using index notation.

We can also provide calculate expected utilities based on a strategy where choices are chosen at random according to some probability distribution. The syntax is the same as for the deterministic case described previously, except we provide a vector of probabilities for each choice. We compute the expected utilities based on the probability that you choose Python 90% of the time, while your colleague chooses Python 50% of the time. The expected speeds are 2.45 and 2.05 for you and your colleague, respectively.

There's more...

There is an alternative to computational game theory in Python. The Gambit project is a collection of tools that's used for computation in game theory that has a Python interface (`http://www.gambit-project.org/`). This is a mature project built around C libraries and offers more performance than Nashpy.

Computing Nash equilibria

A *Nash equilibrium* is a two-player strategic game – similar to the one we saw in the *Analyzing simple two-player games* recipe – that represents a "steady state" in which every player sees the "best possible" outcome. However, this doesn't mean that the outcome linked to a Nash equilibrium is the best overall. Nash equilibria are more subtle than this. An informal definition of a Nash equilibrium is as follows: an action profile in which no individual player can improve their outcome, assuming that all other players adhere to the profile.

We will explore the notion of a Nash equilibrium with the classic game of rock-paper-scissors. The rules are as follows. Each player can choose one of the options: rock, paper, or scissors. Rock beats scissors, but loses to paper; paper beats rock, but loses to scissors; scissors beats paper, but loses to rock. Any game in which both players make the same choice is a draw. Numerically, we represent a win by +1, a loss by -1, and a draw by 0. From this, we can construct a two-player game and compute Nash equilibria for this game.

In this recipe, we will compute Nash equilibria for the classic game of rock-paper-scissors.

Getting ready

For this recipe, we will need the NumPy package imported as `np`, and the Nashpy package imported as `nash`:

```
import numpy as np
import nashpy as nash
```

How to do it...

The following steps show you how to compute Nash equilibria for a simple two-player game:

1. First, we need to create a payoff matrix for each player. We will start with the first player:

```
rps_p1 = np.array([
    [ 0, -1,  1],  # rock payoff
    [ 1,  0, -1],   # paper payoff
    [-1,  1,  0]   # scissors payoff
])
```

2. The payoff matrix for the second player is the transpose of `rps_p1`:

```
rps_p2 = rps_p1.transpose()
```

3. Next, we create the `Game` object to represent the game:

```
rock_paper_scissors = nash.Game(rps_p1, rps_p2)
```

4. We compute the Nash equilibria for the game using the support enumeration algorithm:

```
equilibria = rock_paper_scissors.support_enumeration()
```

5. We iterate over the equilibria and print the profile for each player:

```
for p1, p2 in equilibria:
    print("Player 1", p1)
    print("Player 2", p2)
```

The output of these print statements is as follows:

```
Player 1 [0.33333333 0.33333333 0.33333333]
Player 2 [0.33333333 0.33333333 0.33333333]
```

How it works...

Nash equilibria are extremely important in game theory because they allow us to analyze the outcomes of strategic games and identify advantageous positions. They were first described by John F. Nash in 1950, and have played a pivotal role in modern game theory. A two-player game may have many Nash equilibria, but any finite two-player game must have at least one. The problem is finding all the possible Nash equilibria for a given game.

In this recipe, we used the support enumeration, which effectively enumerates all possible strategies and filters down to those that are Nash equilibria. In this recipe, the support enumeration algorithm found just one Nash equilibrium, which is a mixed strategy. This means that the only strategy for which there is no improvement involves picking one of the choices at random, each with a 1/3 probability. This is hardly a surprise to anyone who has played rock-paper-scissors since for any choice we make, our opponent has a 1 in 3 chance of choosing (at random) the move that beats our choice. Equally, we have a 1 in 3 chance of drawing or winning the game, so our expected value over all these possibilities is as follows:

$$\frac{1}{3} \times 0 + \frac{1}{3} \times 1 + \frac{1}{3} \times (-1) = 0$$

Without knowing exactly which of the choices our opponent will choose, there is no way to improve this expected outcome.

There's more...

The Nashpy package also provides other algorithms for computing Nash equilibria. Specifically, the `vertex_enumeration` method, when used on a `Game` object, uses the *vertex enumeration* algorithm, while the `lemke_howson_enumeration` method uses the *Lemke Howson* algorithm. These alternative algorithms have different characteristics and may be more efficient for some problems.

See also

The documentation for the Nashpy package contains more detailed information about the algorithms and game theory involved. This includes a number of references to texts on game theory. This documentation can be found at `https://nashpy.readthedocs.io/en/latest/`.

Further reading

As usual, the *Numerical Recipes* book is a good source of numerical algorithms. `Chapter 10`, *Miscellaneous Topics*, deals with the maximization and minimization of functions:

- *Press, W.H., Teukolsky, S.A., Vetterling, W.T., and Flannery, B.P., 2017. Numerical recipes: the art of scientific computing. 3rd ed. Cambridge: Cambridge University Press.*

More specific information on optimization can be found in the following books:

- *Boyd, S.P. and Vandenberghe, L., 2018. Convex optimization. Cambridge: Cambridge University Press.*
- *Griva, I., Nash, S., and Sofer, A., 2009. Linear and nonlinear optimization. 2nd ed. Philadelphia: Society for Industrial and Applied Mathematics.*

Finally, the following book is a good introduction to game theory:

- *Osborne, M.J., 2017. An introduction to game theory. Oxford: Oxford University Press.*

10
Miscellaneous Topics

In this chapter, we will look at several topics that don't fit within the categories that we discussed in the previous chapters of this book. Most of these topics are concerned with different ways to facilitate computing and otherwise optimize the execution of our code. Others concern working with specific kinds of data or file formats.

In the first two recipes, we will cover packages that help keep track of units and uncertainties in calculations. These are very important for calculations that concern data that have a direct physical application. In the next recipe, we will look at loading and storing data from NetCDF files. NetCDF is a file format usually used for storing weather and climate data. (NetCDF stands for **network common data form**.) In the fourth recipe, we'll discuss working with geographical data, such as data that might be associated with weather or climate data. After that, we'll discuss how we can run Jupyter notebooks from the terminal without having to start up an interactive session. The next two recipes deal with validating data and working with data streamed from a Kafka server. Our final two recipes deal with two different ways we can accelerate our code using tools such as Cython and Dask.

In this chapter, we will cover the following recipes:

- Keeping track of units with Pint
- Accounting for uncertainties in calculations
- Loading and storing data from NetCDF files
- Working with geographical data
- Executing Jupyter notebooks as a script
- Validating data
- Working with data streams
- Accelerating code with Cython
- Distributing computation with Dask

Let's get started!

Technical requirements

This chapter requires many different packages due to the nature of the recipes it contains. The list of packages we need is as follows:

- Pint
- uncertainties
- NetCDF4
- xarray
- GeoPandas
- Geoplot
- Papermill
- Cerberus
- Faust
- Cython
- Dask

All of these packages can be installed using your favorite package manager, such as `pip`:

```
python3.8 -m pip install pint uncertainties netCDF4 xarray geopandas
    geoplot papermill cerberus faust cython
```

To install the Dask package, we need to install the various extras associated with the package. We can do this using the following `pip` command in the terminal:

```
python3.8 -m pip install dask[complete]
```

In addition to these Python packages, we will also need to install some supporting software. For the *Working with geographical data* recipe, the GeoPandas and Geoplot libraries have numerous lower-level dependencies that might need to be installed separately. Detailed instructions are given in the GeoPandas package documentation at `https://geopandas.org/install.html`.

For the *Working with streaming data* recipe, we will need to install the Kafka server. Detailed instructions on how to install and run a Kafka server can be found on the Apache Kafka documentation pages at `https://kafka.apache.org/quickstart`.

For the *Accelerating code with Cython* recipe, we will need to have a C compiler installed. Instructions on how to obtain the **GNU C compiler** (**GCC**) are given in the Cython documentation at `https://cython.readthedocs.io/en/latest/src/quickstart/install.html`.

The code for this chapter can be found in the `Chapter 10` folder of the GitHub repository at `https://github.com/PacktPublishing/Applying-Math-with-Python/tree/master/Chapter%2010`.

Check out the following video to see the Code in Action: `https://bit.ly/2ZMjQVw`.

Keeping track of units with Pint

Correctly keeping track of units in calculations can be very difficult, particularly if there are places where different units can be used. For example, it is very easy to forget to convert between different units – feet/inches into meters – or metric prefixes – converting 1 km into 1,000 m, for instance.

In this recipe, we'll learn how to use the Pint package to keep track of units of measurement in calculations.

Getting ready

For this recipe, we need the Pint package, which can be imported as follows:

```
import pint
```

How to do it...

The following steps show you how to use the Pint package to keep track of units in calculations:

1. First, we need to create a `UnitRegistry` object:

```
ureg = pint.UnitRegistry(system="mks")
```

2. To create a quantity with a unit, we multiply the number by the appropriate attribute of the registry object:

```
distance = 5280 * ureg.feet
```

3. We can change the units of the quantity using one of the available conversion methods:

```
print(distance.to("miles"))
print(distance.to_base_units())
print(distance.to_base_units().to_compact())
```

The output of these `print` statements is as follows:

```
0.9999999999999999 mile
1609.3439999999998 meter
1.6093439999999999 kilometer
```

4. We wrap a routine to make it expect an argument in seconds and output a result in meters:

```
@ureg.wraps(ureg.meter, ureg.second)
def calc_depth(dropping_time):
    # s = u*t + 0.5*a*t*t
    # u = 0, a = 9.81
    return 0.5*9.81*dropping_time*dropping_time
```

5. Now, when we call the `calc_depth` routine with a minute unit, it is automatically converted into seconds for the calculation:

```
depth = calc_depth(0.05 * ureg.minute)
print("Depth", depth)
# Depth 44.144999999999996 meter
```

How it works...

The Pint package provides a wrapper class for numerical types that adds unit metadata to the type. This wrapper type implements all the standard arithmetic operations and keeps track of the units throughout these calculations. For example, when we divide a length unit by a time unit, we will get a speed unit. This means that you can use Pint to make sure the units are correct after a complex calculation.

The `UnitRegistry` object keeps track of all the units that are present in the session and handles things such as conversion between different unit types. It also maintains a reference system of measurements, which in this recipe is the standard international system with meters, kilograms, and seconds as base units, denoted `mks`.

The `wrap` functionality allows us to declare the input and output units of a routine, which allows Pint to do automatic unit conversions for the input function – in this recipe, we converted from minutes into seconds. Trying to call a wrapped function with a quantity that does not have an associated unit, or an incompatible unit, will raise an exception. This allows runtime validation of parameters and automatic conversion into the correct units for a routine.

There's more...

The Pint package comes with a large list of preprogrammed units of measurement that cover most globally used systems. Units can be defined at runtime or loaded from a file. This means that you can define custom units or systems of units that are specific to the application that you are working with.

Units can also be used within different contexts, which allows for easy conversion between different unit types that would ordinarily be unrelated. This can save a lot of time in situations where you need to move between units fluidly at multiple points in a calculation.

Accounting for uncertainty in calculations

Most measuring devices are not 100% accurate and instead are accurate up to a certain amount, usually somewhere between 0 and 10%. For instance, a thermometer might be accurate to 1%, while a pair of digital calipers might be accurate up to 0.1%. The true value in both of these cases is unlikely to be exactly the reported value, although it will be fairly close. Keeping track of the uncertainty in a value is difficult, especially when you have multiple different uncertainties combined in different ways. Rather than keeping track of this by hand, it is much better to use a consistent library to do this for you. This is what the `uncertainties` package does.

In this recipe, we will learn how to quantify the uncertainty of variables and see how these uncertainties propagate through a calculation.

Getting ready

For this recipe, we will need the `uncertainties` package, from which we will import the `ufloat` class and the `umath` module:

```
from uncertainties import ufloat, umath
```

How to do it...

The following steps show you how to quantify uncertainty on numerical values in calculations:

1. First, we create an uncertain float value of `3.0` plus or minus `0.4`:

   ```
   seconds = ufloat(3.0, 0.4)
   print(seconds)   # 3.0+/-0.4
   ```

2. Next, we perform a calculation involving this uncertain value to obtain a new uncertain value:

   ```
   depth = 0.5*9.81*seconds*seconds
   print(depth)   # 44+/-12
   ```

3. Next, we create a new uncertain float value and apply the `sqrt` routine from the `umath` module in the reverse of the previous calculation:

```
other_depth = ufloat(44, 12)
time = umath.sqrt(2.0*other_depth/9.81)
print("Estimated time", time)
# Estimated time 3.0+/-0.4
```

How it works...

The `ufloat` class wraps around `float` objects and keeps track of the uncertainty throughout calculations. The library makes use of linear error propagation theory, which uses derivatives of non-linear functions, to estimate the propagated error during calculations. The library also correctly handles correlation so that subtracting a value from itself gives 0 with no error.

To keep track of uncertainties in standard mathematical functions, you need to use the versions that are provided in the `umath` module, rather than those defined in the Python Standard Library or in a third-party package such as NumPy.

There's more...

The `uncertainties` package provides support for NumPy, and the Pint package mentioned in the previous recipe can be combined with uncertainties to make sure that units and error margins are correctly attributed to the final value of a calculation. For example, we could compute the units in the calculation from *step 2* of this recipe, as follows:

```
import pint
from uncertainties import ufloat
g = 9.81*ureg.meters / ureg.seconds ** 2
seconds = ufloat(3.0, 0.4) * ureg.seconds

depth = 0.5*g*seconds**2
print(depth)
```

As expected, the `print` statement on the last line gives us `44+/-12 meter`, as we expect.

Loading and storing data from NetCDF files

Many scientific applications require that we start large quantities of multi-dimensional data in a robust format. NetCDF is one example of a format used for data that's developed by the weather and climate industry. Unfortunately, the complexity of the data means that we can't simply use the utilities from the Pandas package, for example, to load this data for analysis. We need the `netcdf4` package to be able to read and import the data into Python, but we also need to use `xarray`. Unlike the Pandas library, `xarray` can handle higher-dimensional data while still providing a Pandas-like interface.

In this recipe, we will learn how to load data from and store data in NetCDF files.

Getting ready

For this recipe, we will need to import the NumPy package as `np`, the Pandas package as `pd`, the Matplotlib `pyplot` module as `plt`, and an instance of the default random number generator from NumPy:

```
import numpy as np
import pandas as pd
import matplotlib.pyplot as plt
from numpy.random import default_rng
rng = default_rng(12345)
```

We also need to import the `xarray` package under the alias `xr`. You will also need to install the Dask package, as described in the *Technical requirements* section, and the NetCDF4 package:

```
import xarray as xr
```

We don't need to import either of these packages directly.

How to do it...

Follow these steps to load and store sample data in a NetCDF file:

1. First, we need to create some random data. This data consists of a range of dates, a list of location codes, and randomly generated numbers:

```
dates = pd.date_range("2020-01-01", periods=365, name="date")
locations = list(range(25))
steps = rng.normal(0, 1, size=(365,25))
accumulated = np.add.accumulate(steps)
```

2. Next, we create an xarray `Dataset` object containing the data. The dates and locations are indexes, while the `steps` and `accumulated` variables are the data:

```
data_array = xr.Dataset({
    "steps": (("date", "location"), steps),
    "accumulated": (("date", "location"), accumulated)
    },
    {"location": locations, "date": dates}
)
print(data_array)
```

The output from the `print` statement is shown here:

```
<xarray.Dataset>
Dimensions: (date: 365, location: 25)
Coordinates:
* location (location) int64 0 1 2 3 4 5 6 7 8 ... 17 18 19 20 21 22
23 24
* date (date) datetime64[ns] 2020-01-01 2020-01-02 ... 2020-12-30
Data variables:
steps (date, location) float64 geoplot.pointplot(cities, ax=ax,
fc="r", marker="2")
ax.axis((-180, 180, -90, 90))-1.424 1.264 ... -0.4547 -0.4873
accumulated (date, location) float64 -1.424 1.264 -0.8707 ... 8.935
-3.525
```

3. Next, we compute the mean over all the locations at each time index:

```
means = data_array.mean(dim="location")
```

4. Now, we plot the mean accumulated values on a new set of axes:

```
fig, ax = plt.subplots()
means["accumulated"].to_dataframe().plot(ax=ax)
ax.set(title="Mean accumulated values", xlabel="date",
ylabel="value")
```

The resulting plot looks as follows:

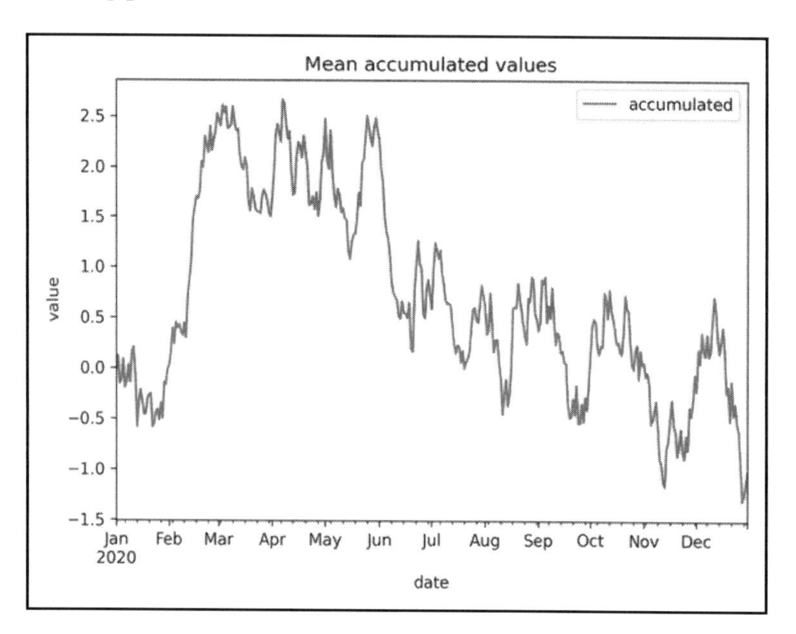

Figure 10.1: Plot of accumulated means over time

5. Save this dataset into a new NetCDF file using the `to_netcdf` method:

```
data_array.to_netcdf("data.nc")
```

6. Now, we can load the newly created NetCDF file using the `load_dataset` routine from `xarray`:

```
new_data = xr.load_dataset("data.nc")
print(new_data)
```

The output of the preceding code is as follows:

```
<xarray.Dataset>
Dimensions: (date: 365, location: 25)
Coordinates:
  * location (location) int64 0 1 2 3 4 5 6 7 8 ... 17 18 19 20 21
22 23 24
  * date (date) datetime64[ns] 2020-01-01 2020-01-02 ... 2020-12-30
Data variables:
    steps (date, location) float64 -1.424 1.264 ... -0.4547 -0.4873
    accumulated (date, location) float64 -1.424 1.264 -0.8707 ...
8.935 -3.525
```

How it works...

The `xarray` package provides the `DataArray` and `DataSet` classes, which are (roughly speaking) multi-dimensional equivalents of the Pandas `Series` and `DataFrame` objects. We're using a dataset in this example because each index – a tuple of a date and location – has two pieces of data associated with it. Both of these objects expose a similar interface to their Pandas equivalents. For example, we can compute the mean along one of the axes using the `mean` method. The `DataArray` and `DataSet` objects also have a convenience method for converting into a Pandas `DataFrame` called `to_dataframe`. We used it in this recipe to convert to a `DataFrame` for plotting, which isn't really necessary because `xarray` has plotting features built into it.

The real focus of this recipe is on the `to_netcdf` method and the `load_dataset` routine. The former stores a `DataSet` in NetCDF format file. This requires the NetCDF4 package to be installed as it allows us to access the relevant C library for decoding NetCDF formatted files. The `load_dataset` routine is a general-purpose routine for loading data into a `DataSet` object from various file formats, including NetCDF (again, this requires the NetCDF4 package to be installed).

There's more...

The `xarray` package has support for a number of data formats in addition to NetCDF, such as OPeNDAP, Pickle, GRIB, and other formats that are supported by Pandas.

Working with geographical data

Many applications involve working with geographical data. For example, when tracking global weather, we might want to plot the temperature as measured by various sensors around the world at their position on a map. For this, we can use the GeoPandas package and the Geoplot package, both of which allow us to manipulate, analyze, and visualize geographical data.

In this recipe, we will use the GeoPandas and Geoplot packages to load and visualize some sample geographical data.

Getting ready

For this recipe, we will need the GeoPandas package, the Geoplot package, and the Matplotlib `pyplot` package imported as `plt`:

```
import geopandas
import geoplot
import matplotlib.pyplot as plt
```

How to do it...

Follow these steps to create a simple plot of the capital cities plotted on a map of the world using sample data:

1. First, we need to load the sample data from the GeoPandas package, which contains the world geometry information:

```
world = geopandas.read_file(
        geopandas.datasets.get_path("naturalearth_lowres")
)
```

2. Next, we need to load the data containing the name and position of each of the capital cities of the world:

```
cities = geopandas.read_file(
        geopandas.datasets.get_path("naturalearth_cities")
)
```

3. Now, we can create a new figure and plot the outline of the world geometry using the `polyplot` routine:

```
fig, ax = plt.subplots()
geoplot.polyplot(world, ax=ax)
```

4. Finally, we use the `pointplot` routine to add the positions of the capital cities on top of the world map. We also set the axes limits to make the whole world visible:

```
geoplot.pointplot(cities, ax=ax, fc="r", marker="2")
ax.axis((-180, 180, -90, 90))
```

The resulting plot of the positions of the capital cities of the world looks as follows:

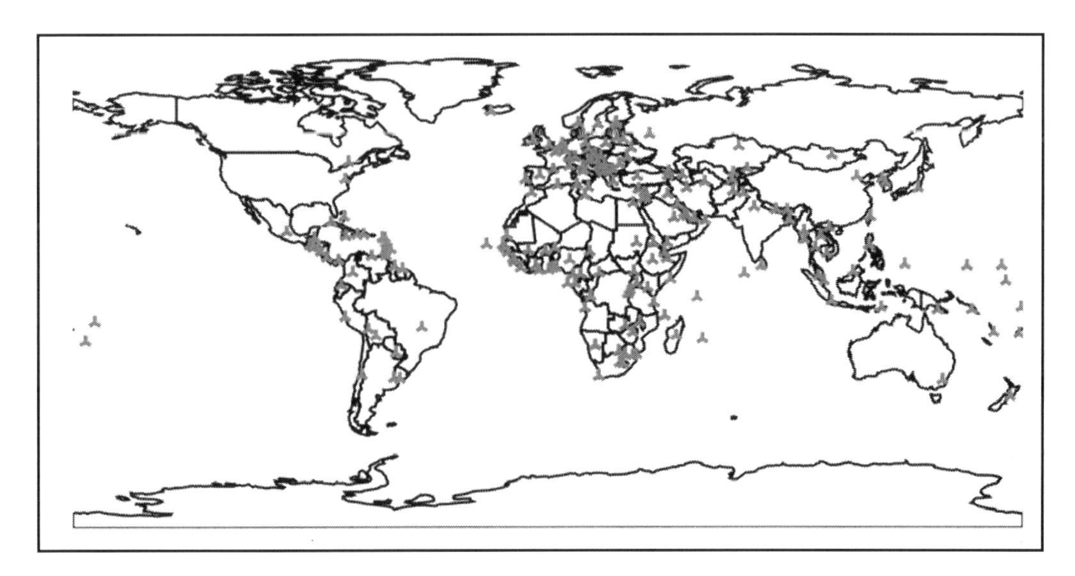

Figure 10.2: Plot of the world's capital cities on a map

How it works...

The GeoPandas package is an extension of Pandas that works with geographical data, while the Geoplot package is an extension of Matplotlib that's used to plot geographical data. The GeoPandas package comes with a selection of sample datasets that we used in this recipe. `naturalearth_lowres` contains geometric figures that describe the boundaries of countries in the world. This data is not very high resolution, as signified by its name, which means that some of the finer details of geographical features might not be present on the map. (Some small islands are not shown at all.) `naturalearth_cities` contains the names and locations of the capital cities of the world. We're using the `datasets.get_path` routine to retrieve the path for these datasets in the package data directory. The `read_file` routine imports the data into the Python session.

The Geoplot package provides some additional plotting routines specifically for plotting geographical data. The `polyplot` routine plots polygonal data from a GeoPandas DataFrame, which might describe the geographical boundaries of a country.
The `pointplot` routine plots discrete points on a set of axes from a GeoPandas DataFrame, which in this case describe the position of capital cities.

Executing a Jupyter notebook as a script

Jupyter notebooks are a popular medium for writing Python code for scientific and data-based applications. A Jupyter notebook is really a sequence of blocks that are stored in a file in **JavaScript Object Notation** (**JSON**) with the `ipynb` extension. Each block can be one of several different types, such as code or markdown. These notebooks are typically accessed through a web application that interprets the blocks and executes the code in a background kernel that then returns the results to the web application. This is great if you are working on a personal PC, but what if you want to run the code contained within a notebook remotely on a server? In this case, it might not even be possible to access the web interface provided by the Jupyter notebook software. The papermill package allows us to parameterize and execute notebooks from the command line.

In this recipe, we'll learn how to execute a Jupyter notebook from the command line using papermill.

Getting ready

For this recipe, we will need to have the papermill package installed, and also have a sample Jupyter notebook in the current directory. We will use the `sample.ipynb` notebook file stored in the code repository for this chapter.

How to do it...

Follow these steps to use the papermill command-line interface to execute a Jupyter notebook remotely:

1. First, we open the sample notebook, `sample.ipynb`, from the code repository for this chapter. The notebook contains three code cells that hold the following code:

```
import matplotlib.pyplot as plt
from numpy.random import default_rng
rng = default_rng(12345)

uniform_data = rng.uniform(-5, 5, size=(2, 100))

fig, ax = plt.subplots(tight_layout=True)
ax.scatter(uniform_data[0, :], uniform_data[1, :])
ax.set(title="Scatter plot", xlabel="x", ylabel="y")
```

2. Next, we open the folder containing the Jupyter notebook in the terminal and use the following command:

```
papermill --kernel python3 sample.ipynb output.ipynb
```

3. Now, we open the output file, `output.ipynb`, which should now contain the notebook that's been updated with the result of the executed code. The scatter plot that's generated in the final block is shown here:

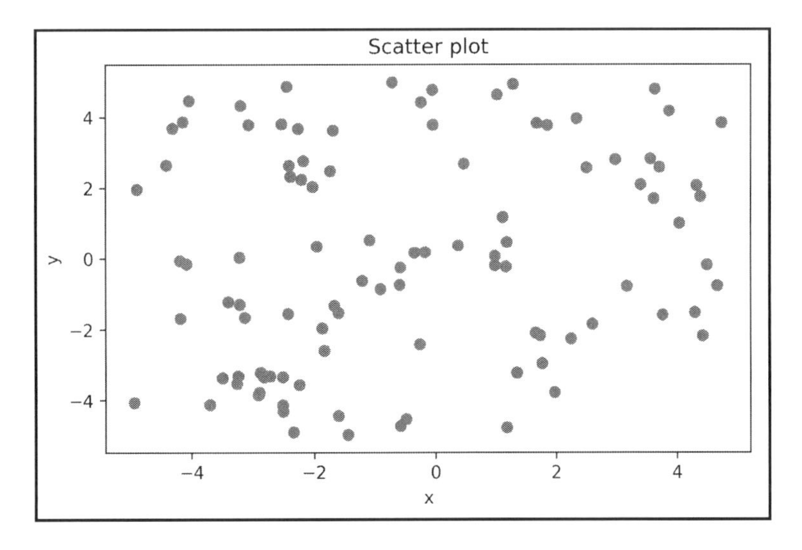

Figure 10.3: Scatter plot of the random data that was generated inside a Jupyter notebook, executed remotely using papermill

How it works...

The papermill package provides a simple command-line interface that interprets and then executes a Jupyter notebook and then stores the results in a new notebook file. In this recipe, we gave the first argument – the input notebook file – `sample.ipynb` and the second argument – the output notebook file – `output.ipynb`. The tool then executes the code contained in the notebook and produces the output. The notebook's file format keeps track of the results of the last run, so these results are added to the output notebook and stored at the desired location. In this recipe, this is a simple local file, but papermill can also store to a cloud location such as **Amazon Web Services** (**AWS**) S3 storage or Azure data storage.

In *step 2*, we added the `--kernel python3` option when using the papermill command-line interface. This option allows us to specify the kernel that is used to execute the Jupyter notebook. This might be necessary to prevent errors if papermill tries to execute the notebook with a different kernel than the one used to write the notebook. A list of available kernels can be found by using the following command in the terminal:

```
jupyter kernelspec list
```

If you get an error when executing a notebook, you could try changing to a different kernel.

There's more...

Papermill also has a Python interface so that you can execute notebooks from within a Python application. This might be useful for building web applications that need to be able to perform long-running calculations on external hardware and where the results need to be stored in the cloud. It also has the ability to provide parameters to a notebook. To do this, we need to create a block in the notebook marked with the parameters tag with the default values. Updated parameters can then be provided through the command-line interface using the `-p` flag, followed by the name of the argument and the value.

Validating data

Data is often presented in a raw form and might contain anomalies or incorrect or malformed data, which will obviously present a problem for later processing and analysis. It is usually a good idea to build a validation step into a processing pipeline. Fortunately, the Cerberus package provides a lightweight and easy to use validation tool for Python.

For validation, we have to define a *schema*, which is a technical description of what the data should look like and the checks that should be performed on the data. For example, we can check the type and place bounds of the maximum and minimum values. Cerberus validators can also perform type conversions during the validation step, which allows us to plug data loaded directly from CSV files into the validator.

In this recipe, we will learn how to use Cerberus to validate data loaded from a CSV file.

Getting ready

For this recipe, we need to import the `csv` module from the Python Standard Library, as well as the Cerberus package:

```
import csv
import cerberus
```

We will also need the `sample.csv` file from the code repository for this chapter.

How to do it...

In the following steps, we will validate a set of data that's been loaded from CSV using the Cerberus package:

1. First, we need to build a schema that describes the data we expect. To do this, we must define a simple schema for floating-point numbers:

```
float_schema = {"type": "float", "coerce": float, "min": -1.0,
    "max": 1.0}
```

2. Next, we build the schema for individual items. These will be the rows of our data:

```
item_schema = {
    "type": "dict",
    "schema": {
        "id": {"type": "string"},
        "number": {"type": "integer", "coerce": int},
        "lower": float_schema,
        "upper": float_schema,
    }
}
```

3. Now, we can define the schema for the whole document, which will contain a list of items:

```
schema = {
    "rows": {
        "type": "list",
        "schema": item_schema
    }
}
```

4. Next, we create a `Validator` object with the schema we just defined:

```
validator = cerberus.Validator(schema)
```

5. Then, we load the data using a `DictReader` from the `csv` module:

```
with open("sample.csv") as f:
    dr = csv.DictReader(f)
    document = {"rows": list(dr)}
```

6. Next, we use the `validate` method on the `Validator` to validate the document:

```
validator.validate(document)
```

7. Then, we retrieve the errors from the validation process from the `Validator` object:

```
errors = validator.errors["rows"][0]
```

8. Finally, we can print any error messages that appeared:

```
for row_n, errs in errors.items():
    print(f"row {row_n}: {errs}")
```

The output of the error messages is as follows:

```
row 11: [{'lower': ['min value is -1.0']}]
row 18: [{'number': ['must be of integer type', "field 'number'
cannot be coerced: invalid literal for int() with base 10:
'None'"]}]
row 32: [{'upper': ['min value is -1.0']}]
row 63: [{'lower': ['max value is 1.0']}]
```

How it works...

The schema that we created is a technical description of all the criteria that we need to check against our data. This will usually be defined as a dictionary with the name of the item as the key and a dictionary of properties, such as the type or bounds on the value in a dictionary, as the value. For example, in *step 1*, we defined a schema for floating-point numbers that limits the numbers so that they're between the values of -1 and 1. Note that we include the `coerce` key, which specifies the type that the value should be converted into during the validation. This allows us to pass in data that's been loaded from a CSV document, which contains only strings, without having to worry about its type.

The `Validator` object takes care of parsing documents so that they're validated and checking the data they contain against all the criteria described by the schema. In this recipe, we provided the schema to the `Validator` object when it was created. However, we could also pass the schema into the `validate` method as a second argument. The errors are stored in a nested dictionary that mirrors the structure of the document.

Working with data streams

Some data is received in a constant stream from various sources. For example, we might have a situation where multiple temperature probes are reporting values at set intervals via a Kafka server. Kafka is a streaming data message broker that passes messages to different processing agents based on topics.

Processing streaming data is the perfect application for asynchronous Python. This allows us to process larger quantities of data concurrently, which could be very important in applications. Of course, we can't directly perform long-running analysis on this data in an asynchronous context, since this will interfere with the execution of the event loop.

For working with Kafka streams using Python's asynchronous programming features, we can use the Faust package. This package allows us to define asynchronous functions that will act as processing agents or services that can process or otherwise interact with a stream of data from a Kafka server.

In this recipe, we will learn how to use the Faust package to process a stream of data from a Kafka server.

Getting ready

Unlike most of the recipes in this book, this recipe cannot be run in a Jupyter notebook since we will run the resulting app from the command line.

For this recipe, we will need to import the Faust package:

```
import faust
```

We will also need an instance of the default random number generator from the NumPy package:

```
from numpy.random import default_rng
rng = default_rng(12345)
```

We will also need to run an instance of a Kafka service on our local machine so that our Faust application can interact with the message broker.

Once you have downloaded Kafka and decompressed the downloaded source, navigate to the folder that the Kafka application can be found in. Open this folder in the terminal. Start the ZooKeeper server using the following command for Linux or Mac:

```
bin/zookeeper-server-start.sh config/zookeeper.properties
```

If you're on Windows, use the following command instead:

```
bin\windows\zookeeper-server-start.bat config\zookeeper.properties
```

Then, in a new terminal, launch the Kafka server using the following command for Linux or Mac:

```
bin/kafka-server-start.sh config/server.properties
```

If you're on Windows, use the following command instead:

```
bin\windows\kafka-server-start.bat config\server.properties
```

In each terminal, you should see some logging information that will indicate that the server is running.

How to do it...

Follow these steps to create a Faust app that will read (and write) data to a Kafka server and do some simple processing:

1. First, we need to create a Faust `App` instance that will act as the interface between Python and the Kafka server:

    ```
    app = faust.App("sample", broker="kafka://localhost")
    ```

2. Next, we will create a record type that mimics the data we expect from the server:

    ```
    class Record(faust.Record):
        id_string: str
        value: float
    ```

3. Now, we'll add a topic to the Faust `App` object that sets the value type to the `Record` class that we just defined:

```
topic = app.topic("sample-topic", value_type=Record)
```

4. Now, we define an agent, which is an asynchronous function wrapped in the `agent` decorator on the `App` object:

```
@app.agent(topic)
async def process_record(records):
    async for record in records:
        print(f"Got {record.id_string}: {record.value}")
```

5. Next, we define two source functions that will publish records to the Kafka server on the sample topic we set up. These are asynchronous functions wrapped in the `timer` decorator with an appropriate interval set:

```
@app.timer(interval=1.0)
async def producer1(app):
    await app.send(
        "sample-topic",
        value=Record(id_string="producer 1", value=
            rng.uniform(0, 2))
    )

@app.timer(interval=2.0)
async def producer2(app):
    await app.send(
        "sample-topic",
        value=Record(id_string="producer 2", value=
            rng.uniform(0, 5))
    )
```

6. At the bottom of the file, we start the application's `main` function:

```
app.main()
```

7. Now, in a new terminal, we can use the following command to start a worker for the application (assuming our application is stored in `working-with-data-streams.py`):

```
python3.8 working-with-data-streams.py worker
```

At this stage, you should see some output that's been generated by the agent printed into the terminal, as shown here:

```
[2020-06-21 14:15:27,986] [18762] [WARNING] Got producer 1:
0.4546720449343393
[2020-06-21 14:15:28,985] [18762] [WARNING] Got producer 2:
1.5837916985487643
[2020-06-21 14:15:28,989] [18762] [WARNING] Got producer 1:
1.5947309146654682
[2020-06-21 14:15:29,988] [18762] [WARNING] Got producer 1:
1.3525093415019491
```

This will be below some application information that's been generated by Faust.

8. Press *Ctrl* + *C* to close the worker and make sure to close both the Kafka server and the Zookeeper server in the same way.

How it works...

This is a very basic example of a Faust application. Ordinarily, we wouldn't generate the records and send them through the Kafka server and process them within the same app. However, this is fine for the purposes of this demonstration. In a production environment, we'd probably connect to a remote Kafka server that is connected to multiple sources and publishing to multiple different topics simultaneously.

The Faust app controls the interaction between the Python code and the Kafka server. We use the `agent` decorator to add a function to process information published to a particular channel. This asynchronous function will be executed each time new data is pushed to the sample topic. In this recipe, the agent that we defined simply prints the information contained within the `Record` objects into the terminal.

The `timer` decorator defines a service that regularly performs some action at a specified interval. In our case, the timer sends a message to the Kafka server through the `App` object. These messages are then pushed to the agent for processing.

The Faust command-line interface is used to start a worker process running the application. These workers are what actually perform the processing in reaction to events on the Kafka server or locally in the process, such as the timer services defined in this recipe. Larger applications might use several worker processes in order to cope with vast quantities of data.

See also

The Faust documentation provides far more details about the capabilities of Faust, along with various alternatives to Faust: `https://faust.readthedocs.io/en/latest/`.

More information about Kafka can be found on the Apache Kafka website: `https://kafka.apache.org/`.

Accelerating code with Cython

Python is often criticized for being a slow programming language – a statement that is endlessly debatable. Many of these criticisms can be addressed by using a high-performance compiled library with a Python interface – such as the scientific Python stack – to greatly improve performance. However, there are some situations where it is difficult to avoid the fact that Python is not a compiled language. One way to improve performance in these (fairly rare) situations is to write a C extension (or even rewrite the code entirely in C) to speed up the critical parts. This will certainly make the code run faster, but it might make it more difficult to maintain the package. Instead, we can use Cython, which is an extension of the Python language that is transpiled into C and compiled for great performance improvements.

For example, we can consider some code that's used to generate an image of the Mandelbrot set. For comparison, the pure Python code – which we assume is our starting point – is as follows:

```
# mandelbrot/python_mandel.py

import numpy as np

def in_mandel(cx, cy, max_iter):
```

```
        x = cx
        y = cy
        for i in range(max_iter):
            x2 = x**2
            y2 = y**2
            if (x2 + y2) >= 4:
                return i
            y = 2.0*x*y + cy
            x = x2 - y2 + cx
        return max_iter

    def compute_mandel(N_x, N_y, N_iter):
        xlim_l = -2.5
        xlim_u = 0.5
        ylim_l = -1.2
        ylim_u = 1.2
        x_vals = np.linspace(xlim_l, xlim_u, N_x, dtype=np.float64)
        y_vals = np.linspace(ylim_l, ylim_u, N_y, dtype=np.float64)

        height = np.empty((N_x, N_y), dtype=np.int64)
        for i in range(N_x):
            for j in range(N_y):
                height[i, j] = in_mandel(x_vals[i], y_vals[j], N_iter)
        return height
```

The reason why this code is relatively slow in pure Python is fairly obvious: the nested loops. For demonstration purposes, let's assume that we can't vectorize this code using NumPy. A little preliminary testing shows that using these functions to generate the Mandelbrot set using 320 × 240 points and 255 steps takes approximately 6.3 seconds. Your times may vary, depending on your system.

In this recipe, we will use Cython to greatly improve the performance of the preceding code in order to generate an image of the Mandelbrot set.

Getting ready

For this recipe, we will need the NumPy package and the Cython package to be installed. You will also need a C compiler such as GCC installed on your system. For example, on Windows, you can obtain a version of GCC by installing MinGW.

How to do it...

Follow these steps to use Cython to greatly improve the performance of the code for generating an image of the Mandelbrot set:

1. Start a new file called `cython_mandel.pyx` in the `mandelbrot` folder. In this file, we will add some simple imports and type definitions:

```
# mandelbrot/cython_mandel.pyx

import numpy as np
cimport numpy as np
cimport cython
ctypedef Py_ssize_t Int
ctypedef np.float64_t Double
```

2. Next, we define a new version of the `in_mandel` routine using the Cython syntax. We add some declarations to the first few lines of this routine:

```
cdef int in_mandel(Double cx, Double cy, int max_iter):
    cdef Double x = cx
    cdef Double y = cy
    cdef Double x2, y2
    cdef Int i
```

3. The rest of the function is identical to the Python version of the function:

```
    for i in range(max_iter):
        x2 = x**2
        y2 = y**2
        if (x2 + y2) >= 4:
            return i
        y = 2.0*x*y + cy
        x = x2 - y2 + cx
    return max_iter
```

4. Next, we define a new version of the `compute_mandel` function. We add two decorators to this function from the Cython package:

```
@cython.boundscheck(False)
@cython.wraparound(False)
def compute_mandel(int N_x, int N_y, int N_iter):
```

5. Then, we define the constants, just as we did in the original routine:

```
cdef double xlim_l = -2.5
cdef double xlim_u = 0.5
cdef double ylim_l = -1.2
cdef double ylim_u = 1.2
```

6. We use the `linspace` and `empty` routines from the NumPy package in exactly the same way as in the Python version. The only addition here is that we declare the `i` and `j` variables, which are of the `Int` type:

```
cdef np.ndarray x_vals = np.linspace(xlim_l, xlim_u,
    N_x, dtype=np.float64)
cdef np.ndarray y_vals = np.linspace(ylim_l, ylim_u,
    N_y, dtype=np.float64)
cdef np.ndarray height = np.empty((N_x, N_y), dtype=np.int64)
cdef Int i, j
```

7. The remainder of the definition is exactly the same as in the Python version:

```
for i in range(N_x):
    for j in range(N_y):
        height[i, j] = in_mandel(x_vals[i], y_vals[j], N_iter)
return height
```

8. Next, we create a new file called `setup.py` in the `mandelbrot` folder and add the following imports to the top of this file:

```
# mandelbrot/setup.py

import numpy as np
from setuptools import setup, Extension
from Cython.Build import cythonize
```

9. After that, we define an extension module with the source pointing to the original `python_mandel.py` file. Set the name of this module to `hybrid_mandel`:

```
hybrid = Extension(
    "hybrid_mandel",
    sources=["python_mandel.py"],
    include_dirs=[np.get_include()],
    define_macros=[("NPY_NO_DEPRECATED_API",
       "NPY_1_7_API_VERSION")]
)
```

10. Now, we define a second extension module with the source set as the `cython_mandel.pyx` file that we just created:

```
cython = Extension(
    "cython_mandel",
    sources=["cython_mandel.pyx"],
    include_dirs=[np.get_include()],
    define_macros=[("NPY_NO_DEPRECATED_API",
       "NPY_1_7_API_VERSION")]
)
```

11. Next, we add both these extension modules to a list and call the `setup` routine to register these modules:

```
extensions = [hybrid, cython]
setup(
    ext_modules = cythonize(extensions, compiler_directives=
       {"language_level": "3"}),
)
```

12. Create a new empty file called `__init__.py` in the `mandelbrot` folder to make this into a package that can be imported in Python.
13. Open the terminal inside the `mandelbrot` folder and use the following command to build the Cython extension modules:

```
python3.8 setup.py build_ext --inplace
```

14. Now, start a new file called `run.py` and add the following import statements:

```
# run.py

from time import time
from functools import wraps
import matplotlib.pyplot as plt
```

15. Import the various `compute_mandel` routines from each of the modules we have defined: `python_mandel` for the original; `hybrid_mandel` for the Cythonized Python code; and `cython_mandel` for the compiled pure Cython code:

```
from mandelbrot.python_mandel import compute_mandel
    as compute_mandel_py
from mandelbrot.hybrid_mandel import compute_mandel
    as compute_mandel_hy
from mandelbrot.cython_mandel import compute_mandel
    as compute_mandel_cy
```

16. Define a simple timer decorator that we will use to test the performance of the routines:

```
def timer(func, name):
    @wraps(func)
    def wrapper(*args, **kwargs):
        t_start = time()
        val = func(*args, **kwargs)
        t_end = time()
        print(f"Time taken for {name}: {t_end - t_start}")
        return val
    return wrapper
```

17. Apply the `timer` decorator to each of the imported routines, and define some constants for testing:

```
mandel_py = timer(compute_mandel_py, "Python")
mandel_hy = timer(compute_mandel_hy, "Hybrid")
mandel_cy = timer(compute_mandel_cy, "Cython")

Nx = 320
Ny = 240
steps = 255
```

18. Run each of the decorated routines with the constants we set previously. Record the output of the final call (the Cython version) in the `vals` variable:

```
mandel_py(Nx, Ny, steps)
mandel_hy(Nx, Ny, steps)
vals = mandel_cy(Nx, Ny, steps)
```

19. Finally, plot the output of the Cython version to check that the routine computes the Mandelbrot set correctly:

```
fig, ax = plt.subplots()
ax.imshow(vals.T, extent=(-2.5, 0.5, -1.2, 1.2))
plt.show()
```

Running the `run.py` file will print the execution time of each of the routines to the terminal, as follows:

```
Time taken for Python: 6.276328802108765
Time taken for Hybrid: 5.816391468048096
Time taken for Cython: 0.03116750717163086
```

The plot of the Mandelbrot set can be seen in the following image:

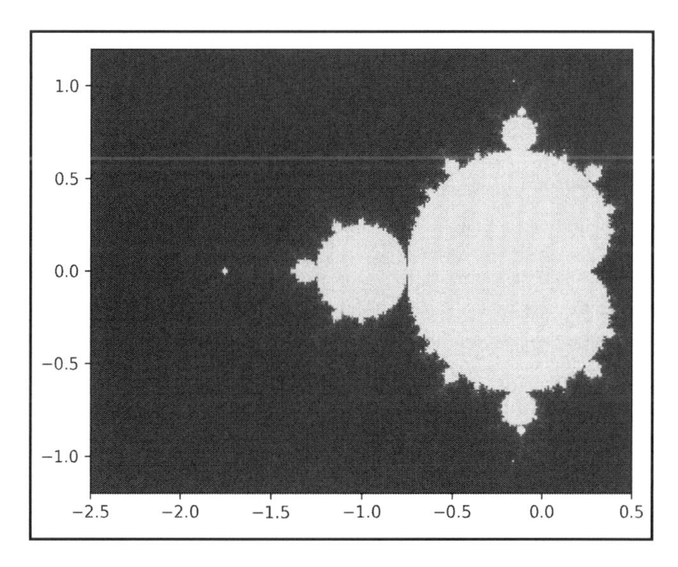

Figure 10.4: Image of the Mandelbrot set computed using Cython code

This is what we expect for the Mandelbrot set.

How it works...

There is a lot happening in this recipe, so let's start by explaining the overall process. Cython takes code that is written in an extension of the Python language and compiles it into C code, which is then used to produce a C extension library that can be imported into a Python session. In fact, you can even use Cython to compile ordinary Python code directly to an extension, although the results are not as good as when using the modified language. The first few steps in this recipe define the new version of the Python code in the modified language (saved as a `.pyx` file), which includes type information in addition to the regular Python code. In order to build the C extension using Cython, we need to define a setup file, and then we create a file that we run to produce the results.

The final compiled version of the Cython code runs considerably faster than its Python equivalent. The Cython compiled Python code (hybrid, as we called it in this recipe) performs slightly better than the pure Python code. This is because the produced Cython code still has to work with Python objects with all of their caveats. By adding the typing information to the Python code, in the `.pyx` file, we start to see major improvements to performance. This is because the `in_mandel` function is now effectively defined as a C-level function that has no interaction with Python objects, and instead operates on primitive data types.

There are some small, but very important differences, between the Cython code and the Python equivalent. In *step 1*, you can see that we imported the NumPy package as usual but that we also used the `cimport` keyword to bring some C-level definitions into the scope. In *step 2*, we used the `cdef` keyword instead of the `def` keyword when we defined the `in_mandel` routine. This means that the `in_mandel` routine is defined as a C-level function that cannot be used from the Python level, which saves a significant amount of overhead when calling this function (which happens a lot).

The only other real differences regarding the definition of this function are the inclusion of some type declarations in the signature and in the first few lines of the function. The two decorators we applied here disable the checking of bounds when accessing elements from a list (array). The `boundscheck` decorator disables checking if the index is valid (between 0 and the size of the array), while the `wraparound` decorator disables the negative indexing. Both of these give a modest improvement to speed during execution, although they disable some of the safety features built into Python. In this recipe, it is OK to disable these checks because we are using a loop over the valid indices of the array.

The setup file is where we tell Python (and therefore Cython) how to build the C extension. The `cythonize` routine from Cython is the key here as it triggers the Cython build process. In *steps 9* and *10*, we defined extension modules using the `Extension` class from `setuptools` so that we could define some extra details for the build; specifically, we set an environment variable for the NumPy compilation and added the `include` files for the NumPy C headers. This is done via the `define_macros` keyword argument for the `Extension` class. The terminal command we used in *step 13* uses `setuptools` to build the Cython extensions, and the addition of the `--inplace` flat means that the compiled libraries will be added to the current directory, rather than being placed in a centralized location. This is good for development.

The run script is fairly simple: import the routines from each of the defined modules – two of these are actually C extension modules – and time their execution. We have to be a little creative with the import aliases and routine names to avoid collisions.

There's more...

Cython is a powerful tool for improving the performance of some aspects of your code. However, you must always be careful to spend your time wisely while optimizing code. Using a profile such as the cProfiler that is provided in the Python Standard Library can be used to find the places where performance bottlenecks occur in your code. In this recipe, it was fairly obvious where the performance bottleneck occurs. Cython is a good remedy to the problem in this case because it involves repetitive calls to a function inside a (double) `for` loop. However, it is not a universal fix for performance issues and, more often than not, the performance of code can be greatly improved by refactoring it so that it makes use of high-performance libraries.

Cython is well integrated with Jupyter notebooks and can be used seamlessly in the code blocks of a notebook. Cython is also included in the Anaconda distribution of Python, so no additional setup is required for using Cython with Jupyter notebooks when it's been installed using the Anaconda distribution.

There are alternatives to Cython when it comes to producing compiled code from Python. For example, the NumBa package (`http://numba.pydata.org/`) provides a **just in time (JIT)** compiler that optimizes Python code at runtime by simply placing a decorator on specific functions. NumBa is designed to work with NumPy and other scientific Python libraries and can also be used to leverage GPUs to accelerate code.

Distributing computing with Dask

Dask is a library that's used for distributing computing across multiple threads, processes, or even computers in order to effectively perform computation at a huge scale. This can greatly improve performance and throughput, even if you are working on a single laptop computer. Dask provides replacements for most of the data structures from the Python scientific stack, such as NumPy arrays and Pandas DataFrames. These replacements have very similar interfaces, but under the hood, they are built for distributed computing so that they can be shared between multiple threads, processes, or computers. In many cases, switching to Dask is as simple as changing the `import` statement, and possibly adding a couple of extra method calls to start concurrent computations.

In this recipe, we will learn how to use Dask to do some simple computations on a DataFrame.

Getting ready

For this recipe, we will need to import the `dataframe` module from the Dask package. Following the convention set out in the Dask documentation, we will import this module under the alias `dd`:

```
import dask.dataframe as dd
```

We will also need the `sample.csv` file from the code repository for this chapter.

How to do it...

Follow these steps to use Dask to perform some computations on a DataFrame object:

1. First, we need to load the data from `sample.csv` into a Dask `DataFrame`:

```
data = dd.read_csv("sample.csv")
```

2. Next, we perform a standard calculation on the columns of the DataFrame:

```
sum_data = data.lower + data.upper
print(sum_data)
```

Unlike with Pandas DataFrames, the result is not a new DataFrame. The `print` statement gives us the following information:

```
Dask Series Structure:
npartitions=1
    float64
      ...
dtype: float64
Dask Name: add, 6 tasks
```

3. To actually get the result, we need to use the `compute` method:

```
result = sum_data.compute()
print(result.head())
```

The result is now shown as expected:

```
0 -0.911811
1 0.947240
2 -0.552153
3 -0.429914
4 1.229118
dtype: float64
```

4. We compute the means of the final two columns in exactly the same way we would with a Pandas DataFrame, but we need to add a call to the `compute` method to execute the calculation:

```
means = data.loc[:, ("lower", "upper")].mean().compute()
print(means)
```

The result, as printed, is exactly as we expect it to be:

```
lower -0.060393
upper -0.035192
dtype: float64
```

How it works...

Dask builds a *task graph* for the computation, which describes the relationships between the various operations and calculations that need to be performed on the collection of data. This breaks down the steps of the calculation so that calculations can be done in the right order across the different workers. This task graph is then passed into a scheduler that sends the actual tasks to the workers for execution. Dask comes with several different schedulers: synchronous, threaded, multiprocessing, and distributed. The type of scheduler can be chosen in the call to the `compute` method or set globally. Dask will choose a sensible default if one is not given.

The synchronous, threaded, and multiprocessing schedulers work on a single machine, while the distributed scheduler is for working with a cluster. Dask allows you to change between schedulers in a relatively transparent way, although for small tasks, you might not get any performance benefits because of the overhead of setting up more complicated schedulers.

The `compute` method is the key to this recipe. The methods that would ordinarily perform the computation on Pandas DataFrames now just set up a computation that is to be executed through the Dask scheduler. The computation isn't started until the `compute` method is called. This is similar to the way that a `Future` is returned as a proxy for the result of an asynchronous function call, which isn't fulfilled until the computation is complete.

There's more...

Dask provides interfaces for NumPy arrays, as well as the DataFrames shown in this recipe. There is also a machine learning interface called `dask_ml` that exposes similar capabilities to the scikit-learn package. Some external packages, such as `xarray`, also have a Dask interface. Dask can also work with GPUs to further accelerate computations and load data from remote sources, which is useful if the computation is distributed across a cluster.

Other Books You May Enjoy

If you enjoyed this book, you may be interested in these other books by Packt:

Python for Finance Cookbook
Eryk Lewinson

ISBN: 978-1-78961-851-8

- Download and preprocess financial data from different sources
- Backtest the performance of automatic trading strategies in a real-world setting
- Estimate financial econometrics models in Python and interpret their results
- Use Monte Carlo simulations for a variety of tasks such as derivatives valuation and risk assessment
- Improve the performance of financial models with the latest Python libraries
- Apply machine learning and deep learning techniques to solve different financial problems
- Understand the different approaches used to model financial time series data

The Python Workshop
Andrew Bird, Dr Lau Cher Han, Mario Corchero Jiménez, Graham Lee, Corey Wade

ISBN: 978-1-83921-885-9

- Learn how to write clean and concise code with Python 3
- Understand classes and object-oriented programming
- Tackle entry-level data science and create engaging visualizations
- Use Python to create responsive, modern web applications
- Automate essential day-to-day tasks with Python scripts
- Get started with predictive Python machine learning

Leave a review - let other readers know what you think

Please share your thoughts on this book with others by leaving a review on the site that you bought it from. If you purchased the book from Amazon, please leave us an honest review on this book's Amazon page. This is vital so that other potential readers can see and use your unbiased opinion to make purchasing decisions, we can understand what our customers think about our products, and our authors can see your feedback on the title that they have worked with Packt to create. It will only take a few minutes of your time, but is valuable to other potential customers, our authors, and Packt. Thank you!

Index

D

E

F

G

H

N

O

P

R

S

Printed in Great Britain
by Amazon

63946851R00203